The
Great
Cultural
Awakening

Other Books by D. Paul Schafer

Culture: Beacon of the Future (1998)

Revolution or Renaissance: Making the Transition from an Economic Age to a Cultural Age (2008)

The Age of Culture (2014)

The Secrets of Culture (2015)

Celebrating Canadian Creativity (2016)

Will This Be Canada's Century? (2017)

The Cultural Personality (2018)

The True North: How Canadian Creativity Changed the World (2019)

The Arts: Gateway to a Fulfilling Life and Cultural Age (2020)

The World as Culture: Cultivation of the Soul to the Cosmic Whole (2022)

THE GREAT CULTURAL AWAKENING

Key to an Equitable, Sustainable, and Harmonious Age

Rock's Mills Press

Rock's Mills, Ontario • Oakville, Ontario
2024

Published by
Rock's Mills Press
www.rocksmillspress.com

For information about trade, library, and bulk orders, please contact the publisher at customer.service@rocksmillspress.com or through our website.

Contents

Contents

Preface

This is a book about the great cultural awakening that is taking place in the world—an awakening that is opening the doors to a cultural age.

I have been thinking about such an awakening ever since I was very young. It all began when my grade six teacher asked me to give a presentation to my classmates at school. After a great deal of searching, I decided to talk about Marco Polo and his trip to China many centuries ago. I was fascinated by his journey along the historic Silk Road through what are now Turkey, Iran, Iraq, Afghanistan, and Pakistan, as well as his experiences in China and elsewhere in Asia, including the several missions to India, Sri Lanka, Indonesia, and Burma (now Myanmar) that he carried out as an emissary of the great Kublai Khan. Over the course of his travels, Marco Polo met many different kinds of people, ate many different types of foods, and enjoyed superb banquets and festivities in the courts of Kublai Khan and other rulers. The terrain he covered, the many different tribes, clans, and peoples he encountered along the way, the numerous places he visited—all these captivated me immensely, as I believe they have many other people. The very names of the places he visited—Constantinople, Trebizond, Kerman, Bukhara, Tabriz, Samarkand, Kashgar, Lanzhou, Suzhow, Khanbaliq, and many others—made such a profound impression on me that I have never forgotten them.

I couldn't help thinking that the world would be a much better place if everyone could experience the kind of cultural awakening that Marco Polo did. I knew even then that I would have to write about the importance of a cultural awakening at some point in my life, although I didn't know how or when.

It took me the better part of thirty years to reach a position where I could think about this task in earnest. When I read somewhere that Gandhi had said, "Be the change you want in the world," I knew the time had come to learn as much as I could about culture and cultures and not just think or dream about them. Nevertheless, it took me *another* twenty-five years before I had broadened and deepened my knowledge of culture and cultures sufficiently to write about them. I published a number of books on culture and cultures in the years to follow, including *Culture: Beacon of the Future, Revolution or Renaissance: Making the Transition from an Economic Age to a Cultural Age, The Age of Culture, The Secrets of Culture, The Arts: Gateway to a Fulfilling Life and Cultural Age, The World as Culture: Cultivation of the Soul to the Cosmic Whole,* and now this book. My deep interest in culture also led to creating the World Culture Project to commemorate the United Nations and UNESCO World Decade for Cultural Development from 1988 to 1997. This Project was founded in 1989 and I still direct it today.

As I delved more deeply into the realm of culture, I came to the conclusion that culture and cultures in the all-inclusive, holistic sense as "complex wholes" and "total ways of life"—the way many anthropologists, sociologists, biologists, cultural historians, and others see them—are the real foundations of human existence. I believe that by understanding culture in this specific sense we come to understand the nature of the world at its core and in its fundamental essence, encompassing not only human beings but other species and the world as a whole. I also believe that the great cultural awakening going on at present will open the doors to the creation and development of a cultural age. Such an age will bring with it more peace, harmony, happiness, sustainability, well-being, and equality, as well as making it possible for all people to enjoy a reasonable standard of living and decent quality of life without straining the globe's resources, ecosystems, and finite carrying capacity to the breaking point.

In order to achieve goals as ambitious and worthwhile as these and enjoy all the benefits that can be derived from them, it is necessary to view the world and everything in it from a cultural perspective. As well, we must consider in detail why culture and cultures should evolve from the ground up and not only the top down if a cultural age is to be realized.

The urgency of this task is reinforced by even the most cursory survey of the difficulties, threats, dangers, and challenges facing humanity and the world that have emerged in recent years, whether it is the steady intensification of climate change, the ongoing COVID-19 pandemic, Russia's war on Ukraine, or, as I write the final words in this book, the outbreak of the calamitous conflict between Israel and Hamas in the Middle East.

In this book, I first read the signs and set the stage in considering the importance of culture. This leads to an examination of the vast constellation of cultures that exist in the world. We then move progressively "up the ladder" in practical terms, from the cultures of individuals, children, parents, homes, families, communities, and schools to those of towns, cities, regions, countries, the entire human world, and those of other species. This is followed by an assessment of several foundational requirements, such as the cultural interpretation of history, the centrality of cultural development and policy, ways of opening the doors to a cultural age, strategies to harmonize crucial relationships and cultivate spirituality and compassion, the prerequisites for living in a cultural age, and, finally, an exploration of why it is so essential to make the transition from the present economic age to a future cultural age.

I would like to express my gratitude to many people who have made valuable contributions to my work over many years. First and foremost, I would like to thank my family—my wife Nancy and daughters Charlene and Susan—for their commitment to my research and writing and always being there for me when this was needed the most. I also wish to thank Réal Bédard for his full support of my work and help with my World Culture Project website and computer requirements. My gratitude goes out to many longtime friends as well, most notably Jack Fobes, Guy Métraux, Prem Kirpal, Mochtar Lubis, Federico Mayor, Ervin Laszlo, Nadarajh Manickam, Joy MacFadyen, Máté Kovács, André Fortier, John Hobday, Max Wyman, Eleonora Barbieri Masini, Biserka Cvjectičanin, Gao Xian, Hans Köchler, Sheila Jans, Walter Pitman, Peter Mousaferiadis, George Simons, Herman Greene, Engelbert Ruoss, Alexander Schieffer, Frank Pasquill, Barry Witkin, Fred Matern, Joyce Zemans, Peter Sever, and many others. I owe a special debt of thanks to several recent friends and colleagues whom I have had the privilege of working closely with more recently, especially Galyna Shevchenko, Mark Riva, Diane Dodd, Susan Magsamen, Ashfaq Ishaq, Brian Holihan, Mira Sartika, Olimpia Niglio, Rana P.B. Singh, Meg Pier, Thomas Legrand, Carmine

Marinucci, and Benno Werlen. Finally, I would like to express my deep appreciation to my friend, editor, and publisher David Stover. Without his support, encouragement, and commitment to publishing many of the books I have written over the last decade, this book and many others would not exist today. I am particularly grateful to him for all his help, kindness, and support during my work on the subjects of culture, cultures, and creativity, as well as in my efforts to make a strong case for a cultural age.

D. Paul Schafer
Markham, Canada
2023

Culture used to look backward in order to understand the world; now, all of a sudden, it is looking forward in order to change it.

—Jean d'Ormesson

The
Great
Cultural
Awakening

Chapter One

Reading the Signs and Setting the Stage

Culture in the future is the crux of the future.
—Eleonora Barbieri Masini[1]

A great cultural awakening is taking place in the world today, an awakening that is opening the doors to a very different kind of age in the future. While this new age is at present barely visible, it holds the potential to create a better world for all people, countries, species, and the world as a whole in the years and decades ahead.

This cultural awakening is manifesting itself in all parts of the world and in many different ways. The most obvious way is the recognition that culture has a crucial role to play in coming to grips with the world's most difficult problems, especially climate change and the environmental crisis, huge disparities in income and wealth, conflicts between different genders, races, tribes, cultures, countries, and civilizations, and many other challenges. Another way is through the realization that culture possesses the potential to produce the new worldviews, values, value systems, lifestyles, and ways of life required to ensure human survival and environmental well-being in the future. Yet a third way is the movement that is occurring among Blacks, Indigenous peoples, and millions of others from colonized countries who are reconnecting with their original cultures, languages, traditions, beliefs, and ways of life after centuries of subjugation, oppression, genocide, injustice, and neglect.

And this isn't all. Far from it. Countless people around the world are discovering that this cultural awakening has a great deal to do with improving their health and well-being, coming to grips with the COVID-19 pandemic and its many variants, connecting with their friends, networks, and communities, and enhancing their personal, local, regional, and national identities and sense of being and belonging. Added to this is the rapidly escalating interest in culture as a complex whole or total way of life; the recent creation of cultural studies as a formal and essential discipline; focusing much more attention on culture and cultures and how they function and are developed; the growing number of films and videos about the cultural achievements of countries and the natural and cultural heritage of humankind; and a new fascination with the evolution of all the different cultures and civilizations in the world.

To this list should also be added the rapid growth of cultural tourism. Millions of people are anxious to travel to other parts of the world to enjoy firsthand experiences with different cultures and enjoy their historical sites, artistic activities, architectural splendors, and culinary delights. As well, an increasing number of people are interested in learning more about the vast panorama of plant and animal cultures that exist throughout the world. And yet more evidence of the growing importance of culture is the competition that now exists between towns and cities around the world vying to be selected as "cultural capitals" or "cities of culture" in order to reap all the economic, social, political, and other benefits that can be realized from this. Put this all together and it is apparent that the great cultural awakening is having a strong impact on virtually everything and everybody in the world in one form or another. This confirms the inescapable fact that culture and cultures have a much more powerful role to play in the world of the future than they did in the past or do at present.

And the implications of the cultural awakening do not end here. More and more people and countries are coming to the conclusion that culture possesses the potential to bring about the changes that are required to set humanity on a very different path in the future. As Joel S. Kahn pointed out in his book *Culture, Multiculture, Postculture*:

> Culture is a word on everybody's lips these days. Hardly a moment seems to pass when we do not hear on the radio or television, see in newspapers and magazines, or read in academic texts some account of the world of the cultural. Governments at all levels announce cultural policies and provide funding for cultural activities; intellectuals announce the need for cultural

initiatives or bemoan the loss of traditional cultural values; famous cultural icons—musicians, artists, novelists—themselves culture makers, are increasingly sought out for their opinions on the state of the world; the new field of cultural studies takes the academy by storm. And small wonder—the image, the representation, things quintessentially cultural have, as cultural theorists like Jean Baudrillard and Fredric Jameson have argued, quite literally taken over our lives.[2]

A great deal has occurred in the cultural field since Kahn's book was published at the end of the twentieth century that serves to confirm his keen insight into the rapidly escalating importance of culture. Many people in the world are now talking about the pressing need to "change the culture" in order to create the new ways of life and living that are required for the future, just as countless organizations are recognizing the necessity of changing their present ways of doing things and modes of operation, from hospitals, retirement homes, and police departments to political, educational, social, and governmental institutions. In recent years, this has been accompanied by the widely held belief that what is most needed in the world today is not piecemeal or partisan change, but rather "systemic cultural change" if humanity is to be successful in dealing with the complex and dangerous problems that threaten us all.

While a surprisingly large fraction of the world's population is involved in the great cultural awakening in one form or another, unfortunately this awakening is not being recognized or given the attention and priority it deserves and needs by the world's most powerful people, governments, corporations, countries, and international institutions. Not only do they continue to deal with culture and cultures in marginal rather than mainstream terms, but they persist in valuing culture primarily as a generator of economic activity and form of entertainment. This is making it difficult to capitalize on the remarkable potential of culture and cultures as well as of the great cultural awakening to set the stage for a very different kind of age and world in the future.

In order to determine why traditional attitudes and practices like this and others persist, it is necessary to delve into the nature, history, significance, and roles of economics and culture, without doubt two of the most powerful activities in the world. Both these activities can be traced back to classical times, when economics was deemed "household management" by the Greeks and culture deemed "cultivation" by the Romans. While both activities have evolved in very different ways since that time, they still retain traces of their original meanings.

Economics provides the most obvious example of this. Over the centuries, it has been expanded enormously as an activity, so much so that it is now seen and treated as the production, distribution, consumption, and administration of goods and services as well as the creation of material and monetary wealth, and therefore the development of all the different economies in the world. Culture, on the other hand, was deemed initially to be "cultivation" by the Romans, and in particular "the philosophy or cultivation of the soul" by Marcus Cicero, the great Roman orator and statesman. Subsequently, culture was seen and treated for many centuries as taking in the arts, humanities, heritage of history, and finer things in life. Then, in the latter part of the nineteenth century, it was defined formally as "the complex whole" or "total way of life of people." This is the way it is seen and defined by most cultural scholars and historians today, as well as by many people and organizations involved in the great cultural awakening.

Since the world has been dominated by economics over the last few centuries, it pays to examine how economics and economies came to play the dominant role in the world and why today we are living in an economic age.

What has brought the need to examine economics, economies, and the economic age to a head is the environmental crisis. When the population of the world was much smaller than it is today, there were enough resources to go around, even if this was not always realized or achieved at the time. Moreover, the Earth's climate was more stable than it is today and there was less pollution, congestion, and waste. Nevertheless, even back then, there were signs that humanity might be in for a rocky ride in the future, especially when the English scholar Thomas Malthus predicted that population growth would eventually outstrip the food supply and means of subsistence.

Fortunately, an event occurred several decades before Malthus's dire prediction that had a much more positive, powerful, and profound effect on the world. It was the publication of Adam Smith's book *The Wealth of Nations* in 1776. This book laid the foundations for the creation and development of the economic age. It set out Smith's belief that people's standards of living and quality of life could be increased enormously if people, institutions, and countries specialized in very specific production functions and looked after their own self-interest. When this was done, Smith claimed that far more material and monetary wealth and countless more goods and services could be produced. In the end, everything would turn out for the best because an "invisible hand" was working to make this happen.

It should be emphasized here that Smith made a fundamental distinction between "productive" and "unproductive" labour. Productive labour was labour that created material goods such as those created by farmers, industrialists, and factory workers. Unproductive labour was labour that did not produce goods like this but, rather, intangible, non-physical services, such as those provided by artists, humanists, teachers, public servants, politicians, and the like.

Such beliefs were strengthened further when David Ricardo, a British economist and politician, arrived on the scene and formalized economics as a discipline. Ricardo claimed that economics and economic development should be awarded the highest priority by governments and take precedence over not only politics but everything else.

By this time, colonialism had been well established in most parts of the world. Vast regions of Africa, Asia, Latin America, the Caribbean, North and South America, and elsewhere were being subjected to the economic needs and practices of countries such as Great Britain, Spain, Portugal, Holland, Belgium, France, Germany, and others. The economic interests and political policies of these countries were imposed on their colonial satellites, through a variety of enticements, inducements, coercion, brutality, slavery, and even warfare if necessary.

The foundations of the western economic system were greatly strengthened when Karl Marx made the compelling case that all countries and societies can be divided into an economic base and a non-economic superstructure. The base takes precedence over the superstructure because it is the *cause* of the superstructure (and everything else). According to Marx, the base is concerned with economic or productive activities, things that came to be known as *the basics in life*—most obviously agriculture, industry, technology, and manufactured products—whereas the superstructure is concerned with non-economic or unproductive activities, things that came to be regarded as *the frills in life*, most often artistic, humanistic, intellectual, and recreational endeavours.

However, Marx went much farther than this. He also developed the economic interpretation of history, which is predicated on the conviction that the division between the economic base and the non-economic superstructure was not only true during his own time—he was living, working, researching, and writing when Great Britain was at the height of the Industrial Revolution, when everything had a highly industrial, material, and economic orientation—but is true at all times and in all places and therefore an "eternal, universal, and inexorable truth."

While Marx's theories in regard to the relationship between capital and labour did much to improve conditions for the working class through the eventual establishment of labour unions and many other developments, his vicious attack on capitalism resulted in the division of the world between capitalism and communism for the better part of the twentieth century and thus was not without its problems. In one of the greatest ironies in history, Marx's economic interpretation of history opened the doors for capitalism to play a much greater and more powerful role in the world than it had up to that point.

Given theories as pervasive, compelling, and well-documented as the ones provided by Smith, Ricardo, and Marx, the most powerful people, corporations, and countries in the world decided that making economics and the development of economies the centrepiece of their efforts was the best way to move forward. As a result, since Adam Smith's day, developing economics and economies, generating economic activity and growth, creating as many goods and services and as much material and monetary wealth as possible, and enjoying all the profuse benefits and rewards that can be derived from this activity were accorded the highest priority and dominant role in the world.

The principal priority was to develop a theoretical and practical system, ideology, and methodology that was based on these convictions and make them concrete realities.

This task was taken up in earnest and carried much farther by what came to be known as the neoclassical economists, especially Alfred Marshall, Carl Menger, William Stanley Jevons, Léon Walras, John Hicks, and many others. Commencing in the latter part of the nineteenth century and extending well into the first half of the twentieth century, the neoclassical economists created a theoretical and practical system predicated primarily on the roles and responsibilities of people and corporations in general and countries in particular. People fulfilled their roles and responsibilities in this system most effectively when they specialized in the production of goods and services, became consumers first and foremost, and maximized their consumer satisfaction in the marketplace. Corporations fulfilled their roles and responsibilities best when they created as many goods and as much material and monetary wealth as possible, based their plans, policies, and practices on the laws of supply and demand, relied on the marketplace to facilitate their transactions and determine prices, and maximized their profits (something which most neoclassical economists believed was *the* most important factor in driving economies and enabling them to function most efficiently). And countries carried out their roles and responsibilities most judiciously when they made developing their economies their highest priority. When Oscar Wilde said somewhat cynically around this time that it is possible to know "the price of everything and value of nothing," his views carried very little weight because most people, companies, and countries were caught up in the ideals and objectives of neoclassical economics.

As a result of developments like this, and many others, virtually all other interpretations of history and views of people's, corporations', and countries' roles and responsibilities ceased except in the most esoteric or obscure places. It was decided by the world's most powerful elites that other ideas, theories, and particularly interpretations of history should be ignored and forgotten because they were no longer relevant or required. Economics and the economic interpretation of history were seen as the most accurate way of looking at the world. The challenge from that point on was to *operationalize* the neoclassical system of economics and make it a concrete and practical reality.

When the stock market crash occurred in 1929, followed by the Great Depression in the 1930s and then the Second World War from 1939 to 1945, governments decided it was time to get more actively involved in the functioning of the economic system. They were concerned by massive unemployment, major fluctuations in levels of economic activity, countless bankruptcies, and numerous other economic and financial difficulties. In order to bring back prosperity, stability, and economic growth, it was concluded that governments should make use of a variety of monetary and fiscal techniques advocated by the British economist John Maynard Keynes and the so-called Keynesian economists who followed in his footsteps.

When governments did get more involved in economic affairs, not only did this achieve a great deal in terms of getting the world economy back on track, but it confirmed the fact that humanity was undoubtedly living in an economic age. Economics, economies, and economic growth took precedence over everything else. This fact was reaffirmed when the economic age was extended from the western world to the entire world through the process known as globalization. This made the economic age a global phenomenon and no longer a western phenomenon.

Developments over the last seven or eight decades have served to confirm the claim that the present age is an economic age and that this is a global rather than just a western phenomenon. The primacy of the economic age is due to something else of fundamental importance—seeing and treating economics as "the whole" and everything else as "a part of the whole" or "part of economics," thereby making Marx's convictions on this matter a self-fulfilling prophecy.

While the tendency to treat economics as the whole rather than part of the whole occurred imperceptibly and largely unconsciously, it eventually resulted in reducing virtually everything else in the world to economics, valuing things primarily if not exclusively for their economic value, and creating a set of quantitative indicators capable of measuring economic activity and performance with exact scientific accuracy and statistical precision. Most notable in this regard are economic indicators such as gross domestic product (GDP), gross national product (GNP), per capita income, and the rate of economic growth. While a few other indicators have been added to this list over the last few decades, including health, education, and general well-being indicators, most people and countries still use quantitative indicators for purposes of comparisons between countries and indications of economic achievement and overall performance and progress. This is confirmed by how closely stock markets and rates of economic growth are followed, assessed, and relied upon in the United States, China, and virtually all other countries in the world.

As a result of these developments and many others, we are all living in an economic age. It is an age that has made economics, economies, and economic growth the centerpiece of countries and principal preoccupation of municipal, regional, national, and international development. It is now assumed and accepted in all parts of the world that if we attend to economics, economies, and economic growth properly, everything else will fall into place and work out for the best.[3]

At least until very recently. What is bringing matters to a head is the environmental crisis and all the studies that have been conducted by numerous scientists and environmentalists on this subject. As a result, many people, institutions, and countries are beginning to have serious reservations and misgivings about the economic age, misgivings intensified by the growing frequency, intensity, and severity of floods, hurricanes, droughts, and fires, excessive carbon emissions, rapidly melting glaciers and ice caps, and numerous other environmental difficulties and ecological disasters. Others are concluding that the "status quo" is no longer acceptable or sustainable because the risks and dangers are too great. And still others feel that things must change and change dramatically if environmental sustainability, human welfare, global harmony, international stability, and the well-being of all species are to be achieved.

Given this situation, it is obvious that an objective assessment of the economic age is imperative at this critical juncture in history.[4] Such an assessment is required for two main reasons. In the first place, it is needed to evaluate the many strengths and benefits as well as the fundamental shortcomings and costs of the economic age, thereby revealing what humanity has done well and done badly. In the second place, it is needed because there is an enormous amount to be learned from this assessment that is helpful in deciding whether the economic age should be maintained in the future, or if a more sustainable, viable, and fulfilling age should be created. If, as John McHale, the well-known futurist, claimed, "people survive, uniquely, by their capacity to act in the present on the basis of *past experience considered in terms of future consequences*,"[5] it only makes sense to determine which direction humanity and the world should be headed in the future based on this assessment of the present and the past.

Without doubt, the creation and development of the economic age is by far the greatest achievement of humanity to date. Not only has it resulted in the production, distribution, and consumption of an astronomical volume of goods and services and the creation of a phenomenal amount of material and monetary wealth, but it has improved living standards and the quality of life very substantially for billions of people throughout the world since it commenced in 1776. It has also produced remarkable advances in virtually all facets of life, from agriculture, industry, science, technology, and communications to health care, medicine, education, the arts, and virtually all other activities and areas of private and public life. This has enabled countless people throughout the world to live much longer and have many more enjoyable experiences—to own beautiful homes and automobiles, enjoy higher levels of income, education, and wealth, benefit from access to health services and medical care, travel widely, work fewer hours, and, in all, live far more pleasant lives than did earlier generations. It is enticing to conclude from this that we should continue living in the economic age and enjoying all its profuse benefits and opportunities.

Regardless of how tempting this is or might be, most indications are that this would be a disastrous mistake. Many of the life-threatening problems that exist in the world today will grow substantially and escalate out of control in the years ahead, especially if humanity continues to place the highest priority on economics, economies, and economic growth, thus consuming the world's scarce resources at an alarming rate and making materialistic demands on nature and the natural environment that expand so rapidly it will soon be impossible to deal with the dire consequences of this. The economic age is designed to produce goods, services, and material and monetary wealth. It is *not* designed to deal with the vast, complex, multidimensional, and dangerous problems that exist throughout the world today.

Consider the devastating effect the economic age is having on the natural environment as the most obvious example. Unfortunately, the natural environment was ignored when the economic age was created and developed in the eighteenth, nineteenth, and twentieth centuries. As a result, it is not possible now to insert the natural environment into the theoretical and practical foundations of the economic age *after the fact*. The architectural equivalent to this would be building a colossal office tower or gigantic condominium on sand or mud. At some point, it is bound to collapse because the stresses and strains are too large and the foundations not strong enough. This conclusion, in and of itself, is sufficient to determine that a very different type of age is required in the future if the environmental crisis and all the other problems facing humanity are to be confronted and resolved.

Countless scientists, environmentalists, and ecologists as well as numerous scientific, environmental, and ecological organizations have been sounding the alarm bell on this problem for a long time now, as well as confirming the fact that there is very little time left to deal with this global crisis before the destruction of the natural environment is inevitable and irreversible. It is now apparent that when people and countries make economics, economies, and economic growth their highest priority and act on their own self-interests, there is no "invisible hand" working to ensure that everything will turn out for the best. Everything depends on us, not on some supernatural power or guiding principle. Not only are we responsible for our own fate, but we are also the perpetrators of our own shortcomings and mistakes.

Lack of ability to deal with the environmental crisis is not the only problem with the economic age that can't be solved. As time goes on, it becomes steadily more apparent that the colossal inequalities that exist in income and wealth throughout the world will not be solved as long as the economic age remains in existence. In fact, they will probably get much worse. This is because the economic age and the theoretical and practical foundations that underlie it are designed largely to benefit wealthy, rich, and powerful classes, corporations, and a small number of countries.

When the economic age was being developed in the first half of the twentieth century, it was commonplace to claim that "welfare economics" and the "trickledown effect" would solve the "distribution problem" by increasing income and wealth for everyone and every country.[6]

Welfare economics was initially created by Alfred Marshall, who in his 1890 book *Principles of Economics* declared that "[p]olitical economy or economics is the study of mankind [humankind] in the ordinary business of life. As such, it examines that part of individual and social behaviour and action which is most closely connected with the production, distribution, and consumption of the material aspects of well-being."[7] Marshall's convictions on this subject were carried much further by Vilfredo Pareto and especially Arthur C. Pigou, who is often regarded as the real founder of welfare economics as an essential component of economics. This is because this component seeks to evaluate how economics affects the welfare and well-being of people, communities, societies, and countries, as well as the development of what is now called the "public sector of economics."

Consistent with convictions like this, there was a great deal of interest in welfare economics before, during, and immediately after the Second World War. As a result, many improvements were made during this time as a result of governmental interventions in the economy that improved people's social welfare and well-being. Such improvements included the creation of income security programs, nutritional assistance programs, and a number of other programs and policies. With Great Britain and the Scandinavian countries taking the lead and capitalizing on the many benefits that accrued from the creation and development of welfare economics, this movement eventually led to the creation of unemployment insurance, workers' compensation, and pension plans, universal health care, and other initiatives that now exist in most countries.

While these developments had a beneficial effect on the distribution of income and wealth at the time and are now permanent fixtures in most countries, interest in welfare economics and commitments like these did not last very long. The importance of such programs is now largely ignored or forgotten. Indeed, much of the recent evidence points in the opposite direction, namely to the fact that over the last few decades wealth has been distributed more and more *unequally* throughout the world. This trend will likely continue if no systemic change or major public intervention is undertaken to prevent it. This is because, as Karl Polanyi pointed out in his book *The Great Transformation: The Political and Economic Origins of Our Time* (1944), the power of the "free-market economy" won out in the end, especially when the "free-market economy" morphed into the "free-market society."[8] Driven largely by the United States as the principal economic powerhouse in the world and by the views of American economists like Milton Friedman, the free market society described by Polanyi now plays a dominant role in the world. In doing so, it contributes to increased inequalities that now exist in the distribution of income and wealth, inequalities that are so evident in all parts of the world.

This problem was confirmed in recent decades ago by the "ninety-nine percent" protests, as well as the escalating evidence showing that the top five percent of the richest people, corporations, and countries in the world now own or control more than ninety percent of the globe's income, wealth, and resources. If this evidence is not compelling enough, think about the fact that in recent years many large corporations have piled up huge profits at the same time many people are struggling to make ends meet in the wake of the COVID-19 pandemic and subsequent price inflation. Or think how difficult it is to argue for an increase in the minimum wage that would amount to only a few hundred dollars a year and how easy it seems to be to raise the annual compensation paid to corporation CEOs by millions of dollars.

Unfortunately, governments have been reluctant to get involved in this problem. Redistributing income and wealth is a very controversial issue and confrontational affair. As a result, they have either ignored the "distribution problem" entirely or claim that this problem will be solved through the trickle-down effect and an even more intense focus on the production and consumption of wealth rather than its distribution. It is claimed that if more wealth is produced, it will eventually filter down to benefit more people. The problem is that the trickle-down effect is not working to any significant extent and more production and consumption means even greater demands will be made on the natural environment and world's scarce resources, thereby broadening and deepening the environmental crisis.

Added to these problems are all the racial, ethnic, tribal, gender, and national conflicts, prejudices, and injustices that exist in the world today. While such things are nothing new, they have become much more pronounced in recent years. Concerns are being voiced by people who have different skin colours and religious beliefs as well as diverse tribal and ethnic origins. Moreover, millions of people were forced to give up their original cultures, languages, identities, and ways of life centuries ago in order to conform to the demands and dictates of colonization and the economic age. Resistance is now manifesting itself in the numerous protests that have taken place in Black, Indigenous, and 2SLGBTQI+ communities. Anger over the slave trade, the creation of residential schools and the burying of Indigenous children in unmarked graves, and the adverse treatment of people of different gender identities displays itself in such actions as pulling down statues dedicated to colonial rulers, and in the unwillingness of colonized people and countries to tolerate colonial procedures and destructive economic and political practices any longer.

What lies at the heart of these problems, and others like them, is that they are increasing at a rapid rate, have outgrown the capacity of the economic age to deal with or contain them, and are threatening to escalate in the future.

Problems like these, and others, indicate that it is necessary to delve even more deeply into the assessment of the economic age. What is it about this age that compels the conclusion that a new type of age is required in the future to deal with all the dangerous and life-threatening problems that exist in the world today?

When the economic age was created in the eighteenth century and developed in the nineteenth and twentieth centuries, economics was unfortunately treated primarily as a free-standing discipline and no consideration was given to its context. As indicated earlier, this was because the natural environment was taken for granted and people were treated as consumers of goods and services and producers of material and monetary wealth rather than as citizens. As a result, not only was the natural environment ignored, but the connection between economics and most other activities and disciplines (apart from agriculture, industry, manufacturing, and technology) was not addressed. This problem was exacerbated by lack of interest in searching for a more accurate interpretation of history, as it was assumed that Marx had solved this problem with his economic interpretation of history. This difficulty was especially evident after economics came to be seen and treated as "the whole" and everything else as a part of the whole or part of economics.

This gave economics a power, prominence, place, and priority in the world and people's and countries' lives that was—and still is—unwarranted. The problem is that economics is *not* the whole in any real or legitimate sense, but rather an extremely important *part* of the whole. While economics plays an essential role in our lives and always will, this does not mean—and should never mean—that economics should take priority over everything.

As a result of today's problems, there has been an incredible outpouring of books, articles, podcasts, newspaper columns, and so forth in recent years about the need to create a different kind of age in the future. For some people, this should be a technological age or an information age or an environmental age. Others call for the dawning of an artistic or spiritual age. While there is a strong feeling throughout the world that a new age is necessary, there is a great deal of uncertainty, debate, and controversy about what *kind* of age it should be.

Is there a way out of this difficult dilemma? Indeed, there is, and the answer lies in the realm of culture, not in the realm of economics. The answer involves seeing and dealing with life from a cultural and holistic perspective rather than an economic and partial perspective, seeing and treating culture rather than economics as the "complex whole" and "total way of life" of people, according culture a central rather than marginal role in the world and people's lives, developing all the diverse cultures of the world and situating them effectively in the natural, historical, global, and cosmic environment, and entering a cultural age and enabling it to flourish in the future.

Just as the origins of the economic age can be traced back to Adam Smith and publication of his book *The Wealth of Nations* in 1776, so the origins of this cultural age can be traced back to Edward Burnett Tylor and the publication of his book *The Origins of Culture* in 1871.[9]

When anthropologists began travelling to different parts of the world in the latter part of the nineteenth and early part of the twentieth century to study different societies, they discovered that people had words for all the specific activities they were involved in as they went about the process of meeting their individual and collective needs and aspirations as well as working out their complex associations with the world. However, what they didn't have and needed desperately was a word that described how all these activities were woven together in different combinations and arrangements to create wholes and total ways of life made up of many interacting parts. Interestingly, the word that was chosen to designate this all-encompassing process and holistic phenomenon was not economics but, rather, **culture**. This was because anthropology as a discipline was seen and defined in terms of *all* aspects and dimensions of people's lives and behaviour, not just some activities such as economics, technology, or politics (among others).

This is why Edward Burnett Tylor, who is regarded as the world's first anthropologist, in 1871 defined culture formally as a discipline and a reality as "that *complex whole* which includes knowledge, belief, art, morals, law, customs, and *any other capabilities and habits acquired by man [woman] as a member of society*."[10] While Tylor defined culture this way for a very specific reason—namely to describe what he and many other anthropologists discovered when they studied people, societies, and countries in depth and on the ground—this definition was largely ignored because the world was preoccupied with the thoughts, ideas, and ideals of economists and all the benefits that could be and were being derived from living in the economic age.

Despite this, culture's holistic ability to focus on the whole and not just a particular part or parts of the whole should not be discounted, ignored, or taken for granted. As Ruth Benedict, the American anthropologist, said in her book *Patterns of Culture*, "The whole, as modern science is insisting in many fields, is not merely the sum of all its parts, but the result of a unique arrangement and inter-relation of the parts that has brought about *a new entity*." She affirmed this statement a few pages later in the book when she stated, "The whole determines its parts, not only their relation but their very nature."[11]

If this idea and definition of culture as the complex whole or total way of life of people had been recognized, adopted, and used when it was first created by Tylor and confirmed by other anthropologists who followed in his footsteps, today's world would be very different. The focus of attention would have been on culture rather than economics. Attention would also have been focused on the fact (revealed by countless anthropologists) that societies and countries that fail to concern themselves with the state of the natural environment run the risk of over-extending themselves, collapsing, and disappearing. The huge statues that stand alone on Easter Island as perpetual reminders of a once vibrant but now vanished civilization serve as a testament to this truth.

What makes ignoring the insights of anthropologists especially unfortunate is the fact that, had they been recognized, developments might have occurred over the past century and a half that would have been not only different in scale or degree but also and more importantly different in substance and kind. Shifting attention from economics and economies to culture and cultures would have directed much more attention to the natural environment. It would also have made it possible to capitalize on Einstein's sage advice that "problems cannot be solved by using the same mode of thinking that caused them in the first place."

Let's not ignore this valuable advice and keen insight into this quintessential problem a second time by failing to recognize the fact that culture has a far more legitimate and authentic claim to being seen and treated as the whole and total way of life of people than does economics. Clearly, we need a different mode of thinking if we are to avoid making this disastrous mistake a second time.

This is not the only advantage to be derived from seeing and dealing with the world from a cultural rather than economic perspective. When culture is perceived and dealt with in the holistic and all-encompassing sense, it is greater than the parts and the sum of these parts because new qualities and capabilities are brought into existence when the whole is created that are not in the parts taken separately or by themselves.

One of the most important of these qualities and capabilities is the ability to see, understand, and deal with the *big picture*, something that was and still is largely missing in the economic age. This all-encompassing capacity of culture not only makes it possible to see the big picture—which is of vital importance to the world of the present and the future—but also all the crucial relationships that exist—*or do not exist*—between the component parts of the big picture. Visualized and dealt with this way, culture provides the context, container, and perspective required to see and come to grips with the major imbalances and disharmonies that exist in the world today, including the relationship between human beings and the natural environment, the material and non-material dimensions of development and life, different genders and races, technology and society, the arts and the sciences, the rich and the poor (whether people or countries), the self and the other, unity and diversity, and many others.

Many of these imbalances and disharmonies have led to devastating swings in the pendulum of power, such as the one between the arts and the sciences which has resulted in demoralizing and painful cuts to many artistic and humanistic activities around the world over the last few decades. While addressing and overcoming imbalances and disharmonies like these will not be easy, obviously the first step lies in seeing these relationships and connections in holistic and harmonious rather than partial, polarized, and disharmonious terms. What partialism, specialization, polarization, and division are and have been to the economic age, holism, the holistic perspective, harmony, and unity must be to the cultural age. This does not mean that economic activities would disappear, since there would always be an essential place for them in the large scheme of things. Rather it means that they would be placed in their proper place by situating them in a much broader, deeper, and more fundamental context.

There is another benefit arising from all this that should also be recognized. It is the fact that when culture and cultures are seen and defined as wholes and total ways of life, it makes it possible to bring things together rather than split them apart—to "unite" rather than "divide"—since this is what *creating wholes and total ways of life is really all about, designed to accomplish, and what is most needed in the world.* This is especially important at the present time because while we have become remarkably skilled at breaking wholes up into parts through specialization, at the same time we have lost our capacity for bringing the parts back together. This explains the enormous amount of fragmentation, division, polarization, and exclusion that exists in today's world.

Looking back over the past, it is now apparent that the holistic perception and definition of culture solves one of the biggest problems of all in the world at present and sets the stage for the creation and development of a cultural age in the future. This is what is meant and understood by the word and idea "culture." While there are many different ways to perceive and define this elusive but evocative word and idea, they can all be boiled down to two very specific manifestations in the end. The first is culture as the arts, humanities, and heritage of history (and much more recently "the cultural industries") that have evolved over more than two thousand years. The second is culture as the "complex whole" or "total way of life" of people, which was perceived and defined originally by Tylor and endorsed by countless anthropologists, sociologists, cultural historians, and practitioners since then.

While there has been much conflict over which of these two perceptions and definitions is the correct one and should prevail in the future, it is evident as a result of the great cultural awakening and many other developments that are taking place in the world that there is really only one basic way to perceive and define culture going forward into the future. It is the all-encompassing, holistic perception and definition of culture as a complex whole or total way of life. However, since culture and cultures as complex wholes and total ways of life in this holistic sense cannot be seen, touched, or handled, this means that the arts, humanities, heritage of history, cultural industries, and certain types of recreational activities such as sports are the principal *gateways* needed to open the doors to culture and cultures in the holistic sense because of their remarkable symbolic significance. This explains the intimate connection between these two related and interconnected ways of seeing, defining, and dealing with culture and cultures.[12]

It is this capacity in culture and cultures to create wholes and total ways of life, see the big picture, and derive the multifarious benefits and rewards that can be reaped from doing so that make it possible to achieve what is most essential of all these days and going forward into the future, namely the need for systemic cultural change, not just partial, piecemeal, or incremental change. What makes matters so promising and exciting is not only the fact that change of this type is possible through viewing culture as a whole and as people's total way of life, but also that more and more people, organizations, and countries throughout the world are realizing this and feel that focusing on culture and cultures in this all-encompassing way makes a great deal of sense. This confirms why culture in this sense is increasingly being seen, understood, recognized, and treated in the world these days as the "change agent" that is necessary to come to grips with the most dangerous and life-threatening problems that exist in the world today.

The impact of developments like this is steadily becoming more evident and relevant in all parts of the world. It is especially apparent, for example, in the systemic change that is going on in the world from elite culture to popular culture, and with this, from the culture of the upper classes to the culture of the masses. It is also evident in the character, coverage, and content of many newspapers, magazines, social media platforms, and other communication media. As this occurs, culture is rapidly becoming more of a mainstream than a marginal activity. As a result, it is more concerned these days with *all* members of societies, countries, and the human family as a whole, and not just *some* members of societies, countries, and wealthy and powerful elites. This is starting to have a profound impact on the world because it is shifting the focus of attention and priority from the "top-down approach to development and life", something which has been in place for many centuries in virtually all parts of the world, to the "bottom-up approach to development and life" that is becoming a more prominent feature of studies and statements like the Jena Declaration on environmental sustainability.[13]

This bottom-up approach provided by culture and cultures possesses the potential to create more peace, harmony, happiness, equality, spirituality, and compassion in the world, as well as to make it possible for all people and all countries to enjoy reasonable standards of living and a decent quality of life without stretching the world's scarce resources and finite carrying capacity to the breaking point. In order to achieve this, culture should no longer be seen or treated as a frill, the icing on the cake, part of the superstructure of societies and countries, or in any other misleading and derogatory fashion. On the contrary, it should be seen and dealt with as the centrepiece of societies, countries, and the world, the foundation of cultural development and policy as well as people's lives, and the vehicle that is needed to create a very different life-course for humanity. Rather than seeing culture as a *consequence of change*—as has traditionally been the case—it should now be seen as the *cause of change* with the capacity to create a cultural age and enable it to flourish in the years, decades, and possibly even centuries ahead.

This does not mean that the very essential role that economics, economies, and economic growth play in our lives will be disregarded or dismissed. What it does mean, however, is that culture and cultures are the real foundations of existence and essence of life and living. This is needed not only to correct the mistakes of the past, but also to ensure that economics, economies, and economic growth are properly situated in a broader and deeper context and serve *environmental, cultural, human, humane, and ecological functions and not just economic, financial, commercial, corporate, and technological requirements.* Without this, the environmental crisis and the other acute and life-threatening problems that exist in the world will not be solved and humanity will continue on its present path towards devastation and destruction rather than renewal and revitalization.

Ever since Tylor visualized and defined culture as the complex whole or total way of life of people, it has become steadily more apparent that culture and cultures are the activities needed to pull everything together and create a great deal more compassion, cooperation, well-being, harmony, and spirituality in the world. Clearly, we have only scratched the surface of the rich potential that culture possesses to create the conditions and lay the foundation for the creation, development, and flourishing of a cultural age.

This is the new narrative that is manifesting itself today as a result of the great cultural awakening that is taking place in the world and opening the doors to a new age. It all starts with people—*all* people and not just some people—as well as with culture as the centrepeice of people's lives. From here, it radiates outwards and upwards from children, parents, homes, families, towns, cities, regions, and countries to the ways of life of other species, the world, the universe, and the need to address a number of crucial cultural requirements. Now that the signs have been read and the stage has been set for the transition from the present economic age to a future cultural age, we can direct our attention to these most important matters.

Chapter Two

Culture as the Centrepiece of People's Lives

People are culture... Culture explains what it means to be
human, and is all the myriad ways we create, communicate,
identify, individuate, and connect with others.
—Meg Pier[1]

After living for decades with a high degree of predictability about
what life would be like in the future, we are now confronted with very
little certainty about the future and what the "new normal" will be.

Now that the COVID-19 pandemic has been brought under control, will we return to our usual jobs, lifestyles, and ways of life? Or will we be compelled to find new jobs and create new lifestyles and ways of life in the years and decades ahead? And what about having to deal on a regular basis with sweltering heat, devastating storms, intense wildfires, and a great deal more social unrest? Will the outbreak of a new pandemic or a resurgence of COVID-19 mean not being able to hold the hands of our loved ones, not being able to embrace our children, parents, and grandparents, and maintaining a safe distance from our friends, neighbours, and colleagues?

Even before the COVID-19 pandemic, there were indications that all was not right in the world. Not only were we losing the battle with climate change and experiencing greater inequalities in income and wealth, but there were also more ethnic, racial, gender, and religious clashes as well as more conflicts between different countries, cultures, and civilizations. These problems, and others, have been growing more acute over the last few years. And always waiting in the wings is the ever broadening and deepening environmental crisis, which will necessitate major changes in our way of life in the years ahead.

Despite this, there are many positive indications that all is not doom and gloom in the world. Countless people, groups, and countries are working diligently and together to come to grips with the dangerous problems and complex challenges confronting us today. Moreover, new strategies, tactics, techniques, and technologies are being designed and cultivated to address these and other issues and concerns, thereby confirming the fact that "necessity is the mother of invention," as it has been on countless occasions over the course of human history.

Added to this is the profuse outpouring of caring, sharing, compassion, and empathy that has been evident in the world, as well as the willingness on the part of millions of people, both health care workers and others, to take major risks and endure incredible hardships and debilitating working conditions to assist people suffering from disease, the ravages of war, and other troubles.

Another development taking place in the world at present is equally reassuring. People in all parts of the world have used this difficult time to assess their lives more intensively than they did previously. Others are deciding that their present ways of life are not sustainable due to the devastating effects they are having on the natural environment and other people, deciding for themselves that dramatic changes are required in their way of life. And still others have realized their lives have not brought them the happiness and fulfillment they expected, and are embarking on new career paths and employment opportunities.

Regardless of what approach we take to the present situation and prospects for the future, one thing is certain. We will never be able to make the changes we feel are needed, or put ourselves in the strongest position to confront the problems, challenges, and opportunities we will be presented with in the future, without taking stock of our lives at a much deeper and more profound level. This includes assessing the overall nature, character, and meaning of our lives, not just specific or selected aspects of our lives, as well as deciding for ourselves what the new normal will be and what we want to achieve in the years ahead.

While most people don't think about such matters very often or in a sustained and systematic way, every person in the world is compelled to combine all the various parts of their lives together to form a "complex whole" or "total way of life" made up of many different parts. It doesn't matter whether they are carpenters or prime ministers, bank presidents or pipefitters, where they live in the world, or what their socio-economic circumstances and educational credentials happen to be. Every person in the world must combine all the various elements of their lives into a meaningful whole, regardless of whether these elements are concerned with their bodies, brains, minds, souls, spirits, and senses, or all the diverse economic, social, political, artistic, scientific, technological, recreational, spiritual, environmental, and other activities they take part in over the course of their lives. There is no escaping it, regardless of whether this examination is done well or badly, what part of the world people live in, or how they deal with the various aspects of their lives.

This holistic requirement that all people must address is obviously not what Edward Burnett Tylor had in mind when he defined culture formally as "that complex whole which includes knowledge, belief, art, morals, law, custom and any other capabilities and habits acquired by man [woman] as a member of society." While Tylor defined culture this way for a specific purpose—to describe what he and other anthropologists encountered when they travelled to different parts of the world to study people, groups, and societies in totality and on the ground—this holistic definition of culture nonetheless applies to all people in the world.

While this all-encompassing definition of culture is not the one most people are familiar with, it is rapidly gaining traction and has powerful implications for everyone. This is because every person in the world lives a *cultural life* in the holistic sense, one made up of myriad parts. They do this not only in their thoughts and ideas, but also in their deeds, actions, and daily practices, even if they are not aware or conscious of it.

Think about it for a moment. Regardless of how much time people devote to developing their faculties and how much they are engaged in different types of activities—some may spend most of their time developing their minds, bodies, souls, spirits, brains, or senses, while others may spend most of their time engaging in activities such as politics, social affairs, the stock market, religion, recreation, science, technology, economic and financial matters, education, the arts, the environment, sports, and so forth—the fact remains that all people are compelled to live cultural lives in this all-encompassing sense. Not only is this consistent with the definition of culture proposed by Tylor, but it is consistent with what James Feibleman had in mind when he said, "The study of culture properly begins with the study of the cultural elements of the individual."[2] It is also in keeping with what Ruth Benedict meant when she said that people and their personalities are really "cultures writ small."[3]

It follows from this that culture in this all-encompassing holistic sense is the centrepiece of people's lives and personalities. Realizing this is *the* most important step we can take as people in developing our lives and personalities if we have not already done so. Our lives as wholes are greater than their parts and the sum of those parts, because new elements and qualities are brought into existence when these wholes are created that do not exist in the parts taken separately. Everything emanates from this fact and depends on it. Admitting this and acting on it is imperative if people want to put themselves in the strongest possible position to come to grips with the complex problems and limitless possibilities they are and will be presented with in life. No other development compares with this. It is foundational in character. A fundamental transformation or paradigm shift in people's lives is required, from seeing and developing one's life as a smorgasbord of separate and independent parts, to seeing and developing it as a complex, organic, dynamic, and integral whole and overall way of life.

No one has recognized the need to understand the importance of culture in this foundational sense more than Meg Pier, founder of the organization People Are Culture (PAC) as well as the Flip the Lens project. Pier's website as well as online magazine and book provide people everywhere in the world and in every walk of life with opportunities to tell their own stores about their lives *as cultures*. In doing so, PAC provides a cultural perspective on life in general and people's lives in particular, presenting stories about how people's own personal cultures have evolved and enabling them to tell these stories in their own voices. In Pier's view, PAC's organizational philosophy is that culture "provides ways to both express our individuality and to see ourselves in others ... [it] is the transmission line that makes possible cooperation, peace, and prosperity." Many of these stories, and more of the underlying philosophy of her valuable organization, are set out in PAC's recently published book, *What is Culture? Why Does It Matter?* as well as on the organization's website. The more recent Flip the Lens project puts the camera in the hands of the subjects of stories rather than storytellers.[4]

Such initiatives not only confirm the fact that culture is the centrepiece of people's lives and essence of their existence, but also that all people are unique and "one of a kind," creating their own individual cultures and stories about them by linking together all their faculties, all the different activities they are involved in, and all their experiences in life, to form a distinct and dynamic whole made up of many parts that is theirs and theirs alone. At the same time, although every person lives a life that is distinctive and unique, culture is common to *all* people and possesses the potential (if handled properly) to bring people together rather than split them apart.

Once culture is recognized as the centrepiece of people's lives and the requisite holistic transformation or paradigm shift has been made (if required), where do we go from here? Surely there is only one place to go and that is to see and understand how essential it is for people to develop their lives not just as wholes—essential as this is—but also as *harmonious* wholes. This is an ideal that all people should be striving to achieve, because it is the key to experiencing a great deal of happiness, fulfillment, good health, creativity, meaning, and authenticity in life. It is also consistent with the ancient Chinese proverb that states, "The beginning of wisdom lies in calling things by their right names."

The nineteenth-century cultural scholar Matthew Arnold is usually credited with being the first person in the world to discuss this matter in some detail, as well as in realistic, idealistic, and holistic terms. When Arnold talked about being a "whole person" in his book *Culture and Anarchy*, it was not just seeing people's lives as wholes that he had in mind, but also achieving the *"harmonious expansion of all the powers which make the beauty and worth of human nature, [which] is not consistent with the over-development of any one power at the expense of the rest."*[5] This makes the development of "harmonious" rather than "disharmonious" wholes in our lives the greatest and most important challenge and requirement in life.

In order to achieve this, Arnold believed it is important for people to avoid falling into the trap of developing only one or two of their faculties, or developing some of their faculties to the detriment or exclusion of others. He also believed that culture is an inward condition of the mind, body, soul, and spirit, and not just an outward condition of mechanical and material civilization, as well as an active rather than passive affair.

If people achieve harmony between all the different facets, factors, forces, and powers that make up their lives—as well as the multiplicity of activities they are involved in on a daily basis and all their human and sensorial faculties, successes, failures, and capabilities—it is very likely that they will experience a great deal of harmony, balance, order, synergy, and synchronicity in their lives in both realistic and idealistic terms. If they are unable to do so, they will still live cultural lives in the holistic sense. However, they may experience disharmonies, imbalances, and disorders and be compelled to deal with all the complications and difficulties that result from this.

It is hard to see how people's lives can be harmonious wholes in the all-encompassing sense without their becoming deeply engaged in the arts, whether in the classical or popular sense or through specific art forms. For the evidence is overwhelming and conclusive.[6] If people want to live happy, healthy, fulfilling, and harmonious lives, it is essential to make the arts a quintessential part of this. For the arts, like culture and cultures, are not frills, luxuries, or the icing on the cake, but rather the elixir that is needed for people to live meaningful, well-rounded, and synchronized lives at each and every stage in the life process, from the earliest signs of life to its final days.

What is it about the arts that makes them so empowering a way for people to live their lives as harmonious wholes? It pays to examine some of the reasons at this stage in the book. The arts make remarkable contributions to people's lives in numerous ways, which helps to explain why there has been an intimate bond between the arts and culture dating back thousands of years, from the dawn of human life on earth and the many drawings etched on the walls and ceilings of caves in France, Indonesia, China, and elsewhere, to the present.

First and foremost, every work of art, like culture and every culture, is a complex whole made up of many different parts, regardless of whether it is a painting, play, musical composition, poem, story, film, or anything else, since all of the various parts are woven together in specific combinations and arrangements to create a whole that is greater than those parts—much like people's lives. New elements are brought into existence when artistic wholes are created that are not in the parts. This makes the arts an ideal vehicle for seeing and understanding things in holistic and harmonious rather than partial or disharmonious terms, because artists are concerned with how the parts are woven together in different combinations and arrangements to form wholes that are blended and balanced rather than partial and polarized.

And this is not all. The satisfaction that is derived from works of art over the course of people's lives is immense, especially if people open their hearts and minds to such works and allow them to penetrate into the interiors of their very being and consciousness. There is simply no substitute for this. Fortunately experiencing the arts does not have to cost a great deal of money. While attending classical concerts or taking dance, singing, or music lessons can be costly, there are many ways to enjoy the arts that are not too expensive if people take the time to search them out and take advantage of them. The fulfillment that comes from the arts is profuse, as confirmed by people's faces whenever we see them enjoying a concert, play, dance, or some other work of art.

Experiencing the arts is much easier to do today than it was in the past, due largely to major developments in contemporary technology and digital communications. There is hardly a person anywhere in the world today who is not able to access the arts through radio, television, film, or some digital device. This ability to gain access to works of art of the highest calibre by virtually every artist and arts organization in the world—past or present, ancient or modern, Asian, African, South American, Caribbean or North American, European, and Middle Eastern—is an achievement of monumental proportions, as people everywhere in the world are discovering to their delight.

People's enjoyment of the arts is enhanced when they become involved as participants and not just as members of the audience or casual observers. The ability to play a musical instrument, sing in a choir, perform in a dramatic production, write a poem or short story, draw or paint a picture, dance in city streets, collaborate in making a film or television program, take evocative photographs, or fashion gifts from small bits of paper is an asset of major proportions. There is simply no substitute for it, and it can be done at any stage in life, as children are learning at home and in school and elderly people are experiencing in seniors' homes and retirement centres.

The arts are also valuable vehicles for developing people's communication skills and abilities. They make it possible for people to speak more clearly, write more convincingly, and express their thoughts and ideas more precisely. This is enriched by the fact that the arts are ideal vehicles for expressing people's feelings and emotions. It is impossible to participate in any artistic activity without learning to express one's feelings and emotions in sensitive, moving, and compelling ways, as well as to connect with other people on a deeper, richer, and more fundamental level. While the arts can be provocative at times—and must be if they are to fulfill their mandate and responsibilities—the feelings and emotions evoked through the arts are usually far more positive than negative. The arts seldom injure people, destroy things, or produce irrational or violent acts of behaviour.

Developing people's communication skills and abilities and helping them express their feelings and emotions are not the only advantages to be derived from involvement and participation in the arts. The potential also exists for developing many other skills and abilities. While some art forms are personal and individual in nature—the visual and material arts or crafts, for example—others are more collaborative and collective. Take drama, music, and opera, for instance. It is impossible to put on a play, perform a symphony, or stage an opera, ballet, or dance without engaging in a great deal of cooperation and teamwork. This cooperation and teamwork extends all the way from working with other people on the creation of sets and props and rehearsing scenes and movements, to practicing parts and putting on final performances. Through the preparation and presentation of works of art, people learn to work collaboratively in the realization of common causes, goals, and concerns, thereby developing cooperative abilities that are in great demand throughout the world today. This also requires a great deal more social cohesion and human inter-action, counteracting the isolation and loneliness that often results from the use of modern technology and is such a real issue in the world today.

There is also much to be learned about life, living, and the world around us from the arts. Not only do the arts open up vast vistas and fertile avenues for exploration, discovery, learning, and education, but they provide an incredible window on the world and everything con-tained in it. Everything is there in one form or another: nature, the human species, other species, countries, cultures, history, geography, time, space, place, past, present, future, the world, the cosmos....

Since the arts engage the mind, body, heart, soul, spirit, brain, in-tellect, and senses, they provide an excellent way to bring all people's faculties together to form a harmonious whole. This makes people more balanced within themselves as well as in tune with other people and the world. This is why artists, arts organizations, and the arts have been and often are seen as "the antennae of the world" as well as in the vanguard of the movement to create "the whole person."

While all arts forms have an essential role to play in helping peo-ple to develop their lives as harmonious wholes, there is a great deal of evidence that music has a special role to play. There is something about music that reaches into the hearts and souls of people. Music broadens, deepens, enhances, and enriches people's personalities and lives in numerous ways, regardless of what type of music they prefer. This belief can be traced back to classical times. The Greek philoso-pher Plato was a strong advocate of the important role of music at all ages and stages in life. Not only did he say, "I would teach children music, physics, and philosophy, but most importantly music, for the patterns in music and all the arts are the keys to learning," but he believed that "musical training is a more potent instrument than any other, because rhythm and harmony find their way into the inward places of the soul, on which they mightily fasten." In *The Republic* Plato stated, "Music is a moral law. It gives soul to the universe, wings to the mind, flight to the imagination, and charm and gaiety to life and to everything." In fact, this book is filled with references to the powerful role music can and does play in the development of people, their personalities, and their lives, as well as the development of societies and the ideal state.

Recognition of the enormous potential of music is not confined to Plato or classical times. Over the course of history, many individuals and institutions have recognized music's unique role and crucial importance. In the nineteenth century, for instance, the American poet Henry Wadsworth Longfellow called music "the universal language of mankind" and the Danish author Hans Christian Andersen declared that "where words fail, music speaks." Both felt that music possesses certain characteristics that make it even more important than language in many ways. Contemporary research is revealing why it is that music plays such a strong role in our lives. Using functional magnetic resonance imaging (fMRI), scientists are discovering that music provides "a total workout for the brain," whereas most other activities in life provide only a "partial workout." Music performs this role by stimulating not only the brain and blood flow, but also the senses and other human faculties. It also reduces anxiety, high blood pressure, and pain, improves sleep, and enhances mood, motivation, mental alertness, and memory. As such, it is an ideal activity for seniors and people suffering from many different types of illnesses and diseases, as well as for children, teenagers, and adults for many of the same reasons.

Findings like these are confirmed by many institutions, such as the International Arts + Mind Lab at the Brain Science Institute at Johns Hopkins University's School of Medicine, which will be discussed in detail later in this book. Similar work has been carried out by Isabelle Peretz at the University of Montreal and Robert Zatorre at McGill University, who together created the International Laboratory for Brain, Music, and Sound Research in order to "study music as a portal into the most complex aspects of human brain functions." And this is not all. Jonathan Burdette, a neuroradiologist at Wake Forest Baptist Medical Center, has conducted numerous studies on the effects of music on people. His studies revealed that "it doesn't matter if it's Bach, the Beatles, Brad Paisley, or Bruno Mars. Your favorite music likely triggers a similar type of activity in your brain as other people's favorites do in their brains. Music is primal. It affects all of us, but in very personal, unique ways. Your interaction with music is different than mine, but it's still powerful."

We have all been so touched by music at certain times and places in our lives that we feel we have transcended the world and entered a very special place. Just as Elizabeth Barrett Browning asked, "How do I love thee? Let me count the ways," so a similar question can be asked (and answered) about music. And the answer is the same: Music affects our personalities and lives in myriad ways and satisfies our every mood, moment, and situation. It also invigorates, stimulates, and motivates us, activates, agitates, and challenges us, soothes and relaxes us, excites and inspires us, enables us to soar to great heights, gives us a sense of awe, wonder, and ecstasy, is nostalgic, helps us express our love, emotions, and compassion, connects us with other people, makes it possible to share experiences, and depicts specific places and events in the world.

We all have our favourite pieces of music. I can't resist mentioning several musical masterpieces that rank very high on my list. They include the second movement of Rachmaninoff's *Piano Concerto No. 2*, Emil von Sauer's *Cavatina* from his *Piano Concerto No. 1*, Chopin's *Étude in A-Flat Major, Op. 25, No. 1 (Aeolian Harp)* and *Ballade No. 1 in G Minor*, Massenet's *Méditation* from *Thaïs*, the second movement of Beethoven's *Violin Concerto*, Wagner's *Prelude* to his opera *Lohengrin*, and Bach's *Prelude No. 1 in C Major*. Whenever I hear the first few bars of any of these pieces, and many others that I could mention, I am immediately reminded of Plato's profound statement on this subject.

While music may play an especially powerful role in people's lives, it is not the only art form that is able to do so. In fact, every art form possesses its own distinct capacities and capabilities: painting through the use of colour and perspective; poetry by stating matters as simply and concisely as possible; other forms of literature as well as drama, opera, television, and film by telling captivating stories; ballet and other modes of dance through movement as well as the use of splendid costumes and sets; and architecture through the use of mass, texture, and interesting shapes.[7] My personal favourites include Claude Monet's painting *The Water Lily Pond*, Boris Pasternak's classic novel *Doctor Zhivago*, Richard Attenborough's memorable movie *Gandhi*, the incredible Pink Mosque in Iran, Maya Angelou's courageous and candid poem *Still I Rise*, and many others. No doubt you have your own personal favourites as well.

Speaking of Angelou's popular poem *Still I Rise*, it is particularly helpful in explaining and understanding the many developments that are taking place at this time in different parts of the world, including the countless artistic activities and achievements of numerous Black and Indigenous people, as well as people from colonized countries going through a period of intense and expressive decolonization. There has been a phenomenal increase in creativity, imagination, and achievement in all areas of the arts as a result of this. This includes artists and arts organizations in Australia, New Zealand, Canada, the United States, Africa, Asia, Latin America, and the Caribbean that are involved in reclaiming their original cultures and cultural identities, learning about and cherishing their traditional languages, costumes, rituals, and dress, and confirming the importance to the world of their sustainable ways of life and spiritual beliefs.

Developments like this are relevant because the arts are essential in people's lives and the cultural age primarily as *ends in themselves*—ends that have an incredible amount to do with people's perceptions of the world, identities, values, value systems, and sense of belonging—but also as *means to other ends* due to their ability to act as gateways to culture and cultures as a result of their symbolic significance and transformational value. Hopefully, this will bring an end to the current tendency to see and treat the arts largely as forms of entertainment, generators of economic activity, and producers of financial and commercial benefits.

With this in mind, let's return to Matthew Arnold and his book *Culture and Anarchy* for a moment longer in order to acquaint ourselves with his conviction that people's lives should not only be wholes and harmonious wholes—essential as this is—but also *altruistic wholes*.

To achieve this, Arnold felt it is necessary for people to get deeply involved in sharing and diffusing the world's best knowledge, wisdom, ideas, and ideals. This was important according to Arnold because knowledge, wisdom, ideas, and ideals possess the power and potential to change the world for the better, and consequently should be shared by all people and countries, not just by wealthy elites and privileged countries. This is also important because altruism is essential in opening the doors to a great deal more spirituality, empathy, and compassion in the world, something which will be discussed in more detail in a later chapter in this book. Here is what Arnold had to say about the importance of altruism in people's lives:

> The great men [and women] of culture are those who have had a passion for *diffusing*, for making prevail, for carrying from one end of society to the other, the best knowledge, the best ideas of their time; who have laboured to divest knowledge of all that was harsh, uncouth, difficult, abstract, professional, exclusive; to humanize it, to make it efficient outside the clique of the cultivated and learned, yet still remaining the *best* knowledge and thought of the time and a true source, therefore, of sweetness and light.[8]

With Arnold's views on this subject in place, let's examine what is needed for people to develop their lives as harmonious and altruistic wholes in idealistic and realistic terms. In regard to the former, it is helpful to focus attention on the thoughts, ideas, and ideals of another prominent cultural scholar—Johan Huizinga—since he had a great deal to say about this matter. This is most apparent in the profound insight he provided into the nature of the world and the development of our personalities and lives:

> The realities of economic life, of power, of technology, of everything conducive to man's [humanity's] material well-being, must be balanced by strongly developed spiritual, intellectual, moral, and aesthetic values.[9]

Huizinga's insight applies not only to the world at large but to people's personalities and lives and how they should be developed and cultivated. Huizinga looked at the world and people's lives and personalities from the holistic perspective provided by culture and then used this to examine many cultures in the world in general and the lives and personalities of people in particular, subjecting them to rigorous evaluation. In making this statement, Huizinga put his finger on one of the most essential challenges facing all of us at present and going forward into the future. Clearly the *more* time, energy, and attention that is devoted individually and collectively to "the realities of economic life, of power, of technology, of everything conductive to man's [humanity's] well-being," the *less* time, energy, and attention is available to devote to creating "strongly developed spiritual, intellectual, moral, and aesthetic values." Over the last century, this has caused the pendulum to swing steadily throughout the world *towards* the development of the material, quantitative, physical, and technological dimensions of life, and steadily *away* from the development of the non-material, qualitative, human, aesthetic, spiritual, and altruistic dimensions of life. This has produced a great deal of disharmony, disorder, and imbalance in the world and in people's lives, regardless of where they live in the world, what they work at, and how they live their lives and develop their personalities.

This has been especially apparent over the last five or six decades. While these developments have produced substantial improvements in the material dimensions of life and living for billions of people, as indicated earlier, they have also had a disastrous effect on the natural environment and the overall development of people's lives. This is confirmed by significant decreases in attendance at religious services and involvement in religious institutions in some parts of the world, and by learning systems that are more concerned with preparing students for consuming goods and services, seeking consumer satisfaction, and producing material and monetary wealth than providing for a well-rounded education, opportunities for life-long learning, and human fulfillment. This has also been accompanied by a decline in ethical values that has been so serious and conspicuous over the last few decades that the World Commission on Culture and Development made the need for a "new global ethics"—rather than the development of the arts, humanities, and cultural industries, as is usually the case—the first chapter and principal priority in its report *Our Creative Diversity* published in 1995.[10] These factors, together with other developments, explain why the global situation has deteriorated a great deal in ethical terms and is threatening to continue to do so in the future.

Fortunately, Huizinga's insight into this situation also provided us with a way out of this predicament and not just an explanation of it, thereby addressing Gregory Bateson's principal concern that "we do not know enough about how the present will lead us into the future."

As Huizinga indicates, more attention should be focused on, and a much higher priority should be accorded to, the creation and development of the spiritual, intellectual, moral, and aesthetic aspects of life, as well as all the diverse activities that are concerned with these aspects. Not only will this cause the pendulum to swing back towards the centre where it rightly belongs, but it also provides the key that is needed to create more balance and harmony in people's lives in the individual sense as well as in the collective and international sense. Coming to grips with the world's most demanding problems, as well as making it possible to achieve sustainable development and assist people with the enhancement of their personalities, characters, and lives in more holistic, altruistic, and harmonious terms, will not be possible, however, without getting more deeply immersed in artistic, humanistic, ethical, and spiritual activities, as well as placing a much higher priority on these activities in the overall scheme of things.

As fortune would have it, Huizinga also provided us with another keen insight into this matter as well as a way out when he observed:

A culture which no longer can integrate the diverse pursuits of men [people] into a whole, which cannot restrain men [people] through a guiding set of norms, has lost its center and has lost its style. It is threatened by the exuberant over-growth of its separate components. It then needs a pruning knife, a human decision to focus once again on the essentials of culture and cut back on the luxuriant but dispensable.... If such harmony of cultural functions is present, it will reveal itself as order, strong structure, style, and rhythmic life of the society in question.[11]

What is true for all the diverse cultures and countries in the world is also true for individuals. Concerted actions of this type will lead to investing a great deal more time, effort, energy, and funding into the development of artistic, humanistic, educational, ethical, and spiritual activities that will yield vital improvements and achievements in altruism, creativity, imagination, innovation, ingenuity, and entrepreneurship. This will also lead to people working cooperatively in the realization of common causes and objectives, and cultivating skills and abilities that are transferable and transportable across a wide spectrum of possibilities. In the long run we might expect to see the creation of many more educational courses on the different cultures and civilizations of the world, a greater appreciation for the diversity of cultural expressions, countless more opportunities for intergenerational, intercultural, cross-cultural, and civilizational dialogues and exchanges, a flowering in international relations, greater commitment to such human values and ideals as caring, sharing, compassion, empathy, and generosity, as well as more equality, justice, order, trust, and stability in the world.

Many events over the last few decades have confirmed that people are capable of manifesting a great deal of altruism and therefore moving in this direction. This was apparent, for example, in the responses people made to the attacks on the Twin Towers in New York City and the Pentagon in Washington on September 11, 2001; in how people came to grips with the COVID-19 pandemic; as well as in the many protests to end systemic racism. During these difficult times, countless people exhibited more concern for other people and their health, welfare, well-being, and safety than their own, put a great deal more emphasis on assisting people who were sick, elderly, in distress, or suffering from deadly diseases, and especially expressed more love, kindness, forgiveness, and sensitivity.

And this is not all. Artists and arts organizations have also brought their heartfelt messages and expressive talents and accomplishments to the attention of others, despite the fact that during the pandemic many of them had lost their sources of income and were compelled to create projects and technologies at their own expense in order to communicate their feelings and passions. And what has been true for artists, arts organizations, and the arts generally is also true of schools, churches, mosques, synagogues, hospitals, seniors' homes, and all the millions of people and organizations that are involved in organizations and activities like these. Many such organizations, as well as countless people in the food and entertainment industries as well as in numerous other fields and walks of life, have given freely of their time, talents, and expertise to provide badly needed services and the basic necessities of life free of charge or at reduced rates to help people who need it most or are experiencing more than their fair share of pain, discomfort, and suffering.

This raises two of the most important questions of all. Will these conspicuous outpourings of kindness, generosity, humanism, altruism, and compassion be sustained and manifested by people and organizations in the future? Or will they fade into the background and possibly even disappear once the pandemic recedes in the rear-view mirror?

The latter possibility explains why it is imperative to keep the pendulum swinging in the direction of more kindness, humanism, altruism, and holism, as well as to make greater commitments to achieving sustainable development and environmental well-being everywhere in the world. This is especially important with respect to people who are concerned about and committed to developing their lives as balanced, harmonious, and altruistic wholes, as well as aspiring to be "whole people" in the fullest and most complete and compelling sense of this term. If people can be holistic, compassionate, altruistic, and humane, as well as manifest these qualities in their lives and personalities on a regular basis, they will send out a strong signal and clear message that the world is moving in the right direction.

In order to achieve this, the first step in the process is obviously to ensure that culture is the centrepiece of people's lives and the cornerstone of their personalities and character development. This will make it possible for people to create more harmony, balance, order, and awareness in their own lives, as well as enable others to enjoy reasonable standards of living, a decent quality of life, and genuine fulfillment, contentment, happiness, and well-being. Margaret Mead expressed this requirement most eloquently and effectively when she said, "Even the small children were collaborators in an undertaking that transcended both me and them—the attempt to understand enough about culture so that all of us, equally members of humankind, can understand ourselves and take our future and the future of our descendants safely in our hands."[12]

What is true for people is also true for other species. As more research takes place in the natural sciences, it is apparent that culture in the holistic sense is not only the centrepiece of our lives, but the centrepiece of their lives as well. Not only are the lives of members of other species wholes in much the same way as our own lives, but much contemporary evidence reveals the lives of members of other species are filled with pleasure and pain as well as happiness and sorrow just as our lives are, and that other species create cultures in much the same way we do—as wholes and total ways of life made up of many parts.

Having dealt with the central role that culture plays in our lives as individuals, we can now climb the next step up the cultural ladder, and consider what culture means for children, parents, homes, families, and the cultures they create. This is without doubt one of—if not *the*—most important steps to take, because it involves getting people's lives off to the best possible beginning.

The distinguished musician and international cultural advocate Yo-Yo Ma provided us with an ideal start in this regard. In an article in *Time* magazine he stated:

> Every generation has a chance—an obligation—to do better, to imagine and create a world that works for all of us.
>
> To me, doing better begins with culture—the point at which the arts, sciences, and society intersect....
>
> If you do not consider yourself a cultural being, I challenge you to think differently: we are all cultural citizens, and culture will be the engine of our reconstruction, as it has always been. We have come back to this first principle again and again in times of fracture, that culture leads us to seek truth, build trust, and act in service of one another. Culture is the foundation on which we will imagine and build a world in which we reaffirm our commitment to equality and safety for all, we act with empathy, and we can always do better.[13]

Chapter Three

Children, Parents, Homes, and Families

Culture is learned as a child, and as children we each learned
from those around us a particular set of rules, beliefs,
priorities, and expectations that moulded our world into a
meaningful whole. *That is our culture.*
—Mary E. Clark[1]

Given all the life-threatening problems that exist in the world, there couldn't be a better time to address one of the most important requirements of all with respect to humanity and the world. It is the lives of children, parents, homes, and families. For how children in all parts of the world are brought up is bound to have a profound influence on the state of the world and prospects for the future. We can't expect to experience more peace, stability, sustainability, harmony, and well-being in the world—and less hostility, anger, conflict, and war—without giving a great deal more attention and awarding a much higher priority to how children are raised.

Many people believe children's first experiences with culture and cultures occur after they are born. However, they actually occur when babies are still in the womb. These experiences are shaped by the customs, traditions, beliefs, and practices that prevail in different communities and cultures with respect to pregnancy and childbirth. This is when mothers provide loving experiences for their as yet unborn babies by playing beautiful music for them, singing songs, reading stories, and whispering heartfelt messages to them.

Once they are born, babies and small children learn many things about the culture and cultures they are born into as well as about their parents, families, and family cultures during the first few years of their lives, due largely to their insatiable appetite for experiences, innate curiosity, ability to soak up information like sponges, and, most notably, pick things up at an astounding rate. By the time they are six or seven, most children have likely inherited, acquired, and cultivated many traits, customs, traditions, languages, values, rituals, and habits of their cultures from their parents, grandparents, other family members, relatives, friends, and others. This results from watching, listening, mimicking, and digesting everything they see, hear, and come into contact with, as well as acquiring specific ways of acting, behaving, and doing things.

This is also true for the likes, dislikes, and attitudes they have towards different people, groups, races, countries, and cultures. This should be constantly borne in mind by parents and other family members when they engage in discussions and conversations in the home because their feelings, emotions, attitudes, and comments on matters like this can be, and often are, picked up by their children at this formative stage in their lives. Like positive experiences and likes, the negative ones are also part of children's heritages, as well as the "cultural baggage" they carry with them for long periods of time and possibly even for the remainder of their lives, especially if this is not recognized and dealt with effectively. This makes children's upbringing and experiences in their homes and with their families and family members during their first few years exceedingly important in the overall scheme of things. We neglect this at our peril. As stated in UNESCO's Constitution, "since wars begin in the minds of men [people], it is in the minds of men [people] that the defenses of peace must be constructed."[2]

Whenever I reflect on matters like this, my thoughts are cast back to my own upbringing and experiences early in life. The bulk of these experiences were created by my parents and at home, as is the case for most children. As I look back on these experiences now, I realize how fortunate I was to have the parents I had and the many valuable experiences and opportunities they provided for me and my brother Murray when we were young.

Although my parents had very little money and no formal education in some of the most important areas in life such as the arts, humanities, and heritage of history, my mother taught herself to play the piano and violin when she was young and ended up playing the violin in a community orchestra and the piano at home and during Sunday school classes at the church we attended on a regular basis when I was very young. My father taught himself to play the piano, too, as well as to paint pictures. He had a natural gift for the visual arts, and produced many beautiful watercolor and pastel paintings that hang in our home today. He also enjoyed listening to classical music a great deal, and would often play the music of Rachmaninoff, Chopin, Beethoven, Schumann, and many other composers on the record player in our living room, as well as listen to Marian Anderson sing "He's Got the Whole World in His Hands," Kathleen Ferrier sing "What Is Life to Me Without Thee," and Jussi Björling and Robert Merrill singing the famous duet *"Au fond du temple saint"* from Bizet's opera *The Pearl Fishers*.

My parents were anxious to see to it that Murray and I had many experiences in the arts when we were young. I can still recall with great fondness my parents taking us to art galleries, museums, concerts, and theatrical productions. I also remember my mother reading bedtime stories to us from *Journeys through Bookland* that were part of a universal anthology created just for children that included some of the finest literary masterpieces from around the world. While neither of my parents had first-generation relatives in Toronto where we lived—they had grown up in western Canada and only moved to Toronto much later in life—my mother made sure that Murray and I had some exposure to more distant relatives who happened to live in or near Toronto in order to provide us with a good sense of our ancestral heritage on her side of the family.

When I was older, my parents provided art classes for Murray and myself at the Art Gallery of Toronto (now the Art Gallery of Ontario), weekly piano lessons paid for in monthly installments, and enrolled us in a choir at Grace Church-on-the-Hill. This turned out to be one of the most important experiences—if not *the* most important—in both our lives. This is confirmed by the fact that Murray became a well-known composer, music educator, and originator of the soundscape concept and the discipline of acoustic ecology later in life, and I have spent the bulk of my life working in the arts and cultural field, making the case that the arts and culture should play a central rather than marginal role in the world and in life, and in 1988 creating the World Culture Project, which I still direct today.

The experiences I had in the choir exposed me to many memorable oratorios and anthems by composers such as Mozart, Haydn, Handel, and others, as well as inspirational hymns including *Abide with Me, He Who Would Valiant Be, Unto the Hills Around Do I Lift Up My Longing Eyes, Jerusalem, Now Thank We All Our God with Heart and Hands and Voices*, and countless others. I also sang in Handel's *Messiah* at Massey Hall in downtown Toronto every Christmas when I was young. Many of these experiences filled me with a deep sense of awe, wonder, ecstasy, reverence, and humility. They lifted me to great heights and produced feelings in me that were sublime and, on some occasions, divine, especially when this was enhanced by singing these pieces and many others like them in sacred surroundings with vaulted architectural features and heavenly characteristics. While most of these musical experiences were intimately connected to religion and religious beliefs and were intended to convey and confirm this, I learned very quickly that many of them also had a great deal to do with developing our personalities and characters as well as living responsible, respectful, and spiritual lives.

These experiences were amplified by many other experiences I had when I was young, such as playing in a beautiful ravine near our home in central Toronto that was filled with exquisite trees, flowering shrubs, and babbling brooks. This was also true for a performance we went to one night that was performed on a lake lit with huge lights and candles and produced by an Indigenous group near Brantford, Ontario. Experiences like these had a spiritual effect on me similar to the ones I had in the choir and music generally. I will simply never forget them, and can still recall them in my mind and memory like it was yesterday.

Combined with these experiences was exposure to a number of cultures and countries that were different from my own. This was because many of the families that lived in our neighbourhood in the central part of Toronto came from countries and cultures in other parts of the world. This was especially true for European cultures and countries such as Ukraine, Poland, Czechoslovakia, Germany, Italy, and France, and occasionally for other cultures in places like Japan, China, and the Middle East. This was because families from these parts of the world came to Canada to escape the horrors of the Second

World War and begin their new lives in Canada in general and Toronto in particular. This made it possible for me to play with children who had different cultural origins and backgrounds than I did, hang around with them at school, and especially spend time in their homes with their families. As a result, I learned a great deal about cultures that had different traditions, beliefs, values, customs, religions, and ways of life than mine. This proved helpful in understanding cultural differences like this at a very early age and counteracting any negative thoughts I had in my mind or had picked up from others about matters like this.

By the time I was nine or ten, I realized it is possible to have spiritual experiences in many areas of life such as the arts, humanities, and culture and not just in religion, despite the fact that there is a strong connection between these two specific areas of life. I also learned that having spiritual experiences and cultivating spirituality is not confined to adults and people in their twilight years, but can be experienced and cultivated at any age in life and often in profound, powerful, and transcendental ways. Thanks largely to my parents, the doors to spirituality were thrust open for me at a very early age. As I look back, I can see that this made it possible for me to have many spiritual experiences over the course of my life that occurred in conscious, natural, and spontaneous ways, enabling me to enjoy "peak experiences" and "spiritual highs" without having to resort to drugs and other dangerous substances.

As I reflect on all these experiences, I realize what my friend George Simons, a well-known cultural scholar and cultural diversity expert, meant when he said to me several decades ago that "parents, homes, and families, like cultures, should provide their children with two basic things in life: one is 'roots'; and the other is 'wings.'"

Roots are needed to make it possible for children and young people to deal with all the practical requirements, basic necessities, and concrete realities they encounter in life, as well as to come to grips with the many complex problems and difficult challenges they will be confronted with over the course of their lives. Wings are required to enable children to soar to great heights, help them realize their full potential, and experience happiness, fulfillment, and contentment. This resonated strongly with me at the time and even more so today because it sums up in a few simple words what my parents, home, and family did for my brother Murray and me when we were young, as well as what parents, homes, and families in general should do for their children.

Parents need to ensure that their children receive a solid grounding and basic exposure to many areas and activities in life that are intimately connected to their roots and wings, such as how to come to grips with their day-to-day problems and issues on the one hand and developing an understanding of and appreciation for the arts, humanities, ethics, religion, and the basic principles and rudiments of science on the other hand. Scientific discoveries and achievements that have occurred in recent years involving other species, planets, galaxies, the universe, and the cosmos, are often particularly intriguing to children.

Childhood is also an ideal time to get involved in a variety of athletic and recreational activities. One of the most important of these activities is playing sports, which were confined for a very long time to boys and men but now involve millions of girls and women. There is a great deal that children can learn about life and living in the practical and spiritual sense by playing on teams that compete with other teams, including the importance of teamwork, cooperation, and working together to achieve common goals and objectives, and especially learning how to win with grace and lose with dignity.

What is true for these activities is also true for learning about one's own culture, heritage, customs, traditions, values, and value systems, as well as the cultures of others. A good start in this regard would be taking children to museums, art galleries, and libraries, attending concerts, dance, and theatrical productions, visiting ethnic and community cultural centres and events, and going to festivals, fairs, and community events organized by people who have different cultural origins, values, rituals, ancestral roots, and ways of life.

These activities should be enhanced and enriched by exposure to the cultural heritages of other countries in the world as well as the tangible and intangible natural and cultural heritage of humankind, and, along with this, the work of such organizations as UNESCO, the International Council on Monuments and Sites (ICOMOS), Culture Digitali, and many others that are now accessible through digital technologies. This should be augmented by exposure to the devastating experiences of the Black, Indigenous, colonized, and marginalized peoples of the world, the Truth and Reconciliation commissions commenced initially by Nelson Mandela and Archbishop Desmond Tutu in South Africa in 1995, and how these and other commissions have been conducted by many other peoples and countries throughout the world since that time and why they are so essential. This should be complemented by exposing children to the cultures of other species, providing them with pets and expecting them to assume responsibility for looking after their pets properly, as well as visiting zoos and animal clinics. This should also include getting children engaged in measures to protect and preserve the natural environment by planting trees, visiting arboretums and flower gardens, learning about gardening and creating a garden of their own and looking after it, taking long walks in local and regional parks and forests, and understanding why it is so imperative to achieve environmental sustainability and ecological well-being in the years and decades ahead.

These activities and many others help to prepare children properly for life, make commitments to life-long learning, and become responsible citizens. This will in turn help to make them feel good about themselves, more confident in their actions, decision-making processes, and relations with other people, and ultimately enable them to live happier, healthier, and more meaningful lives. This is also a very important time to help them create values, lifestyles, and ways of life that enable them to be kinder, more compassionate, tolerant of other people, other cultures, and other species, and committed to preserving the world's scarce resources.

A specific component of this should be teaching children to have decent manners—something that appears to be lacking in many parts of the world today—as well as learning how to deal with people who are aggressive and domineering, have radical forms of behaviour, or are confrontational in their deeds and actions. This is intimately connected to what has become known throughout the world as *character education*, or education that deals with children's sensitivities, sensibilities, and ethical and altruistic development and not only their personalities and commitment to consumerism and materialism. Included in this is the need to cultivate civility, especially when it comes to dealing with other people in a variety of community, casual, and collective settings and relationships. Also important are learning about ethical and moral standards in general, respecting the needs, rights, values, and beliefs of others, learning to compromise and make concessions, acting in a trustworthy and responsible manner, and being adaptable and resilient.

This all has a great deal to do with developing children's wings as well as their roots, thereby making it possible for them to achieve the goals, objectives, and ideals they have set for themselves, as well as to realize that they have fundamental responsibilities to accept and act on, and not only basic rights and freedoms to enjoy. Such developments make it possible for children to achieve a great deal more in life, as well as experience real fulfillment, purpose, and satisfaction in the adult and final stages of their lives and discovering their purpose and calling.

Over the centuries, many prominent scholars and educators have spent an enormous amount of time studying matters like these and designing specific learning methods, models, prototypes, and systems to address them that can be easily accessed by parents to assist them in bringing up and educating their children. This is especially true of scholars such as Shinichi Suzuki, Rudolf Steiner, Maria Montessori, and several others who had children and young people uppermost in mind during the course of their work.

Shinichi Suzuki, for instance, devised a highly successful method for teaching children and young people to play musical instruments such as the piano, violin, and others by convincing them to *listen* to pieces first, then *imitate* them, and finally *practice* and *practice* them over and over again until they get them right. This method was initially very popular in Japan, where it originated, but then spread rapidly to most other parts of the world. Rudolf Steiner, an Austrian artist, scientist, and visionary, devised a method for learning that involved the mind, body, and spirit—and more specifically head, heart, and hands—and was a strong believer that there is a spiritual dimension in every human being. He believed such qualities should be identified and cultivated beginning at a very early age. This method became known as the Waldorf method and now takes in more than 2,000 early childhood programs in more than sixty different countries. To this list should definitely be added Maria Montessori, the Italian physician and teacher, who is undoubtedly the best known of these three innovative scholars as confirmed by the countless Montessori schools that exist throughout the world today. Her approach is based on learning experiences that seek to develop the natural interests and inclinations of children as opposed to formal and traditional teaching and learning. It involves as many "hands-on" and "real-world" experiences as possible, while simultaneously downplaying more conventional methods and practices such as tests, rote-learning, and the like. While both Montessori's and Steiner's methods and approaches place a strong emphasis on experiential learning and the role of the individual in this process, their underlying philosophies diverge in some ways. Montessori's teaching and learning techniques encourage natural curiosity and independent learning, whereas Steiner's techniques emphasize collective and group learning, creativity, imagination, and holistic experiences.

Added to this list of scholars and teachers should be John Dewey, Jean Piaget, and Paulo Freire, who all developed more general types of teaching and learning systems, models, methods and techniques. The American philosopher and educator John Dewey developed a teaching and learning method based largely on concrete and pragmatic experiences. It involves creating opportunities in children's lives and schooling that are thoughtful, reflective, experiential, interactive, interdisciplinary, and socially engaging rather than conventional, passive, and based primarily on memorization. In contrast, Jean Piaget, the French psychologist and epistemologist, focused on cognitive developments and learning experiences that are concerned with how all species—and the human species in particular—adapt to their environment. This helps to explain the popularity of Piaget's techniques today, which also manifest themselves (as noted earlier) in the planting of trees, the creation of gardens, long walks in the countryside, outdoor activities, and concern for conservation, preservation, and ecological harmony between nature and human beings.

Then there is Paulo Freire, the Brazilian educator and philosopher. He advocated an approach to teaching and learning in which children and young people talk and interact freely and openly with each other as well as with their parents, teachers, and others. As far as

Freire was concerned, students should become "active agents" in their own learning experiences, as well as stand up to oppressive teaching and learning techniques based on systems and structures created elsewhere in the world by people committed to imposing their beliefs and practices on other people and other countries. Working largely with marginalized and oppressed peoples, colonized countries, and Indigenous peoples, Freire believed that ultimately teaching and learning should be a dialogue between equals. The importance of liberating poor and oppressed peoples as well as children and young people from oppressive regimes, cultures, and ideologies is spelled out in detail in his book *Pedagogy of the Oppressed* (1968).

Going back much farther in time, scholars and teachers such as Confucius, Mencius, Lao Tzu, and many others have also had a great deal to say about teaching and learning as well as the development of children, families, family lives, and their cultures. This is especially true of Confucius, who is generally regarded as the greatest Chinese teacher and philosopher of all. Among the qualities he emphasized most were personal, professional, and public morality and integrity, correctness in all social relationships and public situations, kindness, benevolence, and family loyalty. His view that "you are what you think" foregrounds the importance of the mind and mindfulness in learning systems—a popular subject in the world today. Many other scholars have made outstanding contributions to what is called "lifelong learning" or "education for life," most notably Jacques Delors, Edgar Morin, and Edgar Faure in France.

If parents can help their children by exposing them to the basics and rudiments of such learning systems and methods of these and possibly others, they can also help their children by exposing them to the lives and achievements of such humanistic and compassion people as Albert Schweitzer, Mahatma Gandhi, Martin Luther King, Jr., Mother Teresa, and many others through all the books, films, and videos that have been created about them and their lives. It is difficult to see how the world will become a better, safer, and more secure and peaceful place—and people will be able to overcome the colossal problems they are confronted with at present and going forward into the future—without exposing children and future generations to people who committed themselves to causes that were greater than themselves and manifested a great deal of caring, sharing, and empathy in their lives and work.

There are millions of people all over the world today who are also doing this and doing it on a daily basis by devoting themselves to a single cause or many diverse causes. This is true regardless of whether they are concerned with helping other people to improve their health, welfare, and well-being, dealing with the COVID-19 pandemic and its many long-term effects, helping Ukraine and Ukrainians in their war with Russia, providing humanitarian aid to victims of conflict in the Middle East, joining protest movements to bring an end to systemic racism, racial violence, and abuse, participating in marches to curb global warming, fighting gender inequalities and injustices, or striving to achieve more stability, sustainability, and order for all people and countries.

While involvement in causes like these and many others can help a great deal in cultivating character, kindness, and compassion, this is not the only way this can be achieved. There are many others as well. One of the most important is to expose children to the diverse cultures of the world in the all-encompassing, holistic sense. While it is not possible for all children, parents, and families in the world to travel to other parts of the world to experience these cultures on the ground, it is possible to do so through all the communications media and devices that now exist. For instance, it is now possible through technological means to fly high and low over most countries and cultures in the world, view their most impressive cultural achievements, monuments, and sites, stroll through their towns, cities, and streets, visit their art galleries, museums, and libraries, enjoy their concerts, theatrical and dance productions, celebrations, parades, and festivals, explore their wineries, be exposed to their cuisines, and a great deal else.

It is capabilities and possibilities like these that make learning a great deal about the diverse cultures of the world so exciting, rewarding, and compelling. This is because many of the signs, symbols, and materials that are needed for this already exist and are accessible through the arts, humanities, heritage of history, cultural industries, and many other means. This includes beautiful music, exquisite paintings, superb plays, enticing architectural masterpieces, fascinating stories, enduring myths, tasty foods, inspiring ideas, worthwhile ideals, and many more. These are the *gateways* that children, parents, homes, and families need to open the doors to the world's diverse cultures, civilizations, and cultural treasures if they take the time and expend the effort that are necessary to have in-depth encounters with them.

From the most exquisite works of art, actions of humanists, and the artistic and humanistic perceptions of culture to the broadest and deepest biological, ecological, and cosmological perceptions of culture, there is no doubt that culture and cultures possess the ability to act as the keys to spirituality in a multitude of ways because everything is there in one form or another when considered in totality. Culture and cultures make it possible to move horizontally and vertically—as well as in breadth and depth—across and around the vast domain of different cultural activities and disciplines, from the human to the non-human, the simple to the profound, the individual to the collective, the local to the global, and the mundane to the magnificent.

This is especially important in today's world with its extremely high levels of human, social, and cultural mobility as well as new transportation and communications developments and an enormous amount of technological change in general. As matters now stand, severe tensions and open conflicts can and often do erupt when parents and grandparents come from different cultures and countries than their children but expect their children or grandchildren to learn about their cultures, maintain their languages, and follow in their footsteps. Their children and grandchildren, however, are born in other countries or come to them early in life, and are struggling to find themselves, develop friendships, and "fit in" where they are living and going to school today. Dealing with significant cultural differences like these can be extremely difficult and demanding for many children, parents, homes, and families.

This was the theme of a 2022 Pixar movie set in Canada called *Turning Red*, directed by Domee Shi. It struck a responsive chord with many young people in Canada, the United States, and other parts of the world because of its relevance. The movie is about a thirteen-year-old Chinese-Canadian girl named Meilin ("Mei") Lee (voiced by

Rosalie Chiang) and the problems she encounters in navigating home and family life on the one hand, and school and community life on the other. In the *Toronto Star*, writer Evelyn Kwong explained how the movie resonated with her own experiences growing up. Kwong's home life was in a world that "consisted of upholding the values that would make my family and ancestors proud, achieving academic excellence, respecting elders, and being a 'good kid,' which meant being obedient and less of a burden." However, she learned very quickly at school that her "home life" would make fitting in at school—her "outside life"—extremely difficult. "Entering kindergarten was a cultural shock from the weird looks I'd get to the questions and comments from others about my appearance, the food I ate and the language I spoke.... I began to rid myself of all things 'Chinese' when I went into the classroom."[3]

Problems like this are not uncommon today, especially in countries like Canada that have large ethnic populations and many diverse immigrant and refugee communities. Not long after *Turning Red* was released, a new musical created by Fatuma Adar and directed and choreographed by Ray Hogg called *Dixon Road* was performed in High Park in Toronto. It dealt with a similar situation but in a totally different way. The musical focused on a family living in Mogadishu, Somalia, whose father, Zaki, had just been appointed minister of culture and heritage by the Somali government. His wife Safiya was living a comfortable life at home, and their daughter Batoul was going to school and doing extremely well. When civil war broke out in Somalia, the family fled to Canada where they eventually found a one-bedroom apartment in a northwest neighbourhood of Toronto called "Little Mogadishu."[4]

(It should be noted here that Toronto has numerous neighbourhoods like this, such as "Little Italy," "Little Portugal," "Little Pakistan," "Greektown," "Chinatown," and many others with large concentrations of various ethnic groups. Canada and Toronto are well known throughout the world not only for their diverse populations, but also for the fact that Canada has an official policy of multiculturalism.)

While Batoul struggled to find her identity and sense of belonging as a result of being positioned between two very different cultures, her father Zaki's experiences and struggles were even more difficult because of discrimination, lack of job opportunities for immigrants, and long periods of unemployment and isolation.

Many other films, plays, and television programs depict situations and problems like this. Among those that were very popular in Canada at one time are *King of Kensington* (1975–80), about the owner of a Jewish delicatessen in the Kensington market area of downtown Toronto, and *Little Mosque on the Prairie* (2007–12), which dealt with the experiences of the Muslim community in a fictional Saskatchewan town. It was created by Zarqa Nawaz and aired not only on the Canadian Broadcasting Corporation (CBC) but in many other countries as well. Even more successful was *Kim's Convenience*, first a play and then a TV sitcom about the lives of a Korean immigrant family who own and operate a Toronto convenience store. Also in this vein was the CBC sitcom *Run the Burbs*, which starred Andrew Phung, who had appeared in *Kim's Convenience*.[5]

As a country with a large number of immigrants, Canada has seen the creation of many organizations that deal specifically with the problems faced by immigrants, refugees, and newcomers. One organization that is doing pioneering work in this area is the not-for-profit Muslim Resource Centre for Social Support and Integration (MRCSSI) in London, Ontario. It is designed to help individuals and families manage conflict, deal with pre-migration experiences such as war trauma, and overcome such challenges in their new country as poverty, unemployment, loss of socio-economic status, unwillingness to recognize their academic credentials, and verbal and physical abuse.

In the course of its work, MRCSSI has discovered that the "primary source of the challenges many migrants ... face is the conflict between the *collectivist* nature of their families and the *individualistic* model of services, support, and intervention of mainstream services and policies."[6] Through its "culturally meaningful approach" to building safe communities and the creation of its new Centre for Culturally Integrative Responses (CCIR), this organization is sharing its knowledge, expertise, and experiences in this complex and difficult field with other ethnic groups and communities across Canada and around the world.

These are not the only problems children, parents, and families are compelled to confront that are deeply rooted in culture and cultures. Just as every culture is a whole composed of many different parts that are constantly changing, interacting, and impacting on one another, so every family is a whole made up of many interconnected parts where exactly the same process takes place on a daily basis. This is apparent as soon as family members transcend their own specific situations, circumstances, and experiences and become aware of the family as a holistic unit or all-encompassing entity. As soon as this happens—and hopefully it *does* happen—it is apparent that families and family cultures are constantly evolving over time as changes take place in the lives of their individual members, as well as all the multifarious relationships between and among them. The similarities to cultures in general are very striking here. In fact, there is a great deal to be learned about all cultures in the world by examining the character, composition, components, operation, and especially functioning of home and family cultures.

In the case of families, there may be both positive and negative experiences for individual members depending on the type of interactions between and among them. This can and often does result in difficult experiences for families as wholes and not just individual family members, especially if one or more members in the family are suffering from problems such as substance abuse, psychological and psychiatric disorders, physical disabilities, or acute diseases. Unfortunately, problems like these can persist for a very long time and make it difficult for families to remain together when other forces are driving them apart.

These problems, and others like them, make it imperative to devote a great deal more time and attention to understanding children's formative years and family experiences. It is essential to ensure that as many experiences as possible are positive rather than negative. Moreover, no individual person, family, or family culture has all the answers to such problems. Every person, family, and family culture in the world has something worthwhile to contribute to this process. This is why learning from other people and cultures early in life is imperative if we want to enrich, enhance, broaden, and deepen the experiences that infants, children, young adults, and all family members and their cultures have over the course of their lives.

There is one final matter that should be addressed here. It is creating *homes for humanity* of many different types. Fortunately, many people in the world are turning their residences into homes for humanity because of their compassion and commitment to helping others who are desperately in need of assistance and help. While this has been evident for centuries in all parts of the world in one form or another, it has become especially important in recent years due to the COVID-19 pandemic and a great deal of poverty, unemployment, and conflict in the world. This is especially true for women who have been badly abused and are being prevented from having jobs and pursuing professions, girls and women who have or are being deprived of educational opportunities, seniors who are living all alone and are totally isolated from other people, millions of people worldwide who are homeless and compelled to live on city streets and in back alleys, children who have been abandoned and neglected, people living in overcrowded, dreadful conditions in refugee camps, victims of disastrous wars such as those in Ukraine, the Middle East, and the civil war in Somalia, and people in countries that have experienced destructive floods, hurricanes, fires, and earthquakes.

Fortunately, many people in far more privileged circumstances and parts of the world are now becoming more aware of this and concerned about those living in situations and conditions like these and are coming to their rescue, as well as opening up their hearts, minds, wallets, and homes to them. Responses to the war in Ukraine provide an excellent illustration of this. People in many different countries are providing emigrants and refugees from Ukraine with food, clothing, blankets, living quarters, and education, as well as opportunities to learn new languages, adjust to different cultures and ways of life, and get a new start in life.

While developments like these are imperative in all parts of the world and hopefully will become one of the most obvious hallmarks of the cultural age, what is especially needed at this time are successful prototypes that can serve as models for this kind of work and these types of developments in the years ahead. One such prototype is Home for Humanity and its many affiliates, which was created several years ago in the Haut Valromey region of France near Lyon. Not only is it training many young people who are committed to a highly humanistic way of life and eager to assist other people in all parts of the world, but it is spreading rapidly in the world and creating co-operative connections and collaborative arrangements with similar organizations elsewhere.

Leading the way among the principal founders of this Home for Humanity movement and its inspirational activities throughout the world are Alexander Schieffer and Rama Mani (co-founders of the aforementioned Home for Humanity in France), A. T. Ariyaratne, Jean Houston, Youssef Mahmoud, and many others. Among their most important goals are creating a regenerative future for all people and countries, renewing culture, cultures, and creativity as well as their vital roles in the world, and especially creating homes for humanity in all major areas and countries in the world. As stated on its website, Home for Humanity believes that human civilization is in peril and needs drastic transformation. As a result, it describes its central mission as calling people home "to the inner home of humanity, to realize our purpose and potential as agents for transformation … to the homes we inherit, to make them seedbeds for ecological and societal regeneration … to the Earth home we share, to uphold each culture and lifeform for its unique contribution to an inclusive Earth civilization, and … together, we can transform our divided world into a united home for the indivisible family of life."

This seminal organization also states in its literature that "an inclusive Earth civilization requires the timeless wisdom of each of our cultures, and the creative expressions of all our fellow human beings to be fully voiced and deeply heard, so we can jointly share a culture of humanity, peace and integrity."[7] The organization's inauguration took place on the International Day of Peace, September 21, 2019, when the Humanity Charter was adopted by a diverse group of people representing all continents. This charter is a "dynamic, living document that crystalizes humanity's timeless wisdom and emerging knowledge across our diverse cultures. It integrates the inputs and echoes of experiences of innumerable pioneers of transformation across all sectors, disciplines, and continents." Also stated in the charter and on the organization's website is a commitment to nurturing "a culture of peace and integrity; we aspire to honour and include the spirit, originality, and creative expressions of all people, cultures, and tribes to jointly shape the integral and sustainable developments of humankind."

With these inspirational developments, commitments, and examples in mind, we can take the next step up the cultural ladder by examining the importance of communities, schools, education, and their cultures.

Chapter Four

Communities, Schools, and Education

Culture and education have no bounds or limits.
—Maria Montessori[1]

As soon as we step outside the door, we are immediately confronted with communities, schools, and education, as well as all the various cultures associated with them. Many developments involving communities, schools, and education are occurring throughout the world, and there are also many people now *connecting* or *reconnecting* with their own community, school, and educational cultures, as well as those of others.

There are also many other changes going on these days in the cultures of communities, schools, and education, as manifested most conspicuously in the changing character and contents of community newspapers and magazines, local radio and television programs, libraries, gender relations, the activities of ethnic groups and cultural centres, and much else. These changes are also manifesting themselves in the use of more locally produced rather than imported products and foodstuffs, meals served in neighbourhood and community restaurants, the focus on the agricultural and culinary achievements of local people and their talents, the lives, stories, and cultural experiences of longtime residents, as well as festivals, fairs, parades, and celebrations of many types. While there are many reasons for all this, one of the most obvious is the shift that is taking place in many parts of the world from internationalism and elite cultures to localism and popular cultures.

What is true of connecting with our culture and cultures is equally true, if not more so, when it comes to *reconnecting* with our culture and cultures. This is especially apparent at present with respect to Black and Indigenous peoples, people in colonized countries, and other oppressed and marginalized groups that were forced to give up their original cultures many centuries ago but are now keenly committed to returning to them and, along with them, their traditional worldviews, values, customs, languages, lifestyles, and ways of life.

No doubt developments such as these will change the lives of countless people throughout the world who are demonstrating an amazing amount of tenacity, courage, and determination to reconnect with their original cultures. This is very much in evidence in the remarkable and robust outpouring of creativity, imagination, and productivity from myriad Indigenous, Black, and colonized peoples as they express their hopes, dreams, aspirations, feelings, fears, and desires in their everyday work, communities, educational institutions, occupational activities, and careers.

While many organizations throughout the world are actively involved in activities like these, one that is making a seminal contribution is Reconnecting With Your Culture (RWYC). This organization was created in 2020 by Olimpia Niglio, a professor of architecture born in Italy, along with her colleagues in other parts of the world such as Rana P.B. Singh in India, Kevin Alexander Echeverry Bucuru in Colombia, and Alberto Blanco-Uribe Quintero in France. They were concerned about the lack of opportunities for children and young people to learn about culture in general and their own cultures and heritages in particular in their own localities and communities.

The creation and development of this organization couldn't have come at a better time. In specific terms, RWYC is designed to assist children and young people in the five-to-seventeen age group in exploring and experiencing their own cultures and heritages and those of their classmates. The pedagogical process for these explorations and experiences is set out clearly and concisely in a *Guide Book* that is available in several languages, divided into three major sections, and which describes this process as a "cultural treasure hunt." Young people are encouraged to explore their own cultures and heritages as a means of broadening and deepening their knowledge, understanding, awareness, and appreciation of those cultures as well as those of their fellow students.

The first stage in this process involves preparing students properly for their treasure hunts. Among other things, this includes selecting a suitable place to begin their hunt, devising an appropriate route and timetable in conjunction with teachers and parents, and gathering such things as cameras, cellphones, notebooks, and sketch pads to document their findings.

The second stage involves recording their encounters in a variety of ways. Goethe said it was largely through the eye that he learned to comprehend the world, so not surprisingly many of the ways the students document their findings are visual, including making sketches, painting pictures, or taking photographs. But other ways of recording the students' findings are used as well. This may include documenting the sounds, aromas, textures, and tastes they discover in their communities, recording local songs and dances, interviewing long-time residents and senior citizens, writing stories, and making maps.

This part of the treasure hunt is an ideal time to help young people understand similarities and differences between the diverse cultures and heritages they experience, including making a distinction between the tangible and intangible aspects of culture. Students and schools can make use of the techniques developed by UNESCO, ICOMOS, Culture Digitali, #DICULTHER, and many other cultural organizations. The system of characterization and classification of "cultural and natural treasures of many different types" that RWYC and other organizations have devised helps students broaden, deepen, and intensify their knowledge, understanding, and awareness of culture and the cultures in their own localities, as well as the tangible and intangible natural and cultural heritages of their communities.

The final stage in the three-stage process involves sharing the findings from the first two stages with their fellow students, parents, and teachers, and others in the community. This includes creating neighbourhood, community, national, and international exhibitions of the visual, oral, olfactory, tactile, emotional, and other experiences the students had during the first two stages, as well as displays and presentations that might include songs, dances, plays, and other types of activities that were created or experienced during this process. In Japan, for example, an international exhibition was created recently by RWYC Japan in collaboration with RWYC International that includes works from participating students, institutions, and countries from all around the world.

In the course of its work, RWYC has developed the "Tokyo Charter." Created in 2021, the charter consists of a general preamble followed by nine articles that include emphasizing and enhancing local concepts of cultures and heritages; respecting the diversity of cultural and heritage expressions in neighbourhoods, communities, and localities; creating responsible citizens and citizenship; dialoguing in such matters as cultural knowledge, understanding, and awareness; creating inclusive and holistic capabilities and competencies; promoting local cultural policies and practices; establishing relationships with municipal governments and educational institutions; and several others.

An excellent complement to RWYC and its work is offered by the International Child Art Foundation (ICAF). This not-for-profit organization was created by Ashfaq Ishaq in 1997 and is still directed by him today. Its mission is "to seed children's imagination, cultivate their creativity, and grow mutual empathy through the arts for a more prosperous, sustainable, and peaceful future." In order to realize this mission, ICAF provides major programs on peace through art, healing arts, and climate change, publishes *ChildArt* magazine, and, most importantly, produces the World Children's Festival and the Arts Olympiad. These two international programs bring young people from more than a hundred countries to the National Mall in Washington, D.C., to explore and express their commitment to creativity, diversity, and unity, as well as to celebrate the "artist-athlete model" through developing creative minds and healthy bodies. Given the success and seminal role Ashfaq has played in the creation and development of this important organization, he is increasingly being recognized as a strong advocate and spokesperson for the needs and interests of children and young people throughout the world.

And this brings us to what is undoubtedly the most important and relevant issue of all in regard to connecting with culture. Why is education in this area so important at this time, and what type of cultural education should be provided to children and young people— and indeed *all* people—in schools and educational institutions throughout the world in the future?

There are many legitimate and compelling reasons for addressing this question and its implications at this crucial time in the history of humanity. In the first place, culture is of growing importance to all people throughout the world as the great cultural awakening continues. Another reason is the growing importance of culture and cultures in municipal, regional, national, and international development and affairs. Yet another is the increased importance that is being accorded to various cultural activities by most governments, especially in terms of passing legislation to protect their heritage as well as formulating and implementing cultural plans and policies designed to increase citizen participation in cultural life. And still another is the increased use in public and private discussions and discourses of such terms as popular culture, elite culture, corporate culture, technological culture, political culture, social culture, youth culture, cancel culture, woke culture, cyberculture, environmental culture, and many others, as well as such powerful phrases as "change the culture," "systemic cultural change," "culture shift," and many others. Use of these terms, which is now occurring with increased frequency in every part of the world, indicates that people are becoming much more *culture-conscious*, more aware of and in tune with the seminal role culture and cultures play in their lives and in the world.

These developments confirm that culture and cultures are destined to play a much more powerful and pervasive role in the world of the future than in the past or at present. Clearly, all cultures in the world are undergoing a period of pronounced and profound change. This is due to many factors, such as all the economic, political, demographic, technological, social, and environmental developments and changes that are taking place in the world. There is hardly anyone in any part of the world today who is not experiencing such developments and changes, and with them the need to be very careful about how they would like their cultures to be developed in the years ahead.

While these developments, and many others, are producing numerous benefits, such as the opportunity to learn more about the cultures, traditions, customs, heritages, lifestyles, and ways of life of people and countries that are different from their own, they also pose risks, uncertainties, threats, and dangers that can result in conflict. This has been demonstrated over the centuries by the experiences of countless Indigenous, Black, Jewish, and colonized people throughout the world as well as many other marginalized and oppressed groups. Without a much better, clearer, and more comprehensive understanding and awareness of this, there is the constant danger that culture and culture will be used for negative rather than positive purposes. *This is why culture should be seen and treated as a "beacon of the future," with the capacity to warn of impending danger and set in place the required safeguards and precautions that are necessary to prevent this, as well as the ability to illuminate a vital, viable, safe, and secure path to the future like all good beacons.* Without this dual capacity, the full potential and reality of culture will not be realized and culture will fall short of the role it can and should play in the world of the future.

If, as many educators, scholars, and statesmen are predicting, the world is entering a period of intense cultural interaction, transformation, and change, it makes a great deal of sense for people in all parts of the world to broaden and deepen their knowledge and understanding of their own culture and the culture of others in both the constructive and destructive sense. While it may never be possible to fully transcend the limits of our own culture and cultural conditioning, surely the world would be a much better, safer, and more peaceful place if people's understanding and awareness of their own culture, other cultures, and especially the reasons for cultural differences were expanded, intensified, clarified, and enhanced. This is especially important for young people and future generations. The well-known cultural scholar Edward Said provided sage advice when he claimed:

> The more one is able to leave one's cultural home, the more easily is one able to judge it, and the whole world as well, with the spiritual detachment and generosity necessary for a true vision. The more easily, too, does one assess oneself and alien cultures with this same combination of intimacy and distance.[2]

Mahatma Gandhi provided wise advice as well when he said, "I do not want my house to be walled in on all sides and my windows to be stuffed. I want the culture of all lands to be blown about my house as freely as possible. *But I refuse to be blown off my feet by any.*"3

Given the need to learn much more about culture and all the diverse cultures of the world, it is imperative to examine the fundamental changes that are going on in the cultural field today, especially with respect to the nature, meaning, and character of culture in general and cultures in particular. Not only are major changes taking place in perceptions and definitions of culture, but also with respect to the perception, characteristics, content, and composition of individual *cultures*.

As noted earlier, culture has been perceived and defined over the course of history in two fundamental but very different ways: first as the arts, humanities, heritage of history, finer things in life, and, much more recently, the cultural industries; and second as the complex whole or total way of life of people, societies, and countries. What is true for culture is also true for individual cultures, since cultures derive their substance and meaning from culture.

The first way of perceiving and defining culture is by far the oldest, which explains why it is deeply entrenched in the policies, practices, and affairs of virtually all people, countries, educational institutions, media agencies, and governments. As noted earlier, the cultural industries (for example, publishing, radio, television, film, sound recordings, social media, and so on) were added to this list very recently due to the crucial role they play as "carriers" and "communicators" of culture and cultures.

There are many advantages to be realized by visualizing and defining culture and cultures in this first way. Not only does such a definition encompass many of humanity's most important activities and worthwhile ideals, but it also emphasizes things that are concrete, tangible, and specific in nature. Paintings can be seen, films, videos, television programs, and dramatic works can be watched, music can be listened to, art galleries and museums can be visited, books can be read, and cultural products can be handled, collected, traded, and bought and sold in the marketplace. This explains why virtually all countries, governments, educational institutions, and media agencies define culture in general and their own cultures in particular in this way for programming, planning, administrative, funding, and educational purposes.

The second way of perceiving and defining culture as the complex whole or the total way of life of people, societies, and countries arose more recently. As indicated earlier, it was created in the latter part of the nineteenth century by Edward Burnett Tylor and has been affirmed by countless other cultural scholars, historians, and practitioners since that time. This holistic definition of culture was not designed or intended to downplay the various elements of culture and cultures such as the arts, humanities, heritage of history, finer things in life, and the cultural industries, but rather to include all these elements along with countless other activities in an all-encompassing or comprehensive definition of culture and cultures.

The importance of both these perceptions and definitions of culture and cultures—and especially the relevance of the first perception and definition as the *gateway* that is needed to understand the second perception and definition—should not be ignored. They are intimately related and are both of crucial importance at present and going forward into the future. However, at this particular time in human and world history, the second perception and definition of culture and cultures is especially important. The reason for this is not difficult to understand. As long as people and countries are in no danger of losing their culture and cultures, it is easy to see and define them the first way. Nevertheless, as soon as culture and their cultures are threatened, it is amazing how quickly people and countries shift to the second perception and definition of culture and cultures as the most important of the two by far. Clearly, there is nothing quite like the threat of foreign domination, invasion, or cultural destruction or extinction to bring about a rapid realization that culture and cultures are complex wholes and total ways of life before anything else.

There is another, even more compelling and legitimate reason for embracing and utilizing the second way of perceiving and defining culture and cultures at this critical stage in the world. This is because the second way includes everything covered by the first definition, as well as a great deal else of crucial importance, such as the natural environment and economics, science and religion, sports and technology, education and social activities, corporate and political activities, and on and on it goes. This is what most people in the world mean today when they say they are the "products of their culture" or products of "their culture as a whole." It is also what Wole Soyinka, the well-known cultural scholar and Nobel Prize-winner, meant when he said, "We need therefore to constantly reinforce our awareness of the primacy of Source, and that Source is the universal spring of Culture. It is nourished by its tributaries, which sink back into the earth, and thereby replenish that common source in an unending, creative cycle."[4] Further confirmation of this same point of view was provided by Fernand Dumont, a well-known Canadian cultural scholar, when he said, "I have always considered a collective project as something mainly cultural. *The economy is not an end in itself, culture is.*"[5]

For centuries, it was commonplace in most countries to view cultures in this holistic sense as homogeneous, uniform, and closed. This was because the focus was on developing cultures that were internally consistent and inclusive, externally delineated and distinct from other cultures, and concerned largely with creating a unique national cultural identity, soul, or spirit. While this led to the creation of many valuable artistic, intellectual, religious, philosophical, and other works, it also produced periods of intense nationalism, rivalry, two major world wars, the slaughter of millions of people, and the clash of many different cultures and civilizations.

World events over the last fifty years have served to dramatically alter this traditional situation. The reason for this is not difficult to determine. As Alfred Kroeber and Clyde Kluckhohn pointed out in their book, *Culture: A Critical Review of Concepts and Definitions*, published in 1963:

> We know by experience that sincere comparison of cultures leads quickly to recognition of their relativity. What this means is that cultures are differently weighted in their values, hence are differently structured, and differ both in part-functioning and total-functioning; and that true understanding of cultures therefore involves recognition of their particular value systems. Comparison of cultures must not be simplistic in terms of an arbitrary or preconceived universal value system, but must be multiple, with each culture first understood in terms of its own particular value system and therefore its own idiosyncratic structure. After that, comparisons can with gradual increasing

reliability reveal to what degree values, significances and qualities are common to the compared cultures, and to what degree distinctive. In proportion as common structures and qualities are discovered, the uniqueness will mean more.[6]

As a result of realizations and developments like these, cultures today are becoming much more heterogeneous, diverse, and open in character. Improvements in communications and transportation are making it impossible to shut out influences from other parts of the world. Moreover, there are many more interactions and exchanges taking place throughout the world these days not only *within* cultures but *between* cultures. There is also more mixing of populations going on because of migration, demographic shifts, interracial marriages, and transformations in social structures and political institutions. As a result, cultures are becoming much more multicultural, pluralistic, multiracial, and diverse in nature, with many different ethnic, religious, and linguistic groups, subcultures, and social, economic, political, and technological activities interacting under one roof. This is bringing with it a new set of circumstances, especially as more tensions and conflicts are occurring not only within countries but also between cultures.

This situation necessitates new understandings of the challenges confronting all people, countries, and cultures today. Whereas the challenge in earlier times was to achieve "unity in uniformity" through homogeneous cultures, ways of life, and a common national cultural identity, the challenge at present and going forward into the future is to achieve "unity in diversity" through heterogeneous cultures, ways of life, and multiple cultural identities. This will require the development of many new cultural symbols, as well as the creation and cultivation of many more links and connections between and among all the diverse cultures, subcultures, racial groups, ethnic and religious communities, and activities in the world. Coexistence, cross-cultural fertilization, dialogue, interaction, communication, and exchange—rather than isolation, separation, exclusion, and delineation—must be the order of the day.

If profound changes are occurring in the composition, character, dynamics, and characteristics of cultures in the internal and domestic sense, profound changes are also taking place in the external and international sense. It would not be far off the mark to say that virtually all cultures in the world, including the smallest, most remote, inconspicuous, and marginalized ones, are becoming "world cultures" in the sense that they are compelled to deal with all the changes that are going on in the world and are unable to tune out developments occurring elsewhere. Whereas in previous decades and centuries it was possible for cultures to be aloof and isolated from each other and the world, today this is no longer possible.

Viewed from the perspective provided by the holistic way of seeing and defining culture and cultures, one of the biggest challenges as far as the future is concerned will be maintaining adequate control over the decision-making processes and policies affecting people's lives and cultures, while simultaneously learning to function effectively in a globalized world. Clearly people know why their cultures must change. What they are opposed to—and opposed to in increasing numbers—is not change, but rather developments that serve the interests of others but not themselves. This is why people everywhere in the world are demanding the right to decide for themselves how they want their cultures to develop and change, as well as how they want to order the component parts of their cultures and cultural lives to form cohesive and coherent wholes.

This means that there is an urgent need for people to learn much more about culture, cultures, and their own cultures in the all-inclusive, holistic sense. This is an exceedingly difficult task in view of the fact that very few schools and educational institutions are able to provide such opportunities today. As a result, if people want to learn more about culture, cultures, or their own culture in this all-inclusive sense, they have to do it through a variety of other means, usually requiring a commitment to self-exploration, self-discovery, lifelong learning, and especially observation and analysis, just as many young people are doing today through organizations such as RWYC, ICAF, and many others.

It is one thing to learn about culture and cultures when they are visualized, defined, and dealt with as the arts, humanities, heritage of history, finer things in life, and the cultural industries, because knowledge and understanding results from concrete, tangible, and material experiences. However, when culture and cultures are visualized, defined, and dealt with as complex wholes and total ways of life, they cannot be grasped in this concrete, tangible, and material sense because they are far too complex, vast, multidimensional, and all-encompassing. Moreover, it is not possible to actually *see* culture and cultures in the holistic sense, *know* all the countless activities, institutions, worldviews, values, value systems, customs, and parts that make them up, and *comprehend* how all these parts are structured, ordered, put together, and connected. This means that people must learn to *sense* how culture and cultures exist, are put together as complex wholes and overall ways of life, and how they function, as well as to piece together general impressions of culture and cultures from a variety of sources, experiences, information, ideas, and possibilities.

For Giles Gunn, a well-known cultural scholar, the best place to start to get to know culture and cultures in this holistic sense is with the parts and the dynamic interplay that is constantly going on between the parts and the whole:

> We cannot understand the parts of anything without some sense of the whole to which they belong, just as we cannot comprehend the whole to which they belong until we have grasped the parts that make it up. Thus we are constantly obliged to move back and forth in our effort to understand something "between the whole conceived through the parts which actualize it and the parts conceived through the whole which motivates them" in an effort "to turn them, by a sort of intellectual perpetual motion, into explication of one another."[7]

It follows from this that if people want to learn about culture and cultures in the holistic sense, the best place to start is with their *own* culture, circumstances, or specific part of the whole, which may be their job, career, geographical location in the world, or their lives. However, this is not their job, career, geographical location, or lives considered in isolation, but rather as part of the substantially larger and more fundamental configuration of their culture as a whole or total way of life. In other words, it is the details of their own specific cultural circumstances and situation examined in terms of the cultural context or container in which they are situated.

For Robert Redfield, an American anthropologist who spent much of his life and career studying cultural and human wholes, the ideal place to start this process is with individuals who are concerned with communicating knowledge, understanding, and insights into wholes in their work, rather than with individuals who are preoccupied with analyzing or comprehending the parts of wholes:

> Still farther from where we just now stand are those who study the relations of parts to parts, of elements abstracted out from the whole in strict and limited relationship to each other generally described.... Over there, on that other side, are all those who strive to present the concrete reality of each human whole as each, in itself, is. They are a various group. Included are novelists, philosophers, historians, philosophers of history, literary people, critics of literature and of art, historians of art, and writers of personal reminiscence. These people describe human wholes—personalities, civilizations, epochs, literature, local cultures—each in its uniqueness.[8]

To progress further in this area, it is helpful and usually necessary to turn to artists and their works. This is a subject Redfield studied in great detail. Here is what he had to say about the ability of artists of all types to help people glean a clearer, simpler, and deeper impression, image, portrait, and understanding of the all-encompassing character of culture in general and cultures in particular by selecting specific parts of culture and cultures—or what are frequently called *cultural symbols*, because they are *symbolic* and *representative* of the structure of feeling of cultures as wholes and total ways of life:

> The characterisations of the artist ... are of course not precise at all; but very much of the whole is communicated to us. We might call them all portraits. They communicate the nature of the whole by attending to the uniqueness of each part, by choosing from among the parts certain of them for emphasis,

and by modifying them and rearranging them in ways that satisfy the "feeling of the portrayer."[9]

In order to learn more about culture and what our own culture and the cultures of other people and countries are really all about in the holistic sense—as well as the worldviews, values, value systems, codes, recipes, and ordering processes that are used to create and underlie these wholes—it is necessary to turn to artistic works and activities. Since these works and activities, like culture and cultures, are also wholes made up of many parts, artists are the people who possess the perceptions, knowledge, understanding, insights, and sensorial skills—as well as the expressive capabilities and communicative techniques—that are required to sense and feel how cultures are created and put together as dynamic wholes and total ways of life, and to communicate this to other people.

They do this largely through their ability to select or create specific parts, such as myths, legends, metaphors, rituals, signs, and especially symbols, that stand for the whole and convey an incredible amount of knowledge and information about the nature and character of cultures in the holistic sense. The old adage that "a picture is worth a thousand words" is a cliché, but it speaks volumes about the ability of artists to create symbols that convey a remarkable amount of information about cultures as wholes that can't be communicated in any other way at all, or, at the very least, can't be communicated nearly as effectively.

While cultures are composed of countless parts, the symbols or parts that are the most symbolic or representative of them in the all-inclusive sense are foods, foodstuffs, and cuisines; pictures, photographs, and paintings; architectural constructions, monuments and historic sites; music, songs, and dances; plays, stories, and poems; craft objects and sports; and so forth, depending on the specific culture in question. Since the use of cultural symbols such as these to broaden, deepen, and intensify our knowledge and understanding of cultures as wholes and total ways of life is a recurring theme in this book, it may be helpful to provide a few obvious examples of this "parts-whole" phenomenon and symbolic process and how they work.

One of the most powerful examples of this is Gandhi's use of "homespun" and "indigenous salt"—two of India's most important domestic resources—as symbols to portray the character, substance, and essence of Indian culture and bring an end to British rule in India. What is true in the case of these two powerful cultural symbols and Indian culture is true as well for food, cuisine, and the Eiffel Tower with respect to the culture of France, soccer and the cultures of Brazil, Argentina, Italy, and Spain, the Great Wall and the culture of China, the Statue of Liberty and American culture, and Charlotte Brontë's *Jane Eyre* and Emily Brontë's *Wuthering Heights* and Victorian culture in England. All these examples, and countless others that could be provided, can be used to create and build images and comprehensive portraits of cultures as wholes and total ways of life, especially if enough symbolic parts, examples, and illustrations of this phenomenon and process are used. This can be a stimulating experience because it involves learning about and using some of the most fascinating, inspiring, and exciting materials and symbols that have ever been created in the world to shed light on the holistic character of many different cultures.

While the works of artists, scholars, historians, architects, critics, athletes, and others are among the best materials to employ in building comprehensive portraits of culture of cultures as wholes, they are not the only ones. The cultural industries play a very useful role in this because they provide the communication channels and distribution mechanisms and networks required to make the works of people like these known to the public. Anthropological, sociological, and historical works are important because they tend to deal with the totality of cultures, and therefore the diverse patterns, themes, customs, traits, traditions, social structures, interrelationships, worldviews, values, and so forth that constitute cultures. Psychological and personality studies are important because, as Ruth Benedict claimed, "cultures are really personalities writ large." Philosophical studies and theological treatises are important because they deal with human conduct and character in a variety of different social settings and circumstances. And biological, ecological, economic, geographical, scientific, and cosmological studies are important because they reveal how all cultures in the world—and not just human cultures—have imprinted their ways of life and structures of feeling on very distinct parts of the global environment.[10]

It is examples, illustrations, and processes like these that Raymond Williams had in mind when he said it is possible to slowly but surely piece together a composite portrait of the "structure of feeling" of cultures as wholes and overall ways of life, especially if enough symbolic parts and the relationships between them are used to convey and enable this:

> More overt and explicit than some underlying collective unconscious but less determinate and intellectualizable than an ideology, a structure of feeling is the "particular and characteristic colour" that the ensemble of the values, beliefs, and practices of a given culture imparts to the experiences of its members. In particular, a given culture's structure of feeling will at least influence if not determine the patterns of response of its members in resolving or coping with the dilemmas and contradictions that confront them in their daily lives. For Williams, the principal aim of cultural analysis is to discern and understand this structure of feeling as it manifests itself throughout the entire range of a given culture's expressions.[11]

This is consistent with what Edward T. Hall, yet another well-known cultural scholar, had in mind when he said:

> One cannot usually transcend one's culture without first exposing its major hidden axioms and unstated assumptions concerning what life is all about—how it is lived, viewed, analysed, talked about, described, and changed. Because cultures are wholes, are systematic (composed of inter-related systems in which each aspect is fundamentally inter-related with all other parts), and are highly contexted as well, it is hard to describe them from the outside. A given culture cannot be understood simply in terms of contents or parts. One has to know how the whole system is put together, how the major systems and dynamisms function, and how they are inter-related.[12]

What is steadily unfolding here are some of the most pertinent and salient ways we can use to increase our knowledge and understanding of culture and cultures in general and our own specific culture in particular in the all-inclusive, holistic sense. When this is combined with other learning possibilities—travelling to other parts of the world to experience the cultures of other countries firsthand and on the ground, searching for books on cultures in libraries, using the internet, joining workshops and study groups, enrolling in lifelong learning, adult education, extension, and foreign language courses, taking advantage of ethnic community centres and new digital technologies, and so forth—a broad spectrum of options and opportunities is opened up for us to learn about culture and all the diverse cultures in the world.

There is much to be gained from this. Through exposure to the diverse cultures of the world, there is exposure to different worldviews, values, and value systems, diverse concepts of space, time, the universe, and the cosmos, the nature and purpose of life, the relationship between human beings and the natural environment, the most worthwhile things in life, and the role that people and different groups play in society. This can also be helpful in "learning a living," as Marshall McLuhan called it, as well as acquiring the skills, abilities, and capabilities that are necessary to function in a variety of cultures as well as different cultural contexts and contents.

Unfortunately, few educational institutions in the world are at present in the position to provide this kind of comprehensive cultural education. There are many reasons for this, such as the lack of well-trained and qualified teachers in this area at the elementary and secondary level as well as the fact that there are very few teaching and learning materials available. While some schools have "multicultural days" that are designed to introduce students to the different cultures of the world through their foods, foodstuffs, cuisines, dances, customs, costumes, dress, and traditions, and others celebrate specific ethnic holidays and events for similar purposes, these activities are usually extracurricular rather than curricular, thereby falling far short of the comprehensive and fully developed cultural education that is necessary to do the job properly.

While it will take a great deal of time, effort, and funding to achieve this objective, cultural education in the comprehensive, holistic sense should be divided into four very distinct and fundamental components if it is to be successful.

The first component should be learning about the *nature and meaning of culture in general and cultures in particular in all their various manifestations and forms*. This is necessary to eliminate the current confusion, controversy, and misunderstandings that exist in the world over the nature and meaning of culture and cultures, as well as to clarify the two basic perceptions and definitions of culture and cultures that exist in the world today and especially the holistic perception and definition that constitutes the real foundation and centrepiece of culture and cultures. In order for this type of education to be effective, it should reveal how culture as an idea and reality has evolved over the course of human history.

The second component should be concerned with *the fundamentals of culture and cultures*. This is imperative because all cultures are based on certain underlying axioms, assumptions, roots, beliefs, themes, worldviews, values, values systems, principles, and ideals that shed light on how these complex entities are structured and put together, as well as on how they function in the world in both theoretical and practical terms. A very important dimension of this will be creating a comprehensive system of classification and cultural indicators for all the different cultures in the world.

In the human domain alone, there is a vast array of cultures in the world that need to be classified in different ways according to the similarities and differences they possess. Included in this comprehensive classificatory system would therefore be such matters as the origins and roots of cultures; the evolution of cultures over time and in space; dynasties and groups that have played dominant or prominent roles in the development of cultures; the most distinctive traits, features, and pace of life in different cultures; the main characteristics of cultures and the most effective indicators to use in identifying and differentiating cultures from each other as well as exposing their greatest strengths and most fundamental shortcomings; the many different layers of cultures that result from their historical development over centuries; the role that cultural development and policy play in the enhancement of cultures; cultures and their specific geographical locations in the world; their ancestral heritages and inheritances; their environmental surroundings and most influential ecological features; their most important achievements; and many others. Where possible, these classification areas should be accompanied by specific cultural indicators that reveal and asses the similarities and differences of cultures.

The third component should focus on examining *the specific contents, parts, and principal relationships of culture and cultures.* This should include all the different activities that make up culture and cultures as wholes and ways of life, how some of these activities act as gateways to broader and deeper understandings and experiences with culture and cultures whereas others do not, and especially what cultural scholars, historians, and practitioners have had to say about the importance of culture and cultures over the centuries and their relevance to humanity and the world at present and going forward into the future. It doesn't take a great deal of imagination to conjure up the pictures, portraits, images, impressions, structures of feeling, and visualizations of all the different cultures in the world and the world as a whole in terms of these aforementioned requirements.

The final component in this comprehensive cultural education should deal with the *context of culture and cultures* as well as *culture and cultures as contexts.* Dealing with the context of culture and cultures involves studying how culture and specific cultures in the world are situated in the natural, historical, global, and cosmic environment, as well as affected by all the powerful forces and factors that exist in the world. Dealing with culture and cultures as contexts involves examining the many different ways culture and cultures can be used to advantage, such as by acting as contexts for all the different activities in the world—from economics, politics, technology, and health care to the arts, humanities, heritage of history, sciences, recreational activities, and many others—in both space and over time. Seen from this perspective, world cultures provide the context for national cultures, just as national cultures provide the context for town, city, and regional cultures, and town, city, and regional cultures provide the context for neighbourhood, community, local, home, and family cultures This should be kept in mind as one of the most crucial aspects of cultural education of all, since, as Ruth Benedict consistently maintained, "context determines contents."

While cultural education should focus initially on the cultures of the countries people are living in at present, ultimately it should fan out and be complemented and enriched by juxtaposing, comparing, and contrasting this with other cultures in the world. A vast amount of information already exists in all these areas at present. What is desperately needed now is to pull all this information together and present it in one place, as well as to classify it in different ways and make it accessible on a sustained and systematic basis.

Just as it is possible to learn a great deal about all the different religions of the world from courses in comparative religions, so it is possible to learn an enormous amount about all the cultures in the world from courses in comparative cultures. If, as the old saying goes, "all is known by comparison," then it makes a great deal of sense to make comparisons between all the diverse cultures in the world. While realizing this objective will take a great deal of collaboration among many cultural scholars, teachers, researchers, practitioners, and educational authorities and institutions, it should help to alleviate some of major tensions, conflicts, and hostilities that exist in the world today, as well as to enlarge and enhance people's cultural consciousness in many ways.

And this is not all. It will also make it possible to cultivate more effective ways of seeing, thinking, acting, interacting, and valuing things, as well as opening the doors to accepting, appreciating, and respecting the cultures of other people and other countries, expanding our awareness and mindfulness, creating more interesting job and employment opportunities, and experiencing more happiness, satisfaction, and contentment in life.

Chapter Five

Towns, Cities, and Regions

In dealing with the urban order, it may be useful to begin
with the sensory, experiential qualities of cities which are
also organized or ordered. Cities, among other things, are
physical artifacts, experienced through all the senses by
people who are in them.... Cities look, smell, sound, and *feel*
different; they have a different character or *ambiance*. This is
easily felt, but is very difficult to describe.
—Amos Rapoport[1]

No sooner do we move beyond communities, schools, education, and
the cultures they manifest than we are confronted with a colossal array of towns, cities, regions, and their cultures. These places and cultures have become much more important, visible, and accessible in
recent years because of incredible improvements in transportation
and communication.

Just as it is important to focus on communities, schools, education, and their cultures in holistic terms, so it is important to focus on
towns, cities, regions, and their cultures in exactly the same way. The
similarities between these two major components of cultures in the
holistic sense are instantly apparent, despite the fact that town, city,
and regional cultures are substantially larger in size and stretch much
farther afield than those of neighbourhoods, localities, and communities. Nevertheless, they are equally striking because, like cultures
at all levels, they are constantly evolving and changing as wholes and
total ways of life made up of many parts.

How often do we take the time or make the effort to delve deeply
into town, city, and regional cultures? Do we assume too much and
explore too little? As soon as we begin to explore cultures at this level, we immediately become aware of the phenomenal number of people, groups, organizations, activities, resources, infrastructures, and so

forth that comprise them. A little curiosity in this respect will produce numerous benefits, learning opportunities, experiences, and rewards. It will also open the doors to a huge swath of possibilities, including understanding the evolution of these cultures through space and time, grasping their many different layers, and coming to terms with the multitude of people, ethnic, and racial groups that live in them. Also noteworthy in respect to such cultures are the countless multicultural activities, events, and celebrations of the different customs, traditions, and languages that are evident in them, not to mention their myriad sights, sounds, smells, textures, and tastes, geological and geographical settings, landscapes, environmental features, and a great deal else. Exposure to such fascinating things helps to enhance and enrich our knowledge, understanding, and awareness of all the different cultures and cultural features that exist in every town, city, and region in the world. It is through explorations like these, as well as the many cultural elements and symbols that epitomize them and give them meaning, significance, and purpose, that it is possible to piece together general and specific impressions, images, and portraits of the character of these cultures as dynamic and organic wholes and fascinating ways of life. And the deeper we go, the more distinct and powerful these impressions, images, and portraits become.

Here, as well, nothing surpasses the arts when it comes to broadening, deepening, and enriching our knowledge and appreciation of different urban and regional cultures in both symbolic and real terms. When we talk about the arts here, as we do throughout this book, we are not only talking about the performing, exhibiting, and literary arts—essential though they are—but also the culinary, architectural, material, decorative, design, photographic, cinemagraphic, recreational, horticultural, environmental, and other arts and all the myriad activities that are manifested in them and emanate from them.

Over the centuries, many artists have been sensitive to the comprehensive and distinctive character of town, city, and regional cultures, and have devoted substantial parts of their lives, careers, and works to depicting these cultures through an incredible variety of aesthetic forms, activities, and idioms. They do so, as illustrated earlier, largely by selecting parts of these cultures that are symbolic of them as wholes and ways of life in a diversity of ways. There are many examples of this. In Europe, for example, Bruegel did it through his paintings of Dutch social scenes and urban life, Canaletto and Guardi through their colourful representations of Venice, Émile Zola through his portrayal of the vivid colours and pungent aromas of Paris, Turgenev through his incredible descriptions of Russian urban life, and Renoir and Whistler through their captivating street scenes and enticing cityscapes. Interestingly, the English composer Eric Coates accomplished this in a substantially broader, deeper, and more fundamental and comprehensive way. He did this by dividing London into six parts that he felt were most symbolic of the culture of this colossal city as a whole in his musical composition *The London Suite*. These parts are Covent Garden, Westminster, Knightsbridge, Oxford Street, Langham Place, and Mayfair. It was a terrific idea, which was and is still enjoyed and appreciated by countless Londoners as well as the flood of visitors who pour into this world-famous city from other parts of the world every minute of every day.

Other authors, filmmakers, and photographers have made similar contributions. Rohinton Mistry powerfully described an unnamed city (most likely Bombay) in *A Fine Balance*; Theodore Drieser did it for Chicago in his book *Sister Carrie*; James Joyce accomplished it for Dublin in *Ulysses*; Joseph O'Neill realized it for Dubai in *The Dog*; Zadie Smith shed light on a specific area of London known as Willesden in her books *NW* and *White Teeth*; and Mikhail Bulgakov captured the sense of Moscow in *The Master and Margarita*. This is also true for filmmakers such as Woody Allen and Martin Scorsese and the Jewish and Italian districts of New York, François Truffaut and Paris, Federico Fellini and Rome, and Wong Kar-Wai and Hong Kong.

To this should be added what may be the most symbolic illustrations of this parts-whole relationship and all-embracing phenomenon of all, namely the many photographs taken by photographers such as Daidō Moriyama of streets in Japan and especially Tokyo which were designed to reveal the conflict between traditional and contemporary cultures and ways of life in this colossal city; Fan Ho and numerous streets in Hong Kong; Eugène Atget, one of the first street photographers in the world, who took thousands of pictures of the streets of Paris at the turn of the twentieth century, much as Robert Doisneau did in Paris fifty years later; Henri Cartier-Bresson, who focused his attention on capturing "decisive moments" in a variety of city and urban settings, neighbourhoods, and contexts throughout Europe; and Vivian Maier, undoubtedly one of the most famous and prolific street photographers of all, who portrayed numerous cities around the world. While these illustrations cover a vast panorama of activities, this is most pronounced in the holistic sense in the case of photographers who have captured images of virtually everything that exists in many urban settings, including the remarkable mixture of people, cherished walks, walkways, and walkers, myriad buildings, bridges, and architectural icons, upscale neighbourhoods and down-trodden districts, people at work and people at play, the diversity of employment pursuits and social situations, and numerous artistic events and cultural celebrations.

When Melina Mercouri, Minister of Culture for Greece, and Jack Lang, Minister of Culture for France, teamed up to create the concept of "cultural capitals" and designated Athens as the first cultural capital in the world in 1985, this idea quickly took hold and spread rapidly throughout Europe and more recently to many other cities in the world. In 2020, for example, Rijeka in Croatia, Galway in Ireland, Porto in Portugal, Pécs in Hungary, Liverpool in England, Vilnius in Lithuania, Umeå in Sweden, Plovdiv in Bulgaria, Košice in Slovakia, and Burgos in Spain were designated as European cultural capitals. This has been augmented in recent years by the United Cities and Local Governments (UCLG) and Culture 21 initiatives and the creation of the Intercultural Cities Index. This index is designed to measure the level of achievement of intercultural policy implementations in cities and their progress over time, as well as facilitate comparisons between and among the world's cities and especially culture's role in sustainable urban development and human societies at large.

Like all cultures in the world, town, city, and regional cultures are situated in a huge variety of contexts of one type or another. Not only are they located in broader cultural contexts such as national and world cultures, but also in very distinct geological, geographical, and environmental contexts. This includes waterfalls such as Niagara Falls, Victoria Falls, Iguazu Falls, and Angel Falls; massive mountains and mountain ranges like Mount Everest, the Matterhorn, the Andes, and the Rockies; millions of small and large lakes including the Great Lakes in North America, Finger Lakes in the United States, the lake district in Italy, and many other lake districts in the world; on or near long, winding, and roaring rivers such as the Amazon, Nile, Yangtze, Mekong, Mississippi, Volga, Danube, Ganges, Congo, and others; and all the oceans and their coastlines. Regrettably, many urban and rural cultures today face challenges created by rapidly rising water levels and powerful floods and storms, as well as severe droughts in some regions, all exacerbated by climate change.

Many of these aforementioned geological, geographical, and environmental features and forces are so powerful and pervasive that they play a dominant role in shaping, determining, or affecting the cultural aspects and characteristics of town, city, and regional cultures, as well as the lives of their inhabitants. This is often compounded by the fact that these features and forces also serve important economic, social, and tourist functions for town, city, and regional cultures, such as providing them with valuable resources, energy sources, and transportation and communication capabilities, as well as affecting the needs, moods, and morals of their residents and therefore serving essential aesthetic, psychological, sociological, and cosmological purposes as well. This is especially evident in many Asian countries where people identify with their urban and rural cultures, environments, and landscapes not only in concrete, practical, and secular terms, but also in many deep spiritual and sacred ways.

What is true for geological, geographical, natural, environmental, and cosmological features and forces is also true for cultural symbols. Since town, city, and regional cultures—like all cultures in the world—cannot be seen in their entirety as wholes or total ways of life, cultural symbols that "stand for these wholes" are essential. Cultural symbols take on enormous significance in this regard and can be incredibly powerful. In fact, some of the most important cultural symbols of all are situated in towns and cities where they are more accessible, more spectacular, and exciting to experience.

While images may possess the most power and potential to achieve this in symbolic or representative terms, they are not the only symbols capable of realizing this. There are many others, such as foods, foodstuffs, and cuisines, plays, buildings, sculptures, monuments, historic sites, music, sounds, songs, dances, stories, poems, crafts, and sports, depending on the specific culture in question. This is also true of flags and anthems, which explains why people get so angry and distraught when people burn flags or talk during the playing of national anthems, as well as crowns, orbs, and other artifacts associated with kings and queens as demonstrated recently as a result of the passing away of Queen Elizabeth II and the coronation of King Charles III in the United Kingdom. Celebrities and athletes like Pelé in Brazil and Lionel Messi in Argentina, cherished animals such as eagles in the United States and cows in India, flowers such as tulips in the Netherlands and sunflowers in Ukraine, trees such as oak, maple, and cherry trees in England, Canada, and Japan also fulfill such symbolic functions. And the list goes on and on.

The same is true of architectural symbols. As the prominent architect I. M. Pei said, "Architecture is the very mirror of life. You only have to cast your eyes on buildings to feel the presence of the past, the spirit of a place; they are the reflection of society." Such is the case, for example, with architectural symbols such as the Leaning Tower in Pisa, Italy, the Guggenheim museum in Bilbao, Spain, the Colosseum in Rome, the Castelli Romani region in Italy, the countless chateaus in the Val de Loire region of France, the Blue Mosque in Istanbul, Turkey, the Taj Mahal in India, and many other structures that say so much about the cultural character and characteristics of these places. Particularly noteworthy, given the theme of this book, is the Mahabodhi Temple, a UNESCO World Heritage site located in Bodh Gaya, Bihar, India. The temple, whose name can be translated into English as "Great Awakening Temple," marks the spot where it is said the Buddha attained enlightenment under the Bodhi Tree, and pilgrims from near and far visit this place to see a descendant of that same tree. The site has been culturally and spiritually significant for more than two millennia.

Also worthy of mention are many other architectural sites, styles, monuments, and dwelling places, such as the circular homes with stucco walls and conical roofs known as "trulli" in the Puglia region of Italy. These are most conspicuous in Alberobella, which is generally regarded as the most precious gem and principal hub of this entire region. Or consider the countless caves that surround and exist in Matera in the Itria Valley in the same region of Italy, which is one of the oldest continuously inhabited urban areas in the world and was designated a European cultural capital in 2019; the half-timbered homes and walled towns that exist in many areas of Europe, the Middle East, and Asia, including Rothenburg ob der Tauber in Germany, Carcassonne in France, Baghdad in the Middle East, and Hangzhou (the City of Lakes) as well as Suzhou (the City of Gardens) in China. Such is also the case of Kyoto, the city of temples in Japan, and the many "hot-spring towns" that are situated in the Kaga Onsen region of Japan and cut a major swath through the centre of the Japanese Alps on the island of Honshu.

This list only scratches the surface of the vast range of habitable structures that exist throughout the world, such as yurts in Mongolia and the incredible rock formations, towers, and dwelling places called "fairy chimneys" that stand out as pinnacles in the valleys and castle-like cliffs of Cappadocia in Turkey. These fascinating lava structures and formations have been hand-carved into thousands of homes, social venues, monasteries, churches and places of worship, and more than 200 underground cities. In the ancient world, it is estimated that 3,500 dwellers lived deep in the caves beneath the earth's surface in this part of the world for safety and security reasons. Inhabitants over the centuries have included the Hittites, Romans, Byzantines, Arabs, Ottomans, and, more recently, primarily the Anatolians. And what is true for these architectural styles, forms, and dwellings is true for all other human-made cultural symbols. Although many may not provide the context for town, city, and regional cultures in the way that geological, geographical, and environmental features and symbols do, they can be very dominating at times.

Added to this are all the town, city, and especially regional cultures (including mixtures of rural and urban areas) that are known in many parts of the world for their natural resources and basic foodstuffs such as petroleum, natural gas, minerals, grapes, wine, olives, tea, coffee, sugar, rice, spices, and so forth. Think, for example, of how many town, city, regional cultures in the world depend on, are affected by, or are known internationally for their foodstuffs and beverages—olives in the case of Spain, Italy, Croatia, and Greece; wines in the Bordeaux,

Burgundy, and Champagne regions of France, the Barossa Valley in Australia, the Mendoza in Argentina, the Maipo in Chile, and Douro Valley in Portugal; tea in specific regions of China, India, Nepal, Bhutan, and Pakistan; coffee in Brazil, Vietnam, Colombia, Indonesia, and southern India; rice in China, India, Indonesia, Bangladesh, and Japan; sugar in the Caribbean and elsewhere in the world; and spices in many Asian countries. All these different products and foodstuffs help shape the character of cultures in specific areas of the world, as well as provide economic benefits and employment opportunities.

Cuisines should definitely be added to this list, since they often play the most prominent role of all as culinary masters such as Anthony Bourdain and many others have revealed in their television programs and books. Many town, city, and especially regional cultures are known first and foremost for the cuisines that symbolize them, such as the Basque Country and Galicia in Spain, Guangdong (formerly Canton), Shandong, and Sichuan in China, the Punjab region and Bengal in south Asia, Togo in Africa, Emilia-Romagna with its capital of Bologna in Italy, the Lyonnais region in France, and myriad others. This is also true for five very specific regions and their cuisines in what are called "blue zones" in Okinawa in Japan, Sardinia in Italy, Nicoya in Costa Rica, Icaria in Greece, and Loma Linda in California. These regions are rapidly becoming well known for the number of people who enjoy good health well into their nineties and in some cases even their hundreds. This results from the fact that their diets are composed largely of local or regional fruits, vegetables, and whole grains, as well as eating less and maintaining better diets and healthier weighs.

Information about these and countless other regions and their distinctive cuisines are documented in detail in numerous books, films, videos, and other publications, as well as maps, championships, and recipes of master chefs and outstanding dishes. This is also the case for numerous guidebooks such as the Michelin guides, which are very popular throughout the world for their famous ratings of restaurants and heritage sites; the Culture Smart Guides; and the International Institute for Gastronomy, Culture, Arts, and Tourism (IGCAT) in Barcelona, Spain. This rapidly expanding organization is becoming well-known for its awards to chefs, a variety of conservation activities, and advocacy of healthy diets. IGCAT's principal aim is to empower local communities, towns, cities, and regions by raising awareness of the importance of promoting and protecting local foods, cuisines, and cultures as part of sustainable and balanced tourist practices and developmental strategies. Founded by Diane Dodd and a number of her colleagues in 2012, this rapidly-expanding not-for-profit organization is working with regional stakeholder consortiums in the various fields under its jurisdiction. IGCAT is also rapidly becoming well-known for its gastronomy awards, as well as the fact that it is the official secretariat for the world and European Regions of Gastronomy platforms, the European Young Chefs Award, the World Food Gift Challenge, and other initiatives.

All these examples, and many others that could be cited, bring to mind the important principle citied by Ruth Benedict earlier that "context determines contents." It is impossible to live in, near, or visit any town, city, or region in the world without recognizing how everything that goes on in these places and their corresponding cultures is strongly influenced by their geological, geographical, environmental, cultural, and human contexts.

Over the last few decades, such developments have generated a great deal of interest in what is called "cultural place-making." In most western and northern countries, this type of activity has often been used to confirm that town, city, and regional cultures are not only valuable for the economic benefits they create and the tourist and employment possibilities they provide, but also for bringing people together, creating identity and a sense of belonging and purpose, and making urban and rural life more meaningful, satisfying, and livable. In many eastern and southern countries, cultural place-making often takes on a much more profound, powerful, and spiritual significance and has far more relevance not only for the places themselves but also for the effect they have on their citizens and inhabitants.

Included among the pioneers in key developments like this in Asia are Rana P. B. Singh, Sung-Kyun Kim, and many others. Kim and Singh wrote about the importance of place-making in Korea:

In Korea, for choosing a site and settlement the Pung-Su principles, which interconnect the spirit of the natural landscape and human sensitivity, are the common practice in making, maintaining, and manifesting, the cultural archetypal as archetypal integrity of habitat. These natural elements are mostly responsible for regulating the cultural notions and traditions in Korean landscapes.... Villagers felt themselves *"being"* here through belonging (existentiality), *"becoming"* there through adjustment (gracefulness), setting them "behind" there to be backing-base (basement), and also *"beholding"* them with contemplation to become beholden (contemporaneous living and being at the same time).[2]

A similar approach to cultural place-making but documented in far more detail and in a highly symbolic place in India was provided by Rana P. B. Singh and Pravin S. Rana in an article published in 2023 entitled "The Riverfrontscapes of Varanasi, India: Architectural Symbolism, Transformation, and Heritagization." In this article, they state:

Varanasi (Banaras, Kashi), is commonly perceived as a site of "vigor and rigor" where religious culture, people, and society get interconnected deeply, and the layers of transformation get absorbed in the landscapes. More visible and distinctively illustrated along the sacred river Gangã the Riverfrontscapes, exemplified with 84 Ghãts (stairways). Of course, the city represents a blending of tradition and modernity; it also records different niches of political interferences and niches of transformations over time, and imbued therein dharmacracy and related resurrection altogether creating landscapes of different worldviews and images for the future, passing on the path of "Succession, Sustenance, and Sustainability." The Ghãts and the associated sacredscapes present examples of the complex story of history, image-making, placemaking, identity formation, involvement of dharmacracy, and superimposing heritagization.[3]

As a result of developments like these, interest and involvement in towns, cities, regions, and their many diverse cultures has escalated enormously in the world over the last few decades. Not only are they assuming greater importance in developmental thinking, planning, policy, practice, and place-making in the total scheme of things, but more people are looking to cultures at the town, city, and regional level to solve their problems and enhance their overall state of health, welfare, and well-being. Whereas the focus of attention immediately after the Second World War and for some time thereafter was on countries, national cultures, international relations, and the world at large, increasingly the focus of attention has been shifting in most parts of the world to towns, cities, regions, and their cultures as more accessible, visible, immediate, and essential spawning grounds for innovative, dynamic, creative, and exciting activity. Clearly this is where the action is at present and may well be for some time in the future, especially as more emphasis is placed on developments from the ground and bottom up rather than the top down, in order to achieve more sustainability in space and over time.

What vortex of factors and forces is at work in the world that is causing the spotlight to shift from countries, national cultures, international relations, and the world at large to towns, cities, regions, and municipal and regional cultures?

It is not difficult to identify some of these factors and forces. In the first place, a large and increasing percentage of the world's population is now living and working in towns, cities, and regions. Whether this is occurring as a result of people being forced out of rural areas due to the lack of sufficient employment opportunities and economic possibilities, or because they are lured by the attractions, thrills, and excitement of municipal and regional life, the results are everywhere much the same. Towns, cities, and regions everywhere in the world have been and are expanding in physical area and population size at a very rapid rate. As this happens, more and more pressure is being exerted on town, city, and regional governments to provide the amenities, infrastructures, resources, and incentives that are required for a healthy, sustainable, and enjoyable existence.

In addition to this, more and more people are realizing that it is the quality of cultural life at the municipal and regional level that is the decisive factor in life. If the cultures where people are living, working, and living for long periods of time lack the basic prerequisites and proper accoutrements for life and living—stimulating and decent paying jobs, excellent housing and accommodation, first-class schools, teachers, and educational systems, fresh water, clean air, a variety of recreational and social amenities, well-equipped hospital and health care facilities, aesthetic ambience and appeal, and especially pride of place—no amount of economic growth, technological change, or commercial development will make up the difference.

Rapidly changing global conditions are also conspiring to make the cultures of towns, cities, and regions more important. Whether it is the break-up of countries, the breakdown of families, the erosion of social values, the quest for identity, the retracing of political, geographical, or cultural boundaries and borders, response to economic uncertainties, major supply chain issues, or the call to "think globally but act locally," more and more people are looking to towns, cities, regions, and their clusters of cultural experiences to make their lives more meaningful and pleasurable.

Finally, and perhaps most importantly, there is the dialectic reaction that is taking place to globalization, the creation of larger trading blocs, the emergence of economic and political superstates, and the increased concentration of industrial, financial, commercial, technological, and military power in fewer and fewer hands. This is manifesting itself in a number of countervailing measures and dialectical reactions aimed at restoring people's sense of personal and collective power and belonging, well-being, and identity, political and social empowerment, community solidarity, control over decision-making process affecting their lives, and protection and preservation of their human rights and fundamental freedoms.

One of the most fascinating things about the development of towns, cities, regions, and their cultures is the way they have evolved historically. For many centuries, the approach that was taken was partial and specialized rather than holistic and total. As a result, these places were usually dominated by a specific activity or particular institution, thereby limiting the perspective from which towns, cities, and regions and their cultures were viewed, assessed, and treated. In medieval times, for instance, this activity was primarily religious and sacred in character. In consequence, a temple, church, cathedral, mosque, basilica, synagogue, or pagoda was usually the dominant architectural feature, principal institution, and major focal point. In the Renaissance, the approach was more secular and social in nature. In consequence, the square replaced religious or spiritual constructions and institutions at the core of urban life. Over the last century or so, the approach and dominant activity has been mostly economic, thereby satisfying the needs of trade, industry, commerce, consumers, producers, and the marketplace. In this case, a huge office tower or a colossal smokestack is usually situated at the centre and hovers over everything else.

The problem here, as noted earlier, is that there are many costs, consequences, and side-effects to developments like these that are far too seldom taken into account in municipal and regional planning, policy, and decision-making. If the benefits are deemed to outweigh the costs, economic change takes place regardless of the environmental, sensory, aesthetic, social, religious, or human consequences. What has far too often been overlooked is the fact that the relationship between citizens and their environmental surroundings and urban settings is interactive and reciprocal. If people don't treat their surroundings with respect or fail to take the environmental costs and ecological consequences of their actions into account, environments can and often do strike back by affecting citizens in some adverse way.

What is needed are cost-benefit evaluations and calculations that include *all dimensions and facets* of town, city, and regional cultural life. In order to do this, perceptions and techniques must be developed and cultivated that are holistic and all-inclusive rather than partial, partisan, or specialized in character.

Where do we commence our search for the clues that are necessary to piece together understandings and portraits of towns, cities, regions, and their cultures that are holistic and all-inclusive? These clues must be capable of encompassing a vast range of economic, political, environmental, social, technological, educational, and spiritual activities, yielding a strong sense of identity, well-being, and belonging, enabling people to get actively engaged in the developmental process, and assuring the value, dignity, and belonging of citizens in municipal and regional development.

Of all the places where such clues can be found, culture possesses more than its fair share of possibilities. Culture contains within itself the all-encompassing perspective and integrative potential that are needed to visualize town, city, and regional cultures as complex and comprehensive wholes and overall ways of life composed of many composite parts, as well as the practical means that are required to deal with the most persistent and important problems confronting their residents.

Rather than situating a cathedral, smokestack, skyscraper, or condominium at the centre of municipal or regional cultures, surely it would make a great deal more sense to make the town's, city's, or region's "cultural statement of itself" the centrepiece and principal focal point of its development and character. In this way, everyone could take collective pride in, and accept individual and collective responsibility for, the cultural statement that every town, city, and region makes to themselves as well as the rest of the world.

It is clear that culture occupies a very different place in municipal and regional development and planning than economics, politics, industry, social affairs, religion, or any other specific activity. Rather than being another ingredient in municipal and regional development, culture is the cement that binds all the various elements, activities, and ingredients together. It is the sum and substance, so to speak, that provides cohesion, continuity, identity, solidarity, a sense of being and belonging, and particularly pride of place. Without this, it will not be possible for people to extricate themselves from their current situation or cross over the threshold to a more exhilarating, exciting, and fulfilling future.

The *culturescape* is a technique that is designed specifically with this purpose in mind. Not only is it capable of engaging citizens, groups, and organizations more actively and fully in the developmental process, but also it is capable of creating a town, city, or region's cultural statement or portrait of itself in the all-encompassing sense, both inwardly and outwardly.[4]

Looked at from the holistic perspective provided by culture in general and the culturescape in particular, there is nothing mysterious about a landscape. A landscape is a *visual* exposition of all the natural and human-made sights, objects, and elements that exist in every urban, rural, or regional area. The concept of the culturescape exposes the way in which the eye surveys these matters, sometimes stopping to focus on distinct features and characteristics that it likes, and, at other times, roving rapidly over features and characteristics that it doesn't like or takes for granted, but always taking mental snapshots and making distinct selections and assessments.

Nor is there anything mysterious about a soundscape. This is the ear's answer to the eye. It is an *aural* exposition of all the different sounds of an environment.[5] It reveals the way in which the human ear samples and assesses natural, mechanical, and human sounds, opening wide to sounds that are pleasing and soothing and closing off to sounds that are unsettling and abrasive. In much the same way, this also holds true for all other sensory abilities, such as those provided by the nose (smells), tongue and mouth (tastes) and hands (tactile experiences) and not just the eyes and the ears. Dealt with in this way, it is possible to create olfactoryscapes, tastescapes, and tactilescapes that are compatible and comparable to landscapes and soundscapes.

As the well-known authority on urban development, Charles Landry, pointed out with respect to the development of cities and their holistic character in his book *The Sensory Landscape of Cities* (2012):

> The city is a communications device. It speaks to us through every fibre of its being. The lived urban experience comes from a circular sensory cycle. *The Sensory Landscape of Cities* sees the city as a 360-degree, enveloping, immersive experience, which has emotional and psychological impacts. It argues that we sense, feel and understand it through increasingly narrow funnels of perception. Living in an impoverished perceptual mindscape makes us operate with a shallow register of experience and understanding about what is important for our cities to survive well. A greater understanding of the importance of environmental psychology is crucial. This focuses on the interplay between people and their surroundings and the degree to which it creates stress or feels restorative.[6]

It follows from insights and examples as powerful, pervasive, and useful as these that culturescapes in this all-encompassing holistic sense are expositions of *all* the different sensory and cultural characteristics and features of environments—natural, historical, sensorial, social, economic, political, aesthetic, human, humane, and so forth.[7] They are environments assaulted by all the human faculties, an explorer's curiosity let loose on the infinite variety and vast panorama of sights, sounds, smells, textures, tastes, objects, structures, institutions, activities, artifacts, and so forth that are encountered in all dimensions and aspects of urban and rural life.

Interestingly, landscapes, soundscapes, olfactoryscapes, tastescapes, and tactilescapes cut down into environments. They are discrete and distinct notions, designed to look at towns, cities, regions, and their cultures through the *vertical* lenses of specialization and partialism. As a result, they are structured to explore, examine, and expose similar facets, facts, and manifestations of urban and regional life. In contrast, culurescapes cut across environments. They are integral, integrative, and *horizontal* notions, designed to convey, reveal, and reflect the infinite and interconnected nature of countless factors and diverse facets of culture in general and cultures in particular. They are designed to bring things together rather than set them apart, and therefore to unite rather than divide.

When this happens, every town, city, and region in the world becomes a precious treasure with all sorts of fascinating gems and secrets in them, some of which are visible and others hidden from view or below the surface. But as citizens, how often do we take the time or expend the energy that is required to delve deeply into our towns, cities, regions, and their cultures and culturescapes in order to become aware of and acquainted with their visible treasures and invisible assets? How often do we take things for granted, assuming that we know what experiences and information they will provide and what programs and products are available to enrich our lives? How much do we really know about the aesthetic state of our urban environments—their captivating or disturbing sights, sounds, smells, textures, tastes, and defining symbols, signs, and characteristics? As I asked earlier, do we assume too much and explore too little?

Respecting people for the valuable contributions they are able to make to urban, rural, and regional developments such as these and many others is the key to the culturescape process. Through respect for people's participation and contributions, many people will be anxious to participate in the transformation of their municipal and regional cultures and culturescapes. Seen from this perspective, every person has something valuable to contribute to this task. For some, it may be itineraries of daily or weekly events or imprints of the cultural patterns they impose on their municipal and regional surroundings. For others, it may be impressions of their likes and dislikes. And for still others, it may be actual materials, such as old photographs, pictures of historical monuments and sites, stories, oral histories, antiques, records, or other memorabilia of municipal or regional interest.

As this information accumulates, it can be classified, codified, and orchestrated in many different ways to produce different results. For example, it can be used to prepare profiles of the different sectors of cultural activity—economic, social, educational, political, environmental, aesthetic, sensory, human, and so forth. Or it can be used to prepare maps, tours, probes, or inventories of specific cultural features and characteristics. It can also be used to assemble citizens' impressions of the aesthetic state of their municipalities and regions, including the things they like best and least about them. It all depends on the objective at hand and the nature of the information received, collected, and required. In this way, culturescapes can be used as vehicles for putting the shattered mirror of town, city, and regional cultures back together and making them more viable, functional, engaging, and inspiring.

If the culturescape process is to fulfil its full mandate, what may be needed more than anything else in towns, cities, and regions around the world are *culturescape centres* where citizens can bring their contributions, acquire basic information about their town, city, and regional cultures as dynamic, organic, and comprehensive wholes, understand how these places should or will evolve in the future, and ensure that they are actively engaged in the planning and development process. As such, these culturescape centres should be concerned with developing the exhibitions, displays, models, replicas, and resources that are needed to illustrate how actual and planned changes affect the sensory, aesthetic, human, social, political, economic, and environmental state of municipalities and regions. When and where this occurs, citizens will have concrete opportunities to ascertain the effect different types of decisions will have on the cultural fabric of their urban and rural cultures, as well as to work alongside professionals, developers, politicians, planners, and civil servants to bring about the requisite cultural changes that are required. The result will be town, city, and regional cultures as well as culturescapes that are shaped less by the dictates and desires of developers and special interest groups and more by the interests and needs of citizens, residents, and community groups.

A large, comfortable, accessible, and informal space capable of presenting exhibitions, mounting maps, providing displays, generating and recording comments, opinions, and feedback, storing memorabilia and artifacts, and dispensing information would be ideal for this purpose. This should be complemented by people who possess specific skills in photography, cartography, documentation, interviewing, creating visual, oral, olfactory, and tactile profiles, and especially making aesthetic assessments and evaluations. Local artists, craftspeople, librarians, historians, photographers, audio-visual and digital experts, geographers, curators, and scholars would all be perfect for such purposes.

Ideally, all this activity should be situated in a separate facility built expressly for this purpose and located at or near the centre of towns, cities, and regions. Failing this, a renovated factory, old warehouse, abandoned office building, dilapidated railroad station, or vacant community centre would all be feasible premises in this respect. A museum, art gallery, community centre, or library could also serve this requirement. However, it should constantly be borne in mind that while these latter institutions possess some of the resources, facilities, equipment, people, skills, and techniques that are needed to engage in culturescape activity, most of them serve other very important functions at present. Their main purpose is not to build or house a town, city, or region's comprehensive cultural statement of itself and project it to the rest of the world, but rather to present artistic, intellectual, and heritage works of great historical and contemporary importance.

It is clear from the foregoing that some fundamental changes are needed in urban and regional administration, planning, and funding if culture is to form the foundation of municipal and regional development and the culturescape process is to become the centrepiece and main focal point of municipal and regional activity.[8]

It is impossible to raise issues and matters as essential as this without raising the related matter of the respective roles and responsibilities of municipal and regional governments, especially as they pertain to culture in general and municipal and regional cultures and culturescapes in particular. Like culture and cultures, issues like this are best seen in context rather than in isolation.

There can be little doubt that determining the respective roles and responsibilities of municipal and regional governments for cultural development and policy constitutes one of the most important but difficult challenges in the political and cultural fields today. This is because people have deep and profound cultural needs at every level—personal, familial, educational, neighbourhood, community, municipal, regional, national, and international—that must be addressed. As a result, it is not advisable to assign roles and responsibilities over culture or cultures to only one level of government because developments in this area are required and affected by culture and cultures at each and every level. As a result, the most important question is not which level of government should be responsible for culture and cultures, but, rather, what are the respective roles and responsibilities of the various levels of government for culture and cultures at each level? Failure to address this question and deal with its implications and consequences opens the door to the possibility of duplication, confrontation, confusion, waste, and the perpetual risk of political and governmental coercion.[9]

While this subject cries out for much more discussion, debate, attention, and clarification at the present time and going forward in the future, common sense suggests that every level of government—municipal, regional, and national—should be involved in cultural development and policy and look after its own needs and requirements in the cultural domain first and foremost, and along with this, the cultural requirements of its constituents and constituencies. This would mean that municipal governments would be responsible for all forms of cultural activity at the neighbourhood, community, town, and city level, and that regional governments would be responsible for all forms of cultural activity at the regional level. Included in this latter requirement, however, would be promoting municipal and regional cultural exchanges and agreements, deepening the sense of regional identity and belonging, confronting the dangers of excessive localism and parochialism, creating constructive connections and fruitful relationships between regional and federal governments, as well as acting as the principal "go between" for these two levels of government as well as all municipal governments in its jurisdiction. Finally, national governments would be responsible for all forms of national cultural activity, the cultural development and policy of countries as wholes, and all international relations and affairs. While this general "rule of thumb" formula may be far removed from the present situation in many countries and parts of the world, it is obviously an objective worth striving for in the future.

Given the rapidly escalating importance of municipalities and regions in general and municipal and regional cultures in particular, it would be foolhardy to underestimate the role that municipal and regional governments should play in this process as a whole. Hence the irony of the present situation. At the time that cultural development and policy are most required at the municipal and regional level, municipal and regional governments are often in the worst possible position to respond to this necessity. Not only do they usually lack the constitutional powers, taxation mandates, and fiscal resources needed to look after the cultural needs of their citizens properly, but they also lack the institutional mechanism and administrative structures, procedures, and funding required to deal with this matter effectively.

In Canada where I live, it is often said that the federal government has the money (due largely to the fact that it possesses the principal taxation power and authority in the country); the provincial and territorial governments have the power (primarily because there are thirteen of them compared to one federal government); and municipal and regional governments have the problems. These problems result from the fact that municipal and regional governments are closest to citizens and their needs. The situation is compounded by the fact that municipal and regional governments in Canada are accountable to the provincial and territorial governments, and therefore have few taxation powers of their own, except for levying property taxes as well as charging for certain types of services. As a result, their revenue capacities are extremely limited and totally inadequate in coming to grips with the needs they are compelled to deal with, especially when they are also required to balance their budgets on an annual basis and must constantly go "cap in hand" to the other levels of government to seek additional revenue injections.

Governments in other parts of the world that find themselves in similar situations to Canada's municipal and regional governments should seek to create different constitutional arrangements and be accorded different (and greater) taxation powers. If, or when, this eventually occurs because of all the changes that are going on in the world today, this should enable municipal and regional governments to increase their funding capacities in key areas of cultural life that are presently being shortchanged or ignored, especially environmental conservation, preservation, and sustainability, affordable housing and infrastructural requirements, health, welfare, education, and employment necessities, and opportunities for oppressed and marginal groups, seniors, and arts organizations. What is also desperately needed are developmental plans, policies, programs, and practices that broaden and deepen citizen participation in cultural life, as well as train cultural animators and administrators who are skilled in acting as catalysts for urban and regional change, revitalization, and elevating and enriching all aspects of municipal and regional cultural life.

Along with these developments should come major improvements in the administrative structures that are required to administer cultural developments and policies at this level. As matters now stand, many municipalities and regions either have no specific administrative structures at all for culture, or they have departments of parks and recreation or economic development where culture is narrowly defined and tacked on as an afterthought. These structures are inadequate to meet present circumstances and future needs. Not only do they lack the necessary resources to do the job properly, but also they marginalize culture and make it an insignificant activity in the overall scheme of things.

If municipal and regional governments are to play a responsible and robust role in cultural development and policy in the future, they must create and develop administrative structures that are equal to the challenge. In other words, they must create departments or ministries of cultural development and policy, community arts and cultural councils, and the like, and endow them with sufficient financial resources and skilled professionals to do the job effectively and without delay. For only in this way will they send out clear signals to citizens, community groups, other levels of government, and corporations, foundations, and educational institutions that they are committed to playing a leadership role in the cultural field in the years and decades ahead.

What can be said about the development of towns, cities, and regions and their cultures, as well as the intimate relationship between and among them, in the final analysis? Surely this. In the past, we have tended to view municipalities and regions largely if not exclusively in economic terms. One consequence of this has been to treat culture and cultures as addendums to the economy and economies. For the future, it is much more appropriate to view municipalities and regions as cultures and possibly even works of art. This would make it possible for them to focus on the qualitative and not just the quantitative side of development and life, as well as make the improvements that are required to enhance and elevate all aspects and dimensions of municipal and regional cultural life. Regardless of whether municipalities and regions are seen as economies or as cultures, however, one thing is certain. Without awarding a much higher priority and substantially more funding to culture, cultures, cultural development and policy, citizen participation in the cultural process and cultivation of pride of place, towns, cities, and regions will not be able to respond to the complex needs, demands, and challenges that are being imposed on them on a daily basis and handicapping their efforts in every respect. This must change and change drastically in the years ahead.

There is no better way to conclude this chapter than by providing information on the *Pact for the Future of Humanity: The Daejeon Political Declaration* that was created and signed at the seventh United Cities and Local Governments (UCLG) World Congress in Daejeon, South Korea, from October 10 to 14, 2022. As stated in the pact's "vision for the future," the future we need includes people, rights and care-centred democracies built on the power of citizens that allow for constructive and mutually beneficial cooperation and solidarity among all spheres of government. A central role of local and regional governments is for a renewed, networked and efficient multilateral system—a multilateralist system that accepts the fact that global challenges can only be dealt with by dealing with local challenges and that in turn local challenges depend on global challenges. An inclusive system that takes into account the multitude of systems of cities and governance that exist to ensure all voices and all spheres of government are included within decision-making processes.[10]

With this in mind, we can take the next essential step up the cultural ladder by dealing with countries, the world, the universe, and the cosmos.

Chapter Six

Countries, the World, Universe, and Cosmos

A nation's culture resides in the hearts and in the soul of its
people.
—Mahatma Gandhi[1]

In the colossal constellation of cultures that exist in the world, from
home, family, town, and city cultures to the cultures of other species,
the cultures of countries stand out and play a very prominent role in
the overall scheme of things.

It would be a mistake to downplay the importance of cultures
at this level. This is because the cultures of countries (or *national
cultures*) constitute the sum, substance, essence, and way of life of
people in the all-encompassing holistic sense.

Cultures at this level are essential because many of the most
important decisions with respect to countries and their citizens
are made at the national level. Not only are national cultures the
summation of all the cultures that exist within countries, but they also
are influenced by developments taking place in other countries and
parts of the world, as well as the policies and practices of international
institutions such as the United Nations, World Bank, International
Monetary Fund, World Trade Organization, UNESCO, World Health
Organization, and many others.

Moreover, many of the most important issues affecting citizens
are dealt with at this level, including citizenship, immigration and
emigration, constitutional arrangements and agreements, supreme
court rulings, human rights abuses and declarations, currency and
taxation measures, and numerous others. Many of these matters are
framed, articulated, and administered at the national level and are
closely monitored by organizations and agencies that are designed

and developed specifically for this purpose. This is not only true for citizens when they are living and working within their own countries, but also when they travel abroad. In this case, they are usually seen and treated as citizens of countries rather than citizens of towns, cities, or regions, and are quick to stress this fact whenever they are asked.

Finally, countries are known throughout the world primarily for their *national* cultures and symbols. These symbols have great cultural significance as well as a great deal to do with citizens' identities at home and abroad. This is most apparent in terms of national flags and anthems, which are without doubt the most powerful national cultural symbols. As such, they are designed to make powerful statements and convey an enormous amount of information, emotion, and feeling about countries and their cultures.

Take the national anthem and flag of the United States as the most obvious and familiar example. The American national anthem, "The Star-Spangled Banner," is sung at virtually every major event that takes place in the United States. Moreover, most Americans hold one hand over their hearts when they sing this anthem in order to convey the heartfelt importance of the anthem and the flag it describes for all Americans despite their differences. The first verse of this anthem and especially its last section—

> And the Rockets' red glare, the Bombs bursting in air,
> Gave proof through the night that our Flag was still there;
> O! say does that star-spangled Banner yet wave,
> O'er the Land of the free and the home of the brave?

—probably convey the importance of both the anthem and flag for Americans and people in other parts of the world better than anything else.

What is true for the American national anthem and flag is also true for the national flags and anthems of all other countries. Every country in the world cherishes its national flag and anthem as the most fundamental symbols and images for its citizens as well as the sense of identity and belonging that is derived from this. This is because these two symbols say "this is who we are" to the rest of the world and therefore represent the essence of a country's culture and way of life.

Most countries use symbols taken from nature for the purpose of bonding people together at home and abroad. This is especially true for flowers, trees, and animals because they can have great cultural significance and appeal as national symbols, especially at a time when so many countries are becoming more multicultural in character and struggling to hold cultures and citizens together when other forces are acting to split them apart.

Consider national flowers. The lily is the national symbol of India, the fleur-de-lis of France, the tulip of Holland and Turkey, and the cherry blossom of Japan. In fact, cherry blossoms and cherry trees can be traced back many centuries in the history of Japan and Japanese culture, where blossoms represent the beauty and fragility of life and serve as a perpetual reminder that life can be very beautiful and long, but also remarkably brutal and short. Despite this, both cherry trees and cherry blossoms are symbolic of Japan, particularly in the spring when they are at their most magnificent and are signs of renewal, revival, rebirth, and revitalization.

Canada, where I live, also has many important elements taken from nature that serve a similar purpose. This is especially true for the maple leaf, which has great cultural significance as a national symbol. It is accorded the dominant position at the centre of the Canadian flag where it is displayed against a white background with a red bar at either end. It is representative of Canada and Canadian culture because the leaves of the maple true are cherished throughout the country for their beauty. As well, maple leaves turn various shades of red, gold, yellow, orange, and brown in the fall, something which corresponds in some ways to the multicultural character of the country's population.

What is true for the maple leaf is also true for the beaver, polar bear, moose, loon, and Canada goose. The beaver symbolizes some of the most valued characteristics of Canada, Canadians, and Canadian culture, such as persistence, determination, and hard work, and appears on the country's five-cent coin, the nickel. The polar bear, moose, loon, and Canada goose signify something quite different. The polar bear and moose signify power and the ability to live in demanding climatic conditions and geographical circumstances, just as many Canadians and especially Indigenous Canadians do. The loon and Canada goose as symbols convey the loneliness and isolation that many Canadians experience due to the colossal size of the country and its relatively small population. This is exemplified by the loon's plaintive and haunting call and by the sight of Canada geese flying overhead in a V-shape.

Regardless of whether it is flowers, trees, or animals, elements drawn from nature perform a valuable function for citizens, their countries, and national cultures, contributing to those cultures' and countries character and cohesion. Many Canadians sew images of the maple leaf or national flag on their backpacks, coats, and sweaters when they travel abroad to identify them and their country and culture in other parts of the world. It is also why many Canadian designers and clothing manufacturers use cultural symbols taken from nature in the design and development of their clothing and winterwear, especially hats, coats, toques, mittens, and parkas.

What is true of Canada is true of other countries and their citizens and national cultures. Just as the beaver is symbolic of Canadians culture, so the kangaroo is symbolic of Australian culture, the panda of Chinese culture, the kiwi of New Zealand culture, the bear of Russian culture, the elephant of Thai culture, and the giraffe of Tanzanian culture. Of these examples, it is probably the bear that is the most powerful and revered national symbol of all in a cultural sense. Not only does it appear frequently in the country's folk tales, sayings, proverbs, and literary works—usually as the protagonist—but also it has been the mainstay of Russian circuses for decades. A bear named Misha was the mascot of the twenty-second Olympic Games in Moscow in 1980, and appeared again in the closing ceremonies at the Winter Olympics in Sochi in 2014.

Many other activities also hold a symbolic significance in national and international terms. Included here are sports such as football and baseball in the United States, hockey, curling, and lacrosse in Canada, cricket in Great Britain and India, ping pong and badminton in China, and soccer (football) in Brazil, Argentina, Spain, Portugal, France, and Italy. Many outstanding athletes are national heroes at home and international heroes abroad. Pelé of Brazil (who passed away in 2022) is generally recognized throughout the world as the greatest football (or soccer) player as well as the greatest athlete of all time. Such athletes as Lionel (Leo) Messi and Diego Maradona in Argentina, Kylian Mbappé and Zinedine Zidane in France, Mia Hamm in the United States, Christine Sinclair in Canada, and Sun Wen in China play similar roles. People who have made outstanding contributions to the sciences, education, and literature, are Nobel Prize winners, or have distinguished themselves in other ways also can symbolize their countries. In the Nobel Prize category, for instance, this would obviously include Marie Curie in medicine, Albert Einstein in physics, Pablo Neruda in poetry, Toni Morrison in literature, and Nelson Mandela, Malala Yousafzai, and the fourteenth Dalai Lama in peace activities. What they and many others have given to the world in real and symbolic terms is remarkable.

The same is true for many artists who have played remarkable roles for their countries, citizens, and cultures through the symbols of national cultures they created and the messages those symbols convey. A number of examples are needed here to convey the magnitude, importance, power, and profundity of such symbols at this crucial time in the historical development of countries, cultures, and the world.

Think, for example, of the role that Claude Joseph Rouget de Lisle played in creating what eventually became "La Marseillaise" and the impact it had on France and its culture; Franz Liszt's *Hungarian Rhapsodies* and especially *Rhapsody Number 2* and the effect they had on Hungary and Hungarian culture; composers such as Xian Xinghai and his *Yellow River* and Chen Gang and He Zhanhao and their *Butterfly Lovers Violin Concerto* (*Liang Zhu* in Chinese) and their impact on China and its culture; Persian architecture and carpets and what they convey about Iran and other Middle Eastern countries and their cultures; and the music of Edward Elgar and his Pomp and Circumstance marches—especially *Pomp and Circumstance Number 1* ("Land of Hope and Glory")—and their impact on England and English culture. Jean Sibelius's musical masterpiece *Finlandia* should also be added to this list. Many people in Finland think this majestic and inspiring piece should be Finland's national anthem (it isn't) because it accomplishes so much in capturing the heart, soul, and character of Finland, its national culture, and the Finnish people.

While these artists have all achieved national and international prominence for their countries, citizens, and cultures because of the national symbols they have created, some of these symbols—for instance, *Pomp and Circumstance No. 1* and *Finlandia*—have gone even further, becoming not only *national* symbols but *nationalistic* symbols, resonating with their populations and countries in so many ways. While England and the United States are perhaps the most prominent examples of this tendency, it is probably the U.S. that has gone further than any other country or culture in creating both national and nationalistic cultural symbols that say a great deal about it as a country and about American culture as a national culture and overall way of life. This is especially true of the military marches of John Philip Sousa, particularly his "Stars and Stripes Forever"; Glenn Miller's "In the Mood"; Louis Armstrong's "What a Wonderful World"; Don McLean's "American Pie"; and "America the Beautiful," the music for which was composed by Samuel A. Ward in 1882 and the lyrics by Katherine Lee Bates in 1893. It has been sung by countless performers but I find Elvis Presley's renditions particularly noteworthy.

The same point could be made about many other American composers and lyricists who were mostly Jewish and were either born in New York in the late nineteenth or early twentieth century or came to the city during this time, when New York was rapidly becoming a major focal point for musical and theatrical activity in the United States. Included in this group are Richard Rodgers and Oscar Hammerstein II and their musicals such as *Carousel* and *The Sound of Music* as well as such popular songs as "You'll Never Walk Alone," "Climb Every Mountain," and "Edelweiss"; George Gershwin and his *Rhapsody in Blue* and *American in Paris*; Aaron Copland's *Appalachian Spring, Rodeo, Billy the Kid*, and *Fanfare for the Common Man*; Max Steiner's film music for *Gone With the Wind*; Jerome Kern's music for *Showboat*; and the music of Erich Wolfgang Korngold, who emigrated from Europe to Hollywood and wrote the music for *Captain Blood, The Adventures of Robin Hood*, and many others. To this list should be added Irving Berlin, who was born in

Russia but came to the United States at a very early age with his family and created a number of America's most popular songs, such as "God Bless America," "White Christmas," and many others. All these pieces have not only had a national and nationalistic impact on American culture and the American way of life, but are now enjoyed by billions of people all over the world.

In recent years, no person has contributed more to America's and the world's understanding, awareness, and appreciation of the importance of this remarkable parts-whole phenomenon and symbolic process than Ken Burns, the American filmmaker. Through his many documentary films, Burns has demonstrated an uncanny knack for selecting specific parts of American culture and the American way of life that are not only symbolic in their own right but also representative of American culture and the American way of life in the holistic sense. This is especially evident in such films as *The Civil War, Jazz, Country Music, Jackie Robinson, Baseball, The Roosevelts, The Statue of Liberty*, and *The National Parks: America's Best Idea*. It is impossible to watch any of these films without learning a great deal about the United States as a country and American culture as a national culture and overall way of life. By identifying and connecting many carefully picked parts, Burns has demonstrated how it is possible to create a comprehensive portrait of American culture that goes right to the heart and soul of what the United States, its culture, and its way of life are all about. His work also provides an excellent illustration of how to apply this parts-whole phenomenon and holistic process to create comprehensive portraits and images of any country, its national culture, and its overall way of life.

What is true for the role artists, composers, lyricists, filmmakers, and many other creative people have played and continue to play in the case of the United States, its culture, and way of life is also true for other countries, their national cultures, and their ways of life. Not only do cultural activities possess the potential to broaden, deepen, and intensify our individual and collective knowledge, understanding, and appreciation of all countries and their cultures in the world in the all-inclusive sense, but they bring people from many different backgrounds, cultures, races, and ethnic groups together and make it possible for them to share cohesive, coherent, and collective experiences.

What makes this matter so essential at present and going forward into the future is the fact that virtually all countries and cultures in the world—and especially their national cultures—are now changing very rapidly. This will necessitate the creation of many *new* and probably *different* national cultural symbols in the future that are capable of bringing countries and citizens together rather than splitting them apart. Although it is impossible to predict where these symbols will come from, if the past is any guide they could well come from people who have experienced injustice and persecution. Interestingly, many people who are Black, Indigenous, marginalized, oppressed, or have been colonized for very long period of time are now seizing opportunities like this and are being inspired to create symbolic works that are bound to have a major impact on the countries where they are living at present or were born in and grew up. While these works and symbols may or may not be related to their own cultures and original languages, heritages, customs, or ways of life, they are desperately needed and could become the new national symbols and cultural masterpieces that all countries and cultures will require and hopefully enjoy and cherish in the future.

These developments and initiatives are coming at a time when the world is in a state of dynamic flux and revolutionary change. This is especially true for homogeneous cultures and the many symbols that people may have shared at one time but don't today, as well as the growing numbers of heterogeneous and hybrid cultures that now exist. Many of the latter have come into existence through major migratory movements and the increasing multiethnic character or multicultural composition of countries' populations.

All this comes at a time when many cultures are manifesting signs of becoming what might be called *world cultures*. This is due to many factors, including transformations in communications technologies and global trade and tourism.

No one understood the importance of developments like these better than T. S. Eliot who declared, "The development of cultures depends on two factors: the ability to go back and learn from domestic sources; and the ability to receive and assimilate influences from abroad."[2] This is the key to building (or rebuilding) all cultures and countries in the world in the years and decades ahead.

It is impossible to address such matters without coming to grips with the nature and functioning of the current system of international relations as well as what relations between countries and cultures can and should be like in the future. Consistent with the ethos of the economic age, the prevailing system of international relations is built to create as much material and monetary wealth as possible and award the highest priority to developing all the diverse economies of the world as well as the multifarious relationships that exist between and among them. This means focusing on creating relations predicated primarily on trade in commodities and resources; negotiating and signing trade agreements that are required to realize this; focusing largely on "hard activities" such as agricultural, industrial, and technological products and natural resources; and establishing the theoretical and practical foundations that are necessary to drive this international system and enable it to function effectively.

While trade has been going on between different parts of the world for thousands of years, the current system of international relations really only got off the ground and was established in a formal and systematic manner when Adam Smith's book *The Wealth of Nations* was published in 1776. Reacting strongly to the system of mercantilism that was in vogue at that time—a system based on massive governmental and political involvement in economic and political affairs—Smith advocated a system of economic and political liberalism in both the domestic and international domain that was predicated on minimal rather than maximal intervention by governments, or, as many people have put it, "the government that governs best governs least."

Smith was convinced that it was essential to base this system on free trade rather than protectionism in order to capitalize on the benefits and opportunities that resulted when countries specialized in the production of products for which they had a "comparative advantage" and then traded these products with other countries that had a comparative advantage in the production of other types of goods. This view was reinforced when Karl Marx claimed that all countries and their international relations can be divided into economic bases and non-economic superstructures (as discussed earlier). The bases consist largely of resources and agricultural, industrial, manufactured, and technological products and the superstructures of a variety of artistic, humanistic, intellectual, and recreational activities. It wasn't long after this that this system of international relations, much like the domestic system, was subdivided into *hard* and *soft* components with the highest priority placed on the hard component and the lowest priority on the soft component.

This is largely where the system of international relations stands at present, despite the fact that it is vastly larger and far more complicated, advanced, and sophisticated than it was in Marx or Smith's day. International trade is now governed, overseen, and monitored by the World Trade Organization (WTO). This system covers trade among virtually all countries and parts of the world. For the most part, "soft" activities (e.g., cultural or artistic exchanges) are treated as vehicles that help to accommodate and enhance trade relations among countries as well as generate more economic activity.

While this international system, like the economic age that gave rise to it and on which it is predicated, produces countless benefits and opportunities for people and countries in all parts of the world, regrettably it comes up short when it is examined in terms of what is going on in the world today and prospects for the future. Given all the life-threatening and dangerous problems that exist in the world, most of which are global in nature, it is apparent that *a new system of international relations* is needed in the future. The need for such a system was advocated and visualized by Paul J. Braisted some time ago when he claimed in his seminal publication *Cultural Cooperation: Keynote to the Coming Age* that:

Anyone who discards the possibility of developing more friendly relations among people should ponder the alternative long and well. The only alternative is continuing and deepening conflict, with its dangers of increasing reliance on violence, and the corrosive effects upon human life of distrust and fear. Is there no better way than the incalculable waste of recurrent strife?[3]

In order to address this challenge, it is necessary to create a great deal more cooperation, compromise, concessions, and interaction—as well as less competition, confrontation, aggression, and conflict—among different countries and cultures. World events over the last few decades have served to heighten awareness of this necessity, especially for national cultures and countries that are homogeneous, inflexible, and closed rather than heterogeneous, pliable, and open. Mircea Malitza, the Romanian cultural scholar, foresaw the need for this new system of international relations as well when he said:

> Cultures in watertight compartments are doomed to oblivion. Dialogue is essential. The choice between the development of a national culture and an increase in exchanges with the outside world is a false one. Interdependence cannot be denied. The cultures that have blossomed are those that have had the advantage of innumerable influences, received and transmitted in accordance with a process of unceasing enrichment.[4]

Developments like these can only be achieved by shifting from the partial and partisan perspective on international relations provided by economics and the economic age to the holistic perspective provided by culture and the cultural age. This means focusing attention on the development of culture and cultures and especially the cultures of countries in the all-inclusive sense first and foremost; doing what is in the best *cultural* interests of countries rather than what is in their best *economic* interests; paying much more attention to the needs of marginalized, oppressed, and poverty-stricken people and countries in the world; ridding the world of the adverse and misleading distinction between "hard" and "soft" activities; aspiring to achieve culture's highest and wisest values and ideals both internationally and domestically; pouring more funding into activities that unite rather than divide people, countries, and cultures; and dealing with international relations and diplomacy in cultural terms. This will not be possible without a dramatic increase in the importance of the arts, sciences, education, and the humanities throughout the world, as well as creating more opportunities for intercultural and cross-cultural dialogue, communication, and exchange.⁵ This is the key to realizing more solidarity, sustainability, harmony, and humanity in the world.

As Paul Braisted concluded when he assessed the nature and functioning of the prevailing system of international relations:

> The advancement of peoples and nations requires a radical subordination of profit-seeking motives to humane impulses. The welfare of people must gradually become the primary concern, and the manifold activities of commerce and business, hasty or careless industrialization, competition for natural resources, labor, and markets, must be adjusted accordingly. Too much of the glib talk about the inevitability of war and the evil nature of men [people] is a thin cloak of justification for unprincipled and unbridled exploitation in utter disregard of the fundamental things of human life. Clearly, subordination of economic motives to the humane interests of people is essential to world order, and to preparation for more fruitful cooperation.⁶

It is universal sharing of culture and cultures and commitment to learning as much as possible about culture and all the diverse cultures in the world from the smallest to the largest that will make it possible to counteract racism, excessive nationalism, imperialism, and xenophobia, as well as reduce the risks and dangers that accompany the current system of international relations. This is what Rabindranath Tagore, the Indian poet, cultural scholar, and sage, had in mind when he said, "We must prepare the field for the cooperation of all the cultures of the world where all will give and take from others. This is the keynote to the coming age."⁷

Thus far, we have been concerned with the incredible array of cultures that exist in the world at present and are apparent when we look downward at the ground, outward at eye level, and upward slightly above eye level.

When we look downward, we see the land and the earth, which are filled with precious natural resources that it is impossible to live without. When we look outward at eye level, we see countless parts of the natural and human environments which make up all human cultures in the world as well as the cultures of other species. And when we look upward, slightly above eye level, we see the tops of all the buildings that human beings have created over the centuries, as well as the tops of tall trees and many birds flying in the sky. In combination, these three ways of viewing all the many different parts of the world enable us to form a comprehensive picture of all the human, animal, and plant cultures that exist throughout the world in the holistic sense, as well as how they are affected by everything that exists under, on, or slightly above the surface of the earth.

However, this is not the end of the story. When we look a bit further upward, we see the sky above with even taller architectural creations such as the Eiffel Tower and all the other tall buildings and structures that have been built over the last few decades, the tops of even more gigantic trees, flocks of birds, and so forth. This view also includes the sky farther above the earth, and with it airplanes, perhaps a few drones, and possibly even an orbiting satellite. These are also part of human cultures. Indeed, steadily evolving today is a rapidly growing network of satellite and extraterrestrial cultures.

It doesn't take much imagination to conjure up an image of the many satellite and extraterrestrial cultures that will eventually exist in outer space due to humanity's insatiable curiosity and appetite for discoveries. Events over the last six or seven decades in this area have been staggering to say the least. While people have been interested in the sky, heavens, and other planets for centuries (as will be discussed momentarily), humanity is now actively involved in the search for extraterrestrial intelligence(s) and also wondering if eventually it might be possible for people to live on other planets and create cultures there. An incredible amount has been achieved in this field since the first artificial earth satellite, *Sputnik I*, was launched by the Soviet Union on October 4, 1957, orbiting the earth 1,440 times before it re-entered the atmosphere and burnt up. This event triggered a space race at first between the USSR (later Russia) and the United States and now involving China, India, and several other countries. It is now apparent that this is merely the beginning of a substantially larger and more active spatial process that will involve more and more countries in the world.

The launch of Sputnik was followed by a remarkable number of real-world events as well as cultural and media activities involving outer space. Among the latter were the creation of the television program *Star Trek*, which first aired on September 8, 1966 and depicted the interstellar voyages of the starship USS *Enterprise* with its captain James T. Kirk (played by William Shatner) and first officer Mister Spock (Leonard Nimoy) as well as other crew members, and the release of George Lucas' film *Star Wars* (1977), the epic space opera that triggered the production of numerous other movies and television programs like it, as well as video games, comic books, and theme parks, and which is now a culture in its own right with a huge following. In the real world, the landing of Apollo 11 on the moon on July 20, 1969 resulted in astronauts Neil Armstrong and Edwin Aldrin walking on the moon's surface. The moon landing was followed by the launch of the first space station, the Soviet Union's Salyut 1, on April 19, 1971; and the assembly and eventual completion of the International Space Station (ISS) between 1998 and 2011. This was a cooperative venture involving Europe, the United States, Russia, Canada, and Japan. As a result of developments like these, it was estimated in May 2023 that nearly 8,000 satellites are now active in orbit.

Once we leave the earth and enter outer space, cultures as wholes and ways of life are very different. Human beings must figure out ways to sustain life in an environment entirely unlike that on the earth's surface. To do so a phenomenal amount of creativity and ingenuity will be required. Despite the challenges posed by weightlessness and the vacuum of space, however, there will obviously be many more public and private space flights taken in the future. Eventually there may be efforts to establish colonies on Mars and other planets. Just as we have relied on the earth beneath our feet for countless centuries to provide us with the resources required for survival, so we will have to rely on looking upward beyond the earth to provide us with knowledge of the universe, and the cosmos, and especially how we can create cultures that can be passed on from one generation to the next and one century to the next in the world of the future.

If we look backward rather than forward in time and space, it is clear that understanding the universe we live in has been a priority for human beings for thousands of years. This began in earnest thousands of years ago with Indigenous peoples around the world. The intensive studies they conducted of the sky were essential to gaining a general impression of how the larger cosmic system operates, including such practical matters as when and where crops should be planted and harvested and what can be expected with respect to weather and climate conditions from season to season and year to year. This work has been carried on over the last two thousand years by too many scientists to mention, as well as other scholars who have tried to see matters like these from a broader and more all-encompassing perspective.

These developments are especially relevant today. While the two terms "universe" and "cosmos" are often used interchangeably, a fundamental distinction can be made between them, in which the universe is considered to be everything that exists in space and time as a "whole," whereas the cosmos can be considered not only as a "whole" but more fundamentally and essentially as a "structured and ordered whole."

Interestingly, cosmology—the discipline or activity that is concerned with the intensive study of the cosmos—is derived from two Greek words: *kosmos*, which means an ordered whole; and *logos* which means the study, discussion, or discourse of a specific subject. It follows from this that the term cosmology means discussion or discourse about the universe *as an ordered whole* and therefore includes all the logical principles and underlying assumptions and procedures that govern the working of the universe or, as the Cambridge Dictionary, puts it, "the universe considered as a system with an order and a pattern."

Unfortunately, cosmology is often confused with astronomy, with which it shares certain similarities. However, whereas astronomy is concerned with the nature and evolution of individual objects and systems in the universe (for instance, stars and planets), cosmology is concerned with the nature and evolution of the universe as an ordered and structured whole:

> Cosmology is thus the all-embracing science, for it deals with the structure and evolution of the entire universe—everything that we now observe and that we can ever hope to observe in the future. Astronomy, by contrast, deals with the properties of individual objects, such as stars and galaxies.[8]

This makes cosmology, like culture, a holistic and integrative discipline rather than a partial and specialized one:

> Cosmology is a joint enterprise by science, philosophy, religion, and the arts that seeks to gain understanding of what is unified and is fundamental. As a science, it is the study of the large-scale structure of the universe.... Cosmology is the one science in which specialization is rather difficult. Its main aim is to assemble the cosmic jigsaw puzzle, not to study in detail any particular jigsaw piece. While all other scientists are pulling the universe apart into more detailed bits and pieces, the cosmologists endeavour to put the pieces together in order to see the picture on the jigsaw puzzle.... The cosmologists, unlike other scientists, take the broad view. *They are like the impressionistic painters who stand well back from their canvas in order not to see too much distracting detail...*
>
> We cannot study cosmology in the broadest terms unless we pay particular heed to the pageantry of world pictures that have shaped the history of the human race.[9]

Unlike many contemporary cosmologists who have tended to emphasize scientific perceptions and studies of the universe and the cosmos, Thomas Berry, the well-known American cultural scholar and historian, was a great believer that the arts have a prominent role to play in the development of the new story of the universe and the cosmos that is needed, but nevertheless working in close conjunction with science rather than against it or separated from it. As David Schenck points out in his article, "Cosmology and Wisdom: The Great Teaching Work of Thomas Berry":

> For Berry cosmology is at once science and poetry, and most fundamentally, a matter of vision and myth and epic. A geologian might then fairly be considered a visionary for the earth.
>
> Thomas Berry, in addition to being our contemporary, is both behind us and ahead—a historian preserving the living core of wisdom traditions of human cultivation—and

a visionary listening towards the future cultivation of human presence on and to the earth.

We need new means of cultivating ourselves if we are to live differently on the earth. Developing and telling the new story is one component of establishing such cultivation. But the grand sweep of the longed-for cultivation is found only in Cosmology envisioned as the comprehensive presentation of the mystery of presence of the universe in myth, ritual and dream; in liturgy, poetry and music; in wisdom, literature and renewed philosophies and theologies; and in the plastic arts of all kinds—painting, sculpture, architecture.[10]

What makes the study of cosmology so captivating is the fact that the cosmos is not only an ordered and structured whole but is also, and far more fundamentally, a *regenerative* and *harmonious* whole. The cosmos's capacity as a regenerative whole is closely related to the need to achieve environmental sustainability. A regenerative whole is able to begin again many things after they are destroyed, such as plants and trees that are consumed by a forest fire and then spring back to life and arise once again. It is much better for the natural environment if, in similar fashion, scarce resources are re-used and recycled rather than being discarded after one use. Governments in countries like Canada, Australia, New Zealand, and the United States are calling on their large Indigenous populations to share their vast knowledge and understanding of how to develop an intimate and viable connection between people, the land, and the natural environment. This is because many Indigenous myths, legends, metaphors, rituals, and the like are intimately connected with environmental conservation, preservation, and sustainability, and, as a result of this, working with nature, the land, the environment, and the world through *permaculture* and activities that work *with* nature rather than *against* it.

And this is not all. Increasingly, the cosmos is being seen and understood these days as a *harmonious* whole. Such an understanding is connected with one of the most worthwhile goals of culture. While this goal will be discussed in detail later in this book, suffice it to say here that creating wholes that are harmonious is one of *the* most quintessential and inspirational ideals of culture and cultures, regardless of how it is applied.

Given the importance of the cosmos and cosmology, the launch in 2021 of the James Webb Space Telescope—the largest optical telescope ever created—could not have come at a better time. The product of collaboration between the U.S. National Aeronautics Space Administration (NASA), the European Space Agency (ESA), and the Canadian Space Agency (CSA), and named after James E. Webb, NASA's administrator from 1961 to 1968 as the agency developed the systems and technology to put human beings on the moon, the telescope has been sending miraculous images back to earth. In 2023, for instance, it sent back images of six galaxies that existed only 540 million to 770 million years after the Big Bang, the event that scientists believe created the universe. It is also achieving many objectives, such as observing primordial stars and galaxies and studying the atmospheres of planets orbiting other stars that might be potentially habitable.

The relevance of these achievements for humanity as a whole were foreshadowed by Milton Munitz when he wrote:

> One of the characteristic, persistent, and irrepressible needs of the human mind is to have a cosmology. It consists in the interest in being able to describe and understand the large-scale global structure of the universe in which we live. An interest in cosmology ... is to be found in virtually every period and culture of recorded history.[11]

Since cosmological questions, like cultural questions, originate in the human mind and people's innate curiosity and incredible imagination, a related set of questions link cosmology and culture together. These questions also have to do with the way human beings see, relate, and connect to the world, the universe, and the cosmos. Munitz confirmed the fundamental importance of this when he stated:

> We wish to know our "place," where we fit in among all the other entities that make up the universe. What forces, powers, and causes brought us into existence and sustain us? What

should be our goals, purposes, and values? Is there some cosmic design of which our lives are a part? Being able to answer these kinds of questions is one way of responding to what is frequently referred to as a search for the meaning of life.[12]

Pierre Pascallon had the same principle in mind when he said that "every culture, every people must discover its own interior cosmology, must arrive at a coherent account of its being in the world, must be able to locate itself in a recognizable world and find for itself the organizing principles of its world."[13]

We would probably be wise to leave the last word on cosmology and the cosmos as a regenerative and harmonious whole and its intimate connection with people, countries, and cultures to ancient and contemporary cosmological and holistic scholars such as Thanu Padmanabhan, Swami Vivekananda, Rana P. B. Singh, and many others in India and elsewhere in the world who have delved deeply into these matters. As Fritjof Capra pointed out in his book *The Tao of Physics*, at its most elementary level, Indian philosophy is predicated on "an awareness of the unity and mutual interrelation of all things and events, the experience of all phenomena in the world as manifestations of a basic oneness. All things are seen as interdependent and inseparable parts of this cosmic whole, as different manifestations of the same ultimate reality."[14]

Given all the conflict that exists in the world today, there may be nothing more important going forward than to capitalize on the sense of harmony, order, unity, and oneness that exists in the cosmos and the potential it possesses to help us bring a new age into existence in the years ahead. In order to do this, we will likely have to look not only downward, straight ahead, or slightly upwards in the future, but increasingly much higher upwards and outward. It is from there that much of our energy and inspiration may have to come if the world's problems are to be addressed and culture's highest, wisest, and most worthwhile and inspiring visions and ideals realized.

Chapter Seven

Behaviour and Ways of Life of Other Species

Culture consists of certain biological activities, neither more or less biological than digestion or locomotion.... Culture is merely a special direction which we give to the cultivation of our animal potencies.
—José Ortega y Gasset[1]

While anthropologists were the first scholars to make the case that cultures are and should be seen as wholes and ways of life, their studies focused on humans and the cultures they created. As a result, not a great deal of attention was paid to other species or the natural environment, except where they connected to anthropology and human beings in important ways.

As a result, it has taken the work of countless biologists, zoologists, botanists, horticulturalists, ecologists, and so forth to expand the realm of culture beyond the human species to include other species, with a focus especially on the similarities and differences that exist between all the diverse species in the world. Most prominent in this regard were the research activities, findings, and publications of Charles Darwin, Gregor Mendel, Louis Pasteur, Carl Linnaeus, George Washington Carver, and Arthur Tansley in earlier times, and Rachel Carson, E. O. Wilson, Desmond Morris, Jane Goodall, Dian Fossey, Eugene Odum, and many others more recently. Through their studies and those of other scholars, numerous questions were raised about the nature and functioning of plants and animals and whether they create cultures as well, or whether culture and cultures are limited to the human species.

It wasn't long before answers emerged to these questions. It soon became apparent that all species including plants and animals and not just human beings create cultures and share much in common in cultural and holistic terms.

The first forms of life on earth were microorganisms, traces of which can be dated to more than 3.7 billion years ago—less than a billion years after the earth itself had formed. For most of the earth's history, bacteria and other one-celled organisms were the predominant form of life, and most living organisms were found in the oceans. Multicellular organisms—first plants, then animals—only emerged onto the land about 450 million years ago. Of the animals we are most familiar with today, amphibians (modern examples of which are frogs and toads) arose about 350 million years ago, and reptiles (snakes and lizards being modern examples) a little more than 300 million years ago. The dinosaurs, historically the most successful reptiles, evolved about 240 million years ago and dominated the animal kingdom until 66 million years ago, when (most scientists now believe) the impact of a comet or asteroid caused worldwide destruction and resulted in their extinction.

Mammals originated about 195 million years ago but lived in the shadow of the dinosaurs until the mass extinction that occurred 66 million years ago. Those mammals that survived rapidly evolved to fill the various ecological niches left open by the vanished dinosaurs. Humans are members of a specific order of animals, the primates, which also includes gorillas, chimpanzees, and gibbons. The first primate fossils date from about 57 million years ago, though there is evidence to suggest the very earliest primates arose while the dinosaurs still roamed the earth, 85 million years ago.

Like human beings, plants and other animals need food, water, and air to exist and survive. They also go through similar stages of life, such as birth, growth, development, decline, and eventually death. They share many physical and social characteristics and functions, such as procreation, consumption and elimination, communication, the development of groups and communities, social interaction, and bonding.

Nevertheless, there are many differences among species. This is especially true for human beings on the one hand and plants and others animals on the other. Many people believe that culture in general—and the ability to create cultures in particular—is primarily, if not exclusively, a human ability and therefore the sole preserve of human beings. Even if other species have culture and are able to create cultures in the holistic sense, critics of this point of view contend that this ability is so limited compared to human beings that it is not worth discussing. For such people, culture and the ability to create cultures is the principal difference between human beings and other species.

This results primarily from the belief sustained over many centuries that only human beings possess the ability to think, reason, and, perhaps most importantly of all, exhibit consciousness and the capacity to engage in self-reflection and critical examination. This led to the conclusion that most human actions are grounded in intelligence—the ability to think things out and act in a logical, rational, conscious, and consistent manner. This contrasted fundamentally, as advocates of this belief were quick to point out, with the behaviour and ways of life of plants and other animals, which they contended are based largely on instinct. Other researchers have a different take on this subject, although it boils down to much the same thing in the end. They see all the different species in the world as forming a gigantic pyramid or hierarchy with human beings at the very top of the pyramid, other animals located below human beings but much farther down, plants farther down yet, and one-celled living organisms such as protozoa, bacteria, and so forth at the bottom.

Views like this were common and often strengthened by many religions and religious institutions because they were based on the belief that human beings were created by one or several gods and were cast in his, her, or their image, granted domination over the earth, and therefore situated in a very privileged position at the apex of the pyramid. This was often interpreted to mean that people could act in any way they wanted towards other species because those species are placed on earth to serve the needs, interests, and aspirations of human beings. This belief is epitomized in the Western tradition by the Biblical verse that states, "Then God said, 'Let us make humankind in our image, according to our likeness; and let them have dominion over the fish of the sea, and over the birds of the air, and over the cattle, and over all the wild animals of the earth, and over every creeping thing that creeps upon the earth'" (Genesis 1:26).

Beliefs like this made it possible for people to create a huge divide between themselves and other species. This helped to ease the sense of guilt they felt for the way they treated other species and especially animals. Humans subjected animals to their will, killed them for their meat, used their hides and fur to make clothing, put them to work carrying heavy loads or lifting awkward objects, and displayed them in circuses, zoos, and cages. And they still do.

Such beliefs have changed dramatically over the last fifty or sixty years. There has been a phenomenal increase in interest in the behaviour and ways of life of other species. With this interest has come much more awareness and acceptance of the fact that other living organisms have culture and create cultures, much as humans do. Moreover, the similarities between human beings, plants, and animals are now deemed to be far greater than was previously assumed. Generally speaking, this has led to the conclusion that the differences between all the different species in the world are primarily differences in degree and extent and not in substance or kind. Every species has its own forms of culture and ability to create cultures that are manifested in its behaviour and ways of life.

This includes not only animals (including humans) and plants, but also microorganisms such as bacteria, archaea, protozoa, algae, and fungi. (Viruses are often included in the list, too, although many scientists do not consider them living organisms as such because they cannot reproduce themselves outside a host cell.) Interestingly, the biggest living organism that has ever existed is not a giant whale, gigantic redwood tree, or dinosaur, as most people may think, but rather a colossal honey mushroom (also known as a shoestring fungus) that exists in the Blue Mountains of Oregon and measures more than three kilometres across.

As living organisms, plants have most of the same needs as human beings and animals. Not only do they need water, air, sunlight, and nutrients, but also they share similar stages in the life process such as birth, development, maturity, and death, consumption and elimination, and the ability to communicate with one another. In fact, current research is revealing that the gap between plants and animals (including humans) is not as great as was once thought.

Nevertheless, there are some basic differences between plants and animals. For instance, most plants can create their own foods and foodstuffs by using water, sunlight, and carbon dioxide through the process known as photosynthesis, while animals including humans must eat other animals or plants in order to exist and survive. Another basic difference between plants and animals turns out to be a real advantage for humans and other animals as well as a real disadvantage for plants. Since animals have specialized nervous and muscular systems, most of them are able to move around and travel from one place to another. This is not the case, however, for plants, which cannot move of their own accord. This difference makes it possible for animals to flee and run when they are in danger or attacked, whereas plants cannot. Despite this obvious difference, some plants are able to warn other plants when they are in danger by emitting certain substances or smells that drive attackers away.

One of the most interesting things about the intimate connection between plants, human beings, culture, and cultures is the fact that the word "culture," which is derived from the Latin word *cultura*, means to plant, grow, nurture, and especially to *cultivate*. The great Roman orator and statesman Marcus Cicero went even further than this by using the word culture for the first time in history more than twenty centuries ago when he said, "*Cultura animi philosophia est*," which can be translated as "Culture is the philosophy or cultivation of the soul."

We owe Cicero a great debt of gratitude for making this connection between plants and human beings. This connection is especially important since all species depend on nature and the natural environment for their survival and well-being, and it is far too important to ignore. We need a world system in the future that is deeply rooted in and connected to nature, cultivation, culture, and cultures if we are to be successful in coming to grips with global warming and other environmental crises. That connection must lie at its very core and be its fundamental essence. Culture possesses the potential to do this when it is seen and dealt with in holistic terms, as Cicero rightly realized more than two thousand years ago.

As far as the natural world is concerned, the idea of culture as cultivation played a crucial role in the development of agriculture thousands of years ago, much as it still does today. This is also true for horticulture, or cultivation of plants, flowers, and gardens; silviculture, or the growth and development of trees, shrubs, and forests; viticulture, or the development of grapes and the production of wine; and most of all, permaculture, or the creation and implementation of activities that work *with* nature rather than *against* it, which is imperative going forward into the future as noted earlier.

According to the Greek historian Thucydides, the importance of culture as cultivation can be traced back to the period when people in the Mediterranean region learned how to cultivate grape vines and olive trees. This occurred sometime between 3000 B.C. and 2000 B.C. in Asia Minor, Greece, the Cyclades Islands, and the Aegean. In fact, recent research has revealed that winemaking began even earlier than this, likely around 6000 B.C. in sites located about 50 kilometres south of the present Georgian capital of Tbilisi.

As time passed, culture began to manifest itself more often in the human domain and not just the natural domain, which is why Cicero was so prophetic when he connected culture to the cultivation of the soul. No person was more committed to the idea of culture as cultivation than Voltaire, the great French scholar and author. He was born François-Marie Arouet in 1694 in Paris, but adopted the pen name "Voltaire." Although he did not use the term "culture" as such, Voltaire was concerned with culture in both the individual and collective sense.

In the individual sense, he felt it was necessary for people to "plant," "build," and "cultivate," since this is the key to achieving a great deal in life, as well as living a full, upright, and responsible life. In a collective sense, he felt that this was the best way of preventing boredom, vice, violence, crime, and sorrow, something Voltaire believed was imperative if societies, countries, and cultures were to be built up rather than torn down. There is an interesting passage on this subject in Voltaire's book *Candide*. It can be paraphrased as follows: *Above all, cultivate! Since this is a matter of conscience and character, it is essential to be constantly asking ourselves such questions as: Do I plant? Do I build? Do I cultivate?*

This is not the only example drawn from nature that Voltaire used to make the case that culture as cultivation is essential for people in general and communities, societies, countries, and cultures

in particular. He also expressed the need to achieve "civilization"—
and to build "civilizations"—which he epitomized by his oft-quoted
phrase, "We must cultivate our garden." By pooling the labour of all
people, Voltaire believed it is possible to build societies, cultures,
and civilizations—human gardens, if you prefer—that are capable of
blending wisdom, morality, material welfare, order, and well-being
together to form dynamic, organic, collective, and harmonious wholes
made up of many different parts. In order to do this, Voltaire felt that
all factors must be present and in balance, since cultures, civilization,
and civilizations require the presence, symbiosis, and synthesis of all
the diverse factors, forces, and activities that constitute these complex
entities.

Consider our own connection with the natural environment as an
excellent illustration of this. Being in tune with nature and bonding
fully with the natural environment are essential because this makes
us more aware of nature's many different elements, cycles, rhythms,
themes, and patterns. Not only do nature and the natural environment
dance to their own drummer and have a life, character, and presence
all their own, but also they are full of all sorts of ingredients that have
been immortalized throughout history for their soothing, relaxing,
and healing properties.

What is true for nature and the natural environment is also true
for the cultivation and functioning of their many diverse elements.
While we have spent a great deal of time over the last few centuries
ignoring the natural world and emphasizing the differences between
human beings and other species—largely for the purpose of making
use of them in economic and materialistic terms—much more time
and attention will now have to be devoted to embracing the natural
world and understanding and appreciating the many similarities that
exist between human beings, nature, the natural world, and other
species. One of the best ways to do this is through creating, studying,
and cultivating gardens.

Indeed, there are striking similarities between plants, flowers,
gardens, people, and cultures when we stop to think about it. As
far as plants and flowers are concerned, there are "early bloomers,"
"mid-bloomers," and "late bloomers." Early bloomers burst forth in
all their glory and magnificence at the first sign of spring. Then there

are mid-bloomers. They tend to hit their stride at different times over the summer. Finally, there are late bloomers, which bloom in the fall. There are even some "non-bloomers," plants that don't bloom because the growing conditions were not right.

What is true for plants and flowers is also true for people. There are early bloomers, mid-bloomers, late bloomers, and—alas—even non-bloomers. Some people bloom very early in life. When they do this, they are often called "child prodigies" because they manifest unusual talents and exceptional abilities at a very early age. Then there are the mid-bloomers. Most people fit into this category because they hit their stride later in life, usually in their thirties, forties, and fifties. These people are followed by the late-bloomers. They bloom much later in life—often in their sixties, seventies, eighties, and possibly even their nineties these days—and may go on to produce things that are very beneficial and worthwhile. Finally, there are the non-bloomers. These are people who don't bloom at all because they received too little attention, recognition, and encouragement during their lives and therefore the growing conditions were not right.

These are not the only similarities between plants and people. Plants come in many different shapes, sizes, colours, and types, just as people do. Some plants are annuals or biennials, blooming once or possibly twice and then—regrettably—never blooming again. However, others are perennials that come back year after year to bless us with their beauty and dependability. Moreover, some plants are tall; others are short. Some grow horizontally and spread along the ground; others grow vertically and stretch towards the heavens. Some are top-heavy and need propping up; others have strong stems and spines and don't require any external assistance.

People are like this, too. They also come in many different shapes, sizes, colours, and types. Some flower once—or possibly twice—and never again. Others flower constantly. Some are seven feet tall; others are four feet short. Some have highly developed minds but need propping up in other areas. Others are fully developed in all areas and require little or no outside assistance. Some are Africans, Asians, and Oceanics; others are Americans, Europeans, Middle Easterners, or South Americans. And this is the point. No two people—like no two plants—are the same. Each one has its own specific qualities and characteristics—qualities and characteristics that make it one of a kind and unique.

And the similarities do not end here. Some plants and flowers love the sun and thrive in it; others prefer the shade. To this must be added the "show-offs" and the "wallflowers." Plants and flowers that grow from bulbs, such as gladiolas, irises, and lilies, are often show-offs. They produce magnificent flowers when they are looked after properly and in full bloom. Others are wallflowers, constantly shrinking from view and attention. People are like this, too. Some like it hot and perform best when they are in the limelight. Others prefer the shade and perform best when these conditions prevail. While show-offs often muscle other people out of the way in order to grab all the attention, recognition, and notoriety for themselves, wallflowers—or "shrinking violets" as they are often called—hold back and stay out of the limelight, thereby providing a great deal of relief from the show-offs.

Skilled gardeners know all about these different capabilities and characteristics of plants and flowers and give them special attention in the design, layout, and cultivation of gardens. If gardens are to delight the eye and soothe the senses and the soul—and if they are to thrive throughout the entire growing season and not just part of it—it is imperative to know an enormous amount about the strengths, shortcomings, and idiosyncrasies of plants and flowers. What would gardens be without their show-offs and wallflowers, annuals, biennials, and perennials, plants that flourish in the sun and plants that thrive in the shade, and plants that bloom at different times during the season?

This is not only because gardens are cultures made up of many different parts just as human cultures are, but also because there are many different kinds of gardens and human cultures in existence throughout the world.

In the case of gardens, some are composed of the same flowers—roses and tulips, for example—and are uniform and homogenous. These gardens are incredibly beautiful when they are in full bloom—think of the rose gardens in England and the tulip gardens in the Netherlands, for instance—but are far less attractive when they are not in bloom. Other gardens are composed of many different flowers, which make them diverse and heterogeneous. These gardens have many different types of plants and flowers in them that bloom at different times throughout the growing season and not all at once. The human equivalent to this would be homogeneous and heterogeneous cultures—monocultures and multicultures, if you like—which is why Voltaire was so committed to the cultivation of many heterogeneous cultures in Europe rather than a single and homogeneous "European culture."

Human cultures, like garden cultures, are also designed and cultivated in many ways and for various reasons. Some cultures, especially western and northern cultures, are designed and cultivated with a great deal of care and attention given to details. As a result, an incredible amount of time, energy, and effort goes into ensuring that every part of these cultures is cultivated properly, from the arts and sciences to politics, economics, education, sports, recreation, technology, social affairs, and numerous others. Many European cultures are like this, especially urban cultures where everything is attended to with a great deal of care to ensure that they serve the purpose for which they are intended. In other cases, cultures may be left more to their own devices, such as some cultures in Africa, South America, the Caribbean, and elsewhere in the world where things are much freer to evolve on their own and in their own particular way or style.

Regardless of what type of garden cultures or human cultures we create, the litmus test is always the same. Do the cultures work? Are needs and aspirations dealt with effectively? Have dynamic and organic wholes been created that achieve balance and harmony between and among the many parts? Without doubt, there is a great deal to be learned from the creation and cultivation of garden cultures that is relevant to the creation and cultivation of human cultures if we are wise enough to realize this and capitalize on it.[2]

One of the best ways to do this is to consider the connection between the cultures of trees and the cultures of human beings. Not only do trees occupy a very prominent place in the natural realm but they have great symbolic significance. They also provide shade, coolness, and relief from the heat, and have been revered from time immemorial as special elements in the natural world. Small wonder one of Handel's most admired and appreciated musical works—*Ombre mai fu*—is an ode to a tree.

This helps to explain why trees are often used as metaphors for culture and cultures. When culture and cultures are defined in this all-encompassing sense, they can be visualized as trees with roots, trunks, branches, leaves, flowers, and fruit. Seen and dealt with this way, myths, mythology, worldviews, ideologies, axioms, cosmologies, and so forth constitute the roots; agricultural and industrial activities, economic and scientific endeavours, technological tools, political pursuits, social processes, behavioural practices, environmental features, and the like comprise the trunk and branches; and artistic creations, ethical beliefs, value systems, intellectual and humanistic achievements, and religious, philosophical, and spiritual ideals are the leaves, flowers, and fruit.

In his book *The Paths of Culture: A General Ethnology*, Kaj Birket-Smith carries this tree metaphor a step further by linking it to human culture and cultures when he states:

Culture is like a tree, a fabulous tree in which each branch is formed differently from its neighbour, each flower has its own color and fragrance, each fruit its special sweetness. This wealth and abundance has developed naturally. Each culture and each people bears its individual stamp; but the branches are all shoots of the same trunk and are fed by the same sap. If the branches are cut and detached from the trunk, the flowers wither. We are all members of the great society of mankind [humankind]; our national cultures are part of the culture of the whole world, which we must continue building up.[3]

Such metaphors are helpful because they provide an effective way of thinking about, visualizing, and understanding how culture and cultures in the human realm function in both the anthropological and biological sense. Not only do they deal with culture and cultures in the all-inclusive and holistic rather than partial and specialized sense—thereby concentrating attention on culture and cultures' inclusive character and integrative potential—but they focus on the fundamental relationships, interdependencies, connections, and links that exist between and among the component parts of culture and cultures. They also depict culture and cultures as dynamic and organic wholes made up of many interacting parts—much like trees— that are constantly evolving, changing, mutating, and adapting over time, just as all living things do.

In their book *Tree Cultures: The Place of Trees and Trees in Their Place*, authors Paul Cloke and Owain Jones confirm the fact that trees have many practical uses in addition to having great symbolic significance and metaphoric potential. Not only do they provide us with wood, bark, fruit, and other types of materials, but they draw carbon dioxide out of the air and therefore constitute one of the best vehicles for fighting global warming. This explains why many countries in the world are planting millions of trees at present and there is so much concern everywhere in the world over the loss of the Amazon rainforests.

And this is not all. Peter Wohlleben, who has spent the bulk of his life analyzing trees in general and forests in particular, confirmed after decades of empirical research that trees like to stand close together, enjoy each other's company, feel pain, have emotions, and experience fear. In his book *The Hidden Life of Trees*, Wohlleben states that there is a great deal of friendship and compatibility among trees. They "bond like an old couple, where one looks after the other," and are therefore not competitive, remarkably social, and have excellent memories. Trees also exchange a great deal of chemical information, not only among members of their own species but also among other trees and even certain other plants and shrubs. When dangers occur or they are threatened by other species, some trees will instantly alert other trees, shrubs, and plants in the vicinity to this threat through the sense of smell, primarily by emitting volatile and often bitter organic substances that boost the tannin levels in their trunks, branches, and leaves. This makes them less attractive to animals and herbivores as well as alerting other plants in the area.

Trees also create cultures together with other trees according to Wohlleben, especially when they grow close together and interact constantly with each other through their root systems. This is especially true in forests, where their massive root systems are submerged underground, not unlike icebergs in oceans. Wohlleben explains this phenomenon this way:

> If you look at roadside embankments, you might be able to see how trees connect with each other through their root systems. On these slopes, rain often washes away the soil, leaving the underground networks exposed. Scientists in the Harz mountains in Germany have discovered that this really is a case of interdependence, and most individual trees of the same species growing in the same stand are connected to each other through their root systems. It appears that nutrient exchange and helping neighbors in times of need is the rule, and this leads to the conclusion that forests are superorganisms with interconnections much like ant colonies.[4]

The root systems of trees are fascinating. They are not unlike cultures in many ways because they are composed of many elements that are constantly growing and interacting with each other and impinging on one another. Tim Flannery, in his introduction to Wohlleben's book, states:

> A tree's most important means of staying connected to other trees is a "*wood wide web*" (this is a phrase created by Suzanne Simard, a forest ecology professor at the University of British Columbia in Canada, in talking about the "language of trees") of soil fungi that connects vegetation in an intimate network that allows the sharing of an enormous amount of information and goods. Scientific research aimed at understanding the astonishing abilities of this partnership between fungi and plant has only just begun.[5]

The fact that trees and other plants share much in common with humans and can create cultures and benefit from them in much the same way that human beings do is very important, especially as far as the future of humanity and life on earth are concerned. Unlike many disciplines that focus largely or entirely on human beings and aspects of the cultures they create, the biological and ecological manifestations of culture do not confine culture and cultures to human beings but include them along with all other types of living organisms and their cultures in the natural realm.

What is true for the intimate connection between the culture and cultures of humans, plants, and trees is also true for the connection between the human species and other types of animal species.

Take bees and bee cultures as one of the most obvious and best illustrations of this. Without the ability of bees to pollinate all the different plants that are required for survival, it is very possible that human beings and many other types of species would not exist today.

Like human beings and human cultures, bees create highly complex and intricately designed cultures that are concerned with their habitation, community living, solidarity, communication, interaction, survival, and well-being. These cultures, with their queen, drone, and worker bees, rigid hierarchies and divisions of labour, finely tuned communications systems, sensing capacities, and productive capabilities, determine how bees live as a species as well as ensure their ongoing procreation, existence, and survival. This is because bees, like human beings, create continuous flows of products, much as human beings do. These products, such as honey, wax, beehives, and honeycombs, are much in demand in the human domain and have both a functional and aesthetic significance. Beehives and honeycombs, for example, are remarkable creations, comparable in their style, design, function, and complexity to many of the cultural creations of human beings, although on a much smaller scale.

Just as bees prefer certain types of habitats and create their homes, so all animal species have habitats and homes of one kind or another. These homes or habitats may be located in towns, cities, forests, deserts, grasslands, wetlands, tundra, or mountainous areas, or, in the case of fish, oceans, seas, lakes, streams, and rivers. Animals live in a variety of accommodations in these places, such as dens, lairs, holes, tree trunks, hollow branches, caves, nests, hills, woods, ponds, meadows, and so forth. We know now that octopuses are capable of using clam and coconut shells to create their homes on the ocean floor. Moreover, the homes of some animals are very elaborate, such as bird nests, beaver dams, and ant hills.

Speaking of ant hills, contemporary research is revealing that ants are much better traffic engineers than people because they never have to endure long traffic jams or gridlocks. Investigations into this matter at the University of Potsdam and the Martin Luther University Halle-Wittenberg in Germany revealed that a nest of black meadow ants had four main trunklines leading to and from their foraging area in a forested area of Saxony. The ants treated each track to and from their ant hill very much like a three-lane highway. When traffic volume was low they travelled down the centre of the track, whereas when it was high they spread out. Similar arrangements were made with respect to leaving and returning to the ant hills; ants searching for food went out on one side of the line or track and returned with food on the other side. There were also strict rules concerning how and when to pass, deal with obstacles and encumbrances, and speed up or slow down depending on the density of the traffic.

In order to compete for survival and ensure their well-being, many animals are compelled to develop, adopt, and cultivate very specific traits, attributes, and sensory capabilities such as this that may not only be on a par with those of human beings, but, in certain cases, far superior to them. This is especially true with respect to the different senses. Elephants, bears, and sharks, for instance, are said to have the strongest sense of smell. Bears can detect a dead carcass twenty miles away, elephants can detect water thirty miles away, and dogs can sniff out drugs and other items in densely packed suitcases and trunks, as well as detect illnesses in people through their highly cultivated sense of smell. When it comes to sight, hawks can see much better than human beings, even though their eyes are substantially smaller. Apparently, moths have the best sense of hearing of all species, largely as a result of having to evade their most dreaded predator, the bat. Moreover, catfish have the best sense of taste, primarily because they have more than 100,000 taste buds situated in their mouths and other parts of their bodies whereas humans have only about 10,000 taste buds.

And this isn't all. Recent research has revealed that animals have many different ways of communicating in general and communicating information related to their survival and well-being in particular. When bees leave the hive to hunt for flowers in order to extract their nectar to produce honey, they dance when they return to their hives in order to communicate this information to their fellow bees. This tells the bees in the hive what direction to fly by following the position of the sun in the sky, how far away the flowers are from their hives, and how large the food supply is in a specific location.

Communication of this type—as well as language in general—is not confined to bees. Every animal species has its own form of language and communication that enables members of a species to communicate with other members of the species and even members of other species on occasion. Birds, for example, have different dialects in song that enable them to communicate information about who they are, where they are, what their territories are, whether or not they want to copulate, and a great deal else. The master of this is without doubt the mockingbird. It was made famous as the principal symbol or metaphor in Harper Lee's novel *To Kill a Mockingbird*. Interestingly, T. Gilbert Pearson called the mockingbird "the song king of the lawn," and, as far back as 1929, the noted ornithologist E. H. Forbush wrote that the mockingbird equals and even exceeds "the whole feathered choir." These birds are renowned for their ability to mimic the sounds of dogs, cats, trucks, and people. They are said to have over two hundred songs, tunes, and words in their repertoires or vocabularies, which is why their scientific name—*Mimus polyglottos*—means "many-tongued mimic." This description might be contested by lyre birds and parrots: lyre birds are able to mimic the sounds of chainsaws, heavy trucks, and so forth; parrots are able to mimic or duplicate the voices and words of people and even talk or sing to them on certain occasions. Small wonder a bird was Mozart's favourite companion, in this case a starling that he loved and was attached to so much that he wrote a musical work, "A Musical Joke," in its honour.

While birds have developed and cultivated many types of language and communication through the variety of sounds they make, this incredible asset is by no means limited to them. Recent research is revealing that fish have also created and cultivated many types of languages and communication through the numerous sounds they make. In an article titled "Chattiest schools are in the sea," journalist Hina Alam claims, "Fish, it turns out, are a chatty lot. They communicate about everything from what area of the sea has the best food to where predators might be lurking or hiding out, and, of course, their desire for a mate."⁶ Through an online portal called FishSounds, Canadian, American, and Brazilian university scholars have created an inventory of sea creature sounds so people can listen to underwater recordings and learn that a sablefish emits a rasp while the orange-lined tigerfish makes a drumroll sound. According to Kieran Cox at Simon Fraser University, "Fish have been singing a lot longer than birds have been singing" from an evolutionary perspective and produce two types of sounds: active and passive. "Active sounds are made intentionally using mouths or other body parts and can involve release of bubbles, maneuvering different muscles to make a certain noise or moving bones around to get a repetitive click. Others make a sound like the beating of a drum with their swim bladers."⁷

When it comes to intelligence, many types of animals are no slouches. There are many examples of this. It is a well-known fact that chimpanzees are very smart, and why not since they share 98 percent of their DNA with human beings? Chimps can easily recognize and remember changing signs and flashing images on computer screens when they are taught to do so. Moreover, dolphins can identify themselves in mirrors when specific markings are made on them, which they immediately attempt to rub off or remove; elephants can tell whether it is a man, woman, or child talking; and some crows, which have long been recognized as being very intelligent and incredibly crafty and creative, were able in one experiment to get a toy floating on top of the water under a tall, narrow glass by dropping pebbles into the glass until enough water was displaced that the toy rose to the top of the glass where it was quickly grabbed by the crow in its beak. But probably the most intelligent feat of all performed by animals should be reserved for raccoons and their ability to figure out how to open garbage cans, bins, and other containers. For years, they have been waging a war with human beings and outsmarting designers by opening ever more complicated and sophisticated garbage cans, bins, and containers that have been designed deliberately to keep them out.

And there is more. Much more. Modern advances in biology and zoology are revealing that animals possess many other capabilities, traits, and characteristics that are similar to those of humans. This includes their capacity to experience joy, happiness, pain, sorrow, and suffering, protect their babies and young ones, respect their elders, and assist other animals that have disabilities or are handicapped or distressed in some way. They also have feelings and emotions such as sympathy, empathy, love, and compassion, engage in acts of kindness, generosity, and reconciliation as well as retaliation and vengeance if required, make concessions and compromises, seek and extend forgiveness, and cooperate when this is necessary. They also make aesthetic judgements and choices, especially during the courting and mating season, appreciate beauty and beautiful things, indulge in play and recreation, recognize and follow rules, act morally in some situations, and have memories. Consistent with the findings of Anne Dagg, Jane Goodall, Dian Fossey, and many others, animals also have personalities and personality traits much like human beings, such as agreeableness, aggression, extroversion, introversion, depression, anxiety, and self-control.

It is impossible to think about the personalities of animals and their various traits and characteristics without mentioning Camille Saint-Saëns' popular musical masterpiece *Carnival of the Animals* and the wonderful description of this evocative piece and the animals in it written by Ogden Nash. While not all animal species may display human characteristics, many do. And why not? Animals are just like people in many ways, and people are just like animals in many ways as well. If animals didn't possess similar qualities, characteristics, and abilities as humans, their lives would be different from ours, and ours from theirs. However, they are similar because humans are animals too, and have evolved from a common ancestor we share with chimpanzees.

Just like humans, animals have many different mating customs, habits, and rituals. These can be very elaborate and even ceremonial in certain situations, extending all the way from puffing up their chests and ruffling their feathers in the case of birds to many different types of dances, hoots, and calls for other animals. Interesting, when swans court and date, they curve their necks towards each other in the shape of a heart, lift their wings, and bow, which explains why swans are often regarded as real courtiers in the animal world.

Much as it is for courting, dating, and mating habits, so it is for "hiving off," procreation, and sexual practices. Some animals spend their entire lives together while others only come together during the mating season, some reuniting with the same partner year after year while others take a new partner every year. Animals that remain together for life or rejoin the same partner every mating season include gibbons, macaroni penguins, sandhill cranes, seahorses, grey wolves, barn owls, bald eagles, beavers, and doves. Of course, sexual practices of animals vary greatly from one species to another. Particularly fascinating in this regard are corals, which are giant colonies of very tiny creatures. Their sexual practices result from mass spawnings tied to seasonally warming water and lunar cycles. They ejaculate collectively in the sense that when one ejaculates all the others follow suit immediately after this, thereby creating a wave-like effect similar to the types of waves produced by crowds and seen at many sporting events.[8]

The way in which animals take care of their offspring following their birth can also vary significantly. Animals that stay together tend to assume parental responsibilities together, although it seems to be more commonplace among many animal species for the male to remain at home while the female goes out foraging for food. Interestingly, this appears to be happening more often in the human domain as well due to all the changes that are going on in the workforce these days and the fact that many more women are working outside the home rather than in the home.

In a study conducted by Paul Zak at Claremont Graduate University, it was found that the feeling of attachment can be very strong in animals, just as it is in human beings. According to Zak, the hormone oxytocin is as strong a bonding agent in other animals' relationships as it is for humans, and "animals are capable of falling in love the same way humans are." And much like humans, this love can extend well beyond one's own species and include members of other species on various occasions. There are many cases where an animal in one species becomes strongly attached to a member of another species. Moreover, everyone knows that humans have great affection and an incredible amount of love for their pets and these pets have an incredible amount of love and affection for their owners as well. This may be especially true for dogs and dog owners. Many dogs have lamented the loss of their owners for long periods of time after their deaths and have gone to the grave sites of their owners every day for years and sometimes decades to show their love, affection, devotion, and remorse. The same holds true for animal owners, who often show the same feelings and emotions when they lose their cherished pets. It often takes years for them to recover from such tragedies, if at all.

Given all the individual traits, attributes, and capabilities of animals, it is not surprising that animals and animal species create cultures just as humans do. Moreover, their culture and cultures can be highly developed and very sophisticated wholes or total ways of life much like ours. Take the culture of elephants as possibly the best-known example of this. Elephants have been known and appreciated for centuries for their symbolism in the human realm, and are greatly admired and even revered in some human cultures for such qualities as wisdom, sensitivity, stability, loyalty, intelligence, reliability, peacefulness, and determination. Often called "gentle giants," these incredible animals show a great deal of affection, care, and compassion towards each other as well as their offspring and elders, thereby acting as excellent role models for other animals and humans as well. Not only do elephants bond with each other in much the same way that humans bond, but also they are each other's keepers. They are very attentive when other elephants are sick, elderly, in distress, or threatened in some way. They also form circles to protect themselves from other animals when they are attacked, much as humans "circle the wagons" and "have each others' backs."

Elephants also look after their young in much the same way that humans do, often doting over them and actively participating in their upbringing, education, and development. It is not surprising in this respect that mother elephants and their children often live together for decades. Elephants also mourn the deaths of loved ones, return to the bodies and bones of deceased elephants, and often leave sticks, stones, or leaves on or at their grave sites. Perhaps more than any other group of animals, elephants have many different ways of communicating with each other, such as trumpeting and creating low and deep sounds that cannot be heard by humans. They also use many different types of gestures, taps, nudges, kicks, grunts, groans, the caressing of trunks, the flapping of ears, and a variety of head movements to express their feelings and emotions. Living in groups of up to four hundred, they are very sensitive as well, consoling other elephants in distress by sticking close together and putting their trunks in the mouths of other elephants to demonstrate their friendship, love, trust, companionship, and devotion.

This contrasts sharply with the culture of meerkats, who gorge themselves during the mating season in order to be and remain dominant. While they live in one of the animal kingdom's most cooperative cultures, the offspring of meerkats are usually raised communally rather than by a single mother (as is the case with elephants and most other animal species), since only one "alpha pair" of parents is permitted to breed. This makes the competition for alpha status fierce, often causing the dominant females to eat the siblings of other meerkats in order to ensure that only their own descendants survive. They may also exile offending meerkats from their colony. Since only the largest and heaviest female meerkats have the right to reproduce, all other meerkats must resign themselves to spending their lives as babysitters because the alpha mothers may give birth to as many as fifty babies over the course of their lives. This is a much better system of reproduction, however, than the ones employed by guinea hens, mother pandas, and African black eagles, which are known to eat some of their siblings and permit their healthier siblings to feed on less physically endowed and weaker siblings in order to exist and survive. They also kick some siblings out of their homes if they are not likely to make it in the "dog eat dog" world of animal survival.

Another good example of animal culture and cultures, and one that has always generated an enormous amount of interest, curiosity, fascination, and attention among humans, involves wolves. In fact, wolf culture and cultures bear a close resemblance to human culture and cultures in numerous ways. Wolves have well-organized social structures, obey strict rules of conduct and behaviour, and are playful when they are well-fed but ferocious and vicious when they are hungry. They live in packs ranging from two to thirty-six, usually averaging about six per pack, which consists generally of a single family with one or perhaps two additional members. The only exception to this general rule is the lone wolf, which decides to go it alone.

Wolf packs generally consist of an alpha male and alpha female, usually the father and mother, but not always the strongest male and female in the pack. Siblings and offspring are organized and ranked in descending order of importance as far as the pack is concerned, and especially in terms of hunting and attacking other packs of animals. This includes beta members—next in line in the hierarchy to the alpha male and alpha female—and zeta members, who are usually the "war generals" of the pack and organize the attacks after the alpha male or alpha female has created the plan and gives the command to attack. Interestingly, the rank of wolves in the pack is often revealed through how they hold their tails. If their tails are held high, they are usually the alpha wolves; if they hold their tails lower or halfway down, they are likely in the middle of the pack; and if they hold their tails between their legs or drag them along the ground, they are likely to be the lowest-ranking members of the pack.

Recent investigations into wolf packs and cultures have revealed that older wolves often share their knowledge, wisdom, experiences, and hunting techniques with younger wolves, maintain lifelong friendships and bonds with them, and often pass on special cultural habits, characteristics, and secrets from one generation to the next, thereby creating a cultural legacy or heritage for the pack that is not unlike the cultural legacies and heritages created by human beings. Moreover, what neighbourhoods, communities, legacies, and heritages are to humans is also true for wolves. It was matters like this that caused Rudyard Kipling to claim that "the strength of the pack is the wolf, and the strength of the wolf is the pack."

This is by no means the end of the story, or why wolves and wolf packs are especially captivating for human beings. In recent years, there has been a tendency in the world and especially some Asian countries to talk about "wolf cultures" and "lamb cultures," as well as to compare and contrast these two cultures in business circles, the functioning of corporations, and especially politics as well as political, governmental, and international affairs. The wolf culture is usually depicted as using any means available to realize a specific objective, disregarding or setting aside ethics and morality in order to achieve a given end, eliminating their competitors, and reigning supreme. Many of these characteristics were set out in a book called *Wolf Totem* and an eight-disc DVD set called *Wolf-like Managers* that were and still are extremely popular.

This is often contrasted with lambs and the "lamb culture." Whereas wolves and the wolf culture represent aggressiveness and often ruthlessness, lambs and the lamb culture represent kindness, gentleness, obedience, trust, serenity, and goodness. These dichotomous and very different types of animal cultures are sometimes used to describe or advocate for different forms of behaviour among humans, especially corporations and businesses but also governments and countries. This is especially true for countries such as China, which helps to explain why China has been moving away from the lamb culture in recent decades and steadily towards the wolf culture in its international dealings and global affairs. In order to even the odds between these two very different types of behaviour and cultures, some people contend that while the wolf culture may be more successful in the short run in business, government, politics, and international relations, the lamb culture may be most successful in the long run. However, the problem with this, as John Maynard Keynes, the British economist, reminded us many years ago, is that "in the long run we are all dead"!

Finally, and likely most relevant of all in terms of animals' behaviour, capabilities, and ways of life that have a great deal of significance for people and human cultures going forward into the future, there is the capacity certain animal species have to lose some of their organs and parts and grow others, and, in some cases, to transform themselves into different forms, manifestations, and species.

Take some sea creatures as informative illustrations of this type. Some sea creatures have the capacity to regrow their hearts and even whole new bodies on occasion if this is necessary, just as some lizards can drop or lose their tails in order to escape from predators when this is required.[9] Moreover, when sea creatures eat certain types of algae, they can photosynthesize their food from oxygen and sunlight, much as plants do. This "regenerative capacity" makes it possible for some sea creatures to create new organs and foods. Understanding how this process works and what is needed to achieve it may perform a very valuable function for humans by enhancing knowledge and understanding of how the molecular mechanisms in human cells and tissues can be used in a similar fashion to repair damage to certain organs or perhaps even replace them.

An excellent example of the transformative capability in certain types of animals is caterpillars. They possess the ability to make the transition from creatures crawling along the ground or on plants, leaves, and tress into exquisite butterflies. This example has great relevance here because the transformative process of caterpillars into butterflies is not unlike the transformation process advocated in this book from one type of age—the economic age—to another: the cultural age.

Here is how this miraculous transformative process works for caterpillars and butterflies. There are four distinct stages to this process: first the eggs, then the larvae, then the pupa or silk-like cocoons, and finally the creation of full-fledged butterflies. This cycle takes about four weeks in total, starting with small jewel-sized eggs that lead to the birth of caterpillars, then, after reaching a certain size and age, the growth of a second head and discarding a number of their skins and developing new ones. When these first two stages are complete, caterpillars develop hard protective shells where their original bodies dissolve and new cells are created that lead to whole new bodies with legs, wings, and other organs that end up in different types of butterflies through this four-stage metamorphosis from beginning to end.

This process first evolved some 65 million to 135 million years ago during the Cretaceous period (the heyday of the dinosaurs). There are now about 17,500 species of butterflies in existence throughout the world, including such exquisite ones as monarchs, rainbow sparkles, painted ladies, swallowtails, spring azures, orange sulfur, and many others. In many North American Indigenous cultures, this evolutionary process of caterpillars turning into butterflies is a symbol not just of transformation, but also of hope, renewal, and rebirth. In Chinese culture, it is symbolic of freedom, beauty, love, and the human soul, which makes this fascinating transformative process an excellent metaphor for this book

It is possibilities and capabilities like this that help to explain why an intimate connection exists between all species in the world in general and between human beings, plants, and animals in particular. Not only have other species had an incredible impact on the development of human species over millions of years, but also there is a great deal to be learned from other species and their cultures that is relevant to human beings. As Frans de Waal pointed out in his book *Are We Smart Enough to Know How Smart Animals Are?*:

Animals should be given a chance to express their natural behaviour. We are developing a greater interest in their variable lifestyles. Our challenge is to think more like them, so we can open up our minds to their specific circumstances and goals and observe and understand them *on their own terms*.[10]

For de Waal, it is time to create a totally new relationship between human beings, animals, and other species—a relationship that is based on equality, dependence, and respect rather than inequality, independence, and dominance. He summed this up best when he said:

Instead of making humanity the measure of all things, we need to evaluate other species by what *they* are. In so doing, I am sure we will discover many magic wells, including some as yet beyond our imagination.[11]

One person who has done a remarkable amount of empirical research on animals and especially the similarities and differences between animals and human beings in general—and their brains, behaviour, characteristics, traits, capabilities, and cultures in particular—is Georges Chapouthier, a neuroscientist, philosopher, and emeritus research director at the National Centre for Scientific Research (CNRS) in France. According to Chapouthier, most of the differences that exist between human beings and other animals can be explained by differences in the size, strength, and capabilities of their brains. Since humans have more powerful brains than other animals, they are able to create and produce many more sophisticated creations and deal with far more complex problems, predicaments, and difficulties.

This is particularly apparent in the ability human beings have to create "super tools" such as computers. This is also evident in the development of languages and language as communication systems that enable people to transmit information from one person or group to another, one generation or century to the next, one country or part of the world to all others. This is also true for converting major documents or human communication in one language into another language or languages in a matter of seconds, thereby opening the doors to countless discussions and meetings between people speaking different languages. And this is not all. Humans also possess the ability to be innovative and imaginative in many other ways, such as the ability to discuss ethics, morality, ideas, and philosophy, create visions and discuss these visions with other people, create highly complex works of art, science, and scholarship, and a great deal else. As a result of abilities like this, and others, Chapouthier contends that the gap between other animals' and humans' brain capabilities is widening rapidly and will likely widen much more in the future.

This is without doubt one of culture's greatest assets and foremost capabilities, not only for human beings but also for other species. Culture and cultures are all-encompassing in the holistic sense because they can be perceived and defined in different ways in many disciplines such as anthropology, sociology, psychology, philosophy, ecology, and biology, and not just in one way which is the case for virtually all other disciplines. This makes it possible for culture to move backward and forward as well as horizontally and vertically across a huge array of disciplines, fields, and possibilities.

As a result, culture is the ideal discipline or activity for coming to grips with global warming and the environmental crisis in general because it encompasses all of the many different human and natural fields that are needed to collaborate on this. We urgently need a discipline of this type if we are to be successful in preserving the natural environment, protecting the biosphere and vulnerable ecosystems, and improving the well-being of humans and other species. This is equally true for achieving sustainable, self-sustaining, and regenerative development, dealing with infectious diseases, and coming to grips with the biggest threat to humanity and the planet of all, namely a global environmental catastrophe. There is no doubt that culture and cultures possess the potential to do this if they are taken seriously and developed fully in the years, decades, and centuries ahead.

Chapter Eight

The Cultural Interpretation of History

Culture constitutes the topmost phenomenal level yet recognized—or for that matter, now imaginable—in the realm of nature. This of course does not compel the prediction that emergence into our consciousness of a new and higher plane is precluded.
—Alfred Kroeber and Clyde Kluckhohn[1]

Now that we have examined the development of culture and cultures from the ground up, starting with individuals, children, parents, homes, and families and ending with the behaviour and ways of life of other species, we can turn our attention to some of the more general and foundational requirements that must also be addressed to open the doors to a cultural age and enable it to flourish.

No issue is more pressing or important in this respect than the need to create a more accurate and authentic interpretation of history. Interpretations of history are of vital importance at all times and in all places. Strange as it may sound, it is to the past and especially interpretations of history that we must look for the signs, signals, and insights that are necessary to pave the way for a future cultural age and lay the theoretical and practical foundations for a more equitable, inclusive, sustainable, peaceful, and harmonious world.

For people who believe history plays a crucial role in the world and possesses an awesome power, interest in history and especially how it is interpreted is very gratifying. For history and the way it is interpreted possess the potential to answer some of humanity's most profound and basic questions, most notably: Where did we come from originally? Why and how have we evolved the way we have over the course of history? Where do we stand today? And, perhaps most important of all in view of the state of the world today and prospects for the future, where do we go from here? It is to history and how it is interpreted, then, that we must turn in times like this.

The first step in this process is to distinguish between history as fact and history as interpretation. History as fact includes all the actual events and developments that took place in the past. Whether these occurred at random or as a result of some divine force or inexorable law is impossible to say in view of our limited knowledge and abilities at present. Indeed, short of some divine miracle or supreme revelation, we may never be able to unravel the mystery of history in this sense.

Then there is history as interpretation. All written and oral history is subject to interpretation because some form of human intervention is needed to size up historical events and experiences, explain them, and give them meaning.

Here a difficult problem arises. If it was possible to interpret these experiences and events free from biases and beliefs, it would be possible to produce an objective reading and impartial assessment of history. However, a totally objective reading or impartial assessment of history is more than we can expect, since it is impossible to transcend the very thing that makes us human. As a result, the most we can hope for, have the right to expect, and struggle to achieve are interpretations of history that are as accurate, authentic, and objective as possible with respect to the true nature and real character of historical evolution. Conversely, what we must guard against and do our utmost to prevent are interpretations of history that are false, distort reality, or are designed to manipulate human behaviour and actions in the present and the future.

Unfortunately, this distinction between history as fact and history as interpretation is seldom made clear to us. As a result, we grow up thinking that historians are dealing with "the truth"—the truth substantiated by decades of research, intensive analysis, and impartial investigations. Viewed from this perspective, how powerful interpretations of history become. They take on superhuman powers and wield an incredible amount of power and influence.

The fact that historical interpretations of history are vital but interpretative presents us with a real dilemma. Much as it is difficult to live with them, it is far more difficult—and often very misleading—to live without them.

By this time you will suspect that I have a particular interpretation of history in mind when I refer to the need to create the most accurate, authentic, impartial, and up-to-date interpretation of history possible. You would be quite right. I am convinced that humanity and the world are locked at present—and have been locked over the last two and a half centuries—in the economic interpretation of history. Since this interpretation of history and the economic age we are currently living in are the two most powerful forces in the world at present, there is much to be learned from this interpretation of history that is pertinent to creating a more accurate, authentic, and impartial interpretation of history going forward into the future.

By the middle of the nineteenth century, conditions were ripe for the economic interpretation of history to begin its ascent to the pinnacle of world power. The Scientific Revolution had produced a strong backlash against metaphysics, spiritualism, and romanticism, thereby paving the way for a much more pragmatic and empirical approach to history and human life on earth. Moreover, the physical interpretation of history, which asserted the primacy of physical elements in historical evolution, was rapidly gaining ground and winning converts. In addition, and surely the most important factor of all, the Industrial Revolution was in full swing by this time and was eclipsing all other factors in the interpretation of history and the past.

Given conditions as powerful and pervasive as this, it didn't take Marx and Engels—the principal architects of the economic interpretation of history—long to formulate it. In a series of incisive statements, Marx laid bare the economic or materialistic interpretation of history in no uncertain terms:

The first premise of all human history is, of course, the existence of living human individuals. The first fact to be established, therefore, is the physical constitution of these individuals and their consequent relations to the rest of Nature...

Men [humans] ... begin the distinguish themselves from animals as soon as they begin to *produce* their means of subsistence, a step which is determined by their physical constitution... What they are, therefore, depends on the material conditions of their production...

This conception of history, therefore, rests on the exposition of the real process of production, starting out from the simple material production of life... From this starting point, it explains all the different theoretical productions and forms of consciousness, religion, philosophy, ethics, etc., and traces their origins and growth, *by which means the matter can of course be displayed as a whole...*

In the social production which men [humans] carry on they enter into definite relations that are indispensable and independent of their will, these relations of production correspond to a definite stage of development of their material powers of production. The totality of these relations of production constitutes the economic structure of society—the real foundation, on which legal and political superstructures arise and to which definite forms of social consciousness correspond. The mode of production of material life determines the general character of the social, political, and spiritual process of life...

Morality, religion, metaphysics, and other ideologies, and their corresponding forms of consciousness, no longer retain therefore their appearance of autonomous existence. They have no history, no development; it is men [humans], who, in developing their material production and their material intercourse, change, along with this their real existence, their thinking and the product of their thinking. *Life is not determined by consciousness, but consciousness by life.*[2]

Since Marx's time, the economic interpretation of history has moved progressively and relentlessly from the wings to centre stage on the world scene. Although it has been greatly simplified to enhance its universal acceptance and mass appeal, it still bears the unmistakable stamp of its creators: the division of life in general and human needs in particular into economic and non-economic components; the belief that all societies are composed of an economic base and a non-economic superstructure; the assumption that all historical change is the product of economic forces; and, last but far from least, the belief that economics should take precedence over all other activities because it is the *cause* of all activities.

Nothing typifies the power of this causality principle better than the idea of the "economic surplus." According to this idea, non-economic activities such as the arts, humanities, religion, education, recreation, and so forth owe their existence to the fact that economic activities generate a surplus over and above consumption. As a result, economic activities are deemed to be the "basics in life" because they constitute the productive forces in societies and countries as stated earlier, whereas all other activities are deemed to be the "frills in life," or the unproductive forces in societies and countries. The conclusion that was drawn from this division of life, societies, and human needs into economic and non-economic components is that the "frills" can only be provided for after the basics have been met and must be cut back or terminated the moment the economic surplus is jeopardized.

In its relentless march to the apex of world power, the economic interpretation of history—or *economic determinism*, as it is sometimes called—was greatly assisted by two major developments. The first was class conflict, exploitation, confrontation, and ultimately revolution, conditions and events that lay at the heart of the economic interpretation and bolstered the conviction of Marx, Engels, and many other Marxian scholars that communism or socialism possessed the best potential to create a more equal world. This belief, in turn, captured the attention of countless people around the world in the twentieth century. The second development was the materialistic revolution that was occurring at the same time, and which reduced life largely to the production, distribution, and consumption of material products and monetary wealth. As a result of these two developments, the economic interpretation of history became so powerful and pervasive that it was eventually taken for granted. As such, it became the foundation of the economic age. Everywhere it is assumed that as economics and economies go, so goes the world. Susan Hunt comments on the power and pervasiveness of this ideology:

The economic ideology, the dominant intellectual framework in the world today, has reduced practically every human value to the categories of economics: production and consumption, basic needs and satisfiers, human rights, scarcity, nature, energy, systems, Cartesian time and space, the assumption that all things are measurable and comparable.[3]

As a result, economics and economies have become the most dominant activities and principal preoccupations in human life. People are seen as economic assets or liabilities according to whether they make a net contribution to or subtraction from the income stream. The concept of "economic man"—the person who is concerned primarily with maximizing his or her economic interests and consumer satisfaction in the marketplace—has become the basic personality type. Communities, cities, regions, countries, and the world as a whole are seen largely in terms of economics and economies where the principal preoccupation is to activate and accelerate economic growth.

Despite the stranglehold the economic interpretation of history has on the world at present, recent developments indicate that it is losing its grip as the most accurate and authentic interpretation of history possible. Not only is it too simplistic, deterministic, and inconsistent with the real nature of the world, but it is also much too dangerous to carry forward into the future.

In theoretical terms, the economic interpretation of history must be rejected for the same reason that all partial or specialized interpretations of history must be rejected: it simplifies the process of historical evolution and change to the point where it is misleading. But we must be careful about exactly what is misleading here. What is misleading is *not* the belief that economics, economic needs, and economies are essential for human survival, well-being, and existence, or that they are exceedingly important in the overall scheme of things. No, what is misleading is the division of people's overall needs and aspirations into rigid economic and non-economic components for the purpose of asserting the priority of the former over the latter. This conviction results from a basic theoretical and practical fallacy, namely that production is a physical and material activity as Smith, Marx, Engels, and many other economists maintained, rather than an integrated physical, mental, spiritual, environmental, and cultural activity, which is actually the case. In fact, it is the inexorable connection between people's physical, mental, spiritual, environmental, and cultural activities that makes it impossible to divide human needs into rigid economic and non-economies components in actual terms, as well as to partition countries into economic bases and non-economic superstructures in order to assert the power of the former over the latter components. Such conclusions, however useful they may be, have no foundation in historical reality or in general observations of human nature, conduct, and character.

If the economic interpretation of history is too simplistic, it is also too deterministic. Many scholars and ordinary people alike seem to be coming to the conclusion that free will rather than determinism lies at the heart of history. If so, we have much more control over the future than we think, insofar as we have the ability to create, change, re-create, or redirect it according to our individual and collective needs, wants, aspirations, wishes, and wills. The fact that we are free to make conscious choices and deliberate decisions about many different possibilities—such as economic and non-economic options— means that we are free to decide for ourselves how the future should unfold and what role we can, should, and will play in this. If this was not the case, there would be no point whatsoever in discussing or interpreting history or preparing for the future since, in deterministic terms, it will unfold according to some preordained law or grand design that we are powerless to prevent.

If the economic interpretation of history has some basic theoretical flaws, it also has some obvious practical inaccuracies and shortcomings. If history actually evolved the way the economic interpretation of history claims, history would be full of examples of countries that developed their economic bases first and only later turned to the development of their artistic, religious, educational, and social superstructures. However, it is impossible to find an example in history where this has been or is the case. In each and every case, all or most of these activities have been developed in concert and therefore *simultaneously* rather than *sequentially*, albeit in different ways and rates depending on the needs, wants, values, aspirations, assumptions, and activities of the diverse peoples and countries in the world at different times and periods in history.

While interpreting history in economic terms has produced major improvements in people's material standards of living and quality of life as well as yielded countless advances in almost every area of human life, thereby making life fuller, richer, and more enjoyable and fulfilling, it has also driven humanity and the world to the brink of disaster. By focusing attention first and foremost on the material and acquisitive side of human behaviour and people's lives, it has produced economic, industrial, commercial, technological, and material demands as well as consumption practices, expectations, and needs that are impossible to fulfill in view of the finite carrying capacity of the earth. It is also having a devastating effect on the natural environment and threatening to escalate out of control, making the earth much less habitable for human beings and other species.

No one was more aware of the potential and actual danger of environmental devastation than Rachel Carson. More than half a century ago, this is what she wrote in her well-known book *Silent Spring*:

> We stand now where two roads diverge. But unlike the roads in Robert Frost's familiar poem ["The Road Not Taken"], they are not equally fair. The road we have long been travelling is deceptively easy, a smooth superhighway on which we progress with great speed, *but at its end lies disaster*. The other fork of the road—the one "less travelled by"—offers our last, our only chance to reach a destination that assures the preservation of our earth.[4]

It follows from Rachel Carson's remarkable insight that the challenge at present and going forward into the future is to create a more authentic, accurate, and contemporary interpretation of history at this crucial stage in human history and humanity's evolution and development. This is the *cultural interpretation of history*. While this task can only be addressed here in general terms due to its incredible size and enormous complexity, it is what is needed at this stage in history to put us on the right path to the future.

While some believe that history and the past are irrelevant today because things are changing so rapidly in the world, nothing could be farther from the truth. As has been confirmed time and again over the course of history, when history and the past are ignored, humanity goes on making the same fundamental and foolish mistakes. Surely we don't want to continue doing so in the future.

With this in mind, standing with our feet planted firmly in the present and casting an objective eye back over the past, what do we see? Surely we see that history is and has been a continuous process over millions—even billions—of years, involving the creation, development, and ebb and flow of countless cultures as *complex wholes* or *total ways of life*, as manifested by all the different species in the world.

Everything began with what many scientists believe marks the origin of the universe 13.8 billion years ago, the "Big Bang" that set this process in motion. In the wake of the Big Bang, stars and galaxies began to form. Our own solar system formed out of a cloud of diffuse gas and dust about 4.6 billion years ago. Life itself emerged no more than a billion years after the formation of the Earth. The earliest life forms were simple one-cell organisms. Over time, more complicated forms of life evolved. Eventually some cells developed the ability to make use of the energy of sunlight through a process called photosynthesis. These were the first green plants.

For more than 85 percent of its existence, life was confined to the oceans, but about half a billion years ago adaptations occurred that allowed living organisms to survive on dry land. Over time, more complex plants and animals appeared. Early in the twentieth century, plants were studied in detail by Sir Jagadish Chandra Bose, a scientist who worked in a variety of other fields as well, including research on microwave radiation. He was able to show that the physiology of plants was in many ways similar to that of animals.

Animals have long been of great interest to humans. The serious study of animals can be traced back more than two thousand years, when Aristotle studied animal life and behaviour and developed the first system of animal classification that we know of.

Over the centuries, and especially over the last two or three centuries, knowledge of the history and nature of plants and animals has increased enormously. As a result, there is now a vast amount of information available in these areas that could provide the requisite historical foundation for the cultural interpretation of history if it was pulled together from all these different sources and situated in one place.

The development of plants and non-human animals and their cultures was followed much later by the development of the first humans and their family, tribal, clan, ethnic, group, and community cultures, and more recently, the creation and development of all the town, city, regional, national, and even several "world cultures" that are evolving in the world today. Oswald Spengler called this miraculous process "a picture of endless formations and transformations or the marvellous waxing and waning of organic forms."[5]

It is important to emphasize that we are talking here about culture and the cultures of all the diverse species in the world in *holistic* terms, which, as we have seen, were understood initially through the anthropological definition of culture developed in the latter part of the nineteenth century. Over the last century and a half, this definition has been expanded and enhanced tremendously with the inclusion of the culture and cultures of other species as well as the development of biological, ecological, and cosmological perceptions of culture and cultures. All these perceptions and definitions provide the foundation of the cultural interpretation of history.

Matters started to move in a more favourable direction in this regard when Jacob Burckhardt, the Swiss cultural historian, carried out pioneering research on the historical development of culture and cultures in the human domain, thereby opening the doors to the cultural interpretation of history in a much broader, deeper, and more all-encompassing sense. He also provided us with an excellent approach to this interpretation of history when he advanced the idea of a *cultural continuum* in his book *Reflections on History* (*Weltgeschichtliche Betrachtungen*). While Burckhardt's concept of this continuum does not include the culture and cultures of other species, it is still valuable in understanding human developments in this particular area. This should be borne in mind in creating a more comprehensive cultural interpretation of history that includes all species and not just humans. Doing so is imperative if the cultural interpretation of history is to be as accurate, authentic, impartial, and factual as possible.[6]

But Burckhardt's contribution to the cultural interpretation of history does not end here. He also believed that "[t]here exists a marvelous, universal, silent promise to bring an objective interest to everything, to transform the entire past and present world into a spiritual possession."[7] Contrary to what he saw as a "barbaric future" marked by excessive materialism, Burckhardt expressed faith in the vision of a "cultural continuum" that focuses on admiration of the "great amidst the perishables." In order to do this, he felt the chief task in life is to take pleasure in worthwhile things, work intensely, and strive to realize the ultimate, harmonious, and absolute in life, just as Voltaire contended before him.

As Karl J. Weintraub points out in his book *Visions of Culture: Voltaire, Guizot, Burckhardt, Lamprecht, Huizinga, and Ortego y Gasset*, Burckhardt made many seminal contributions to the cultural interpretation of history that set the stage for its future development:

> Extensive reading of Burckhardt's writings suggests the central importance of these words: harmony, organic, whole, true measure, and ideal form. His letters attest to the importance which the word "harmony" had for him in a variety of meanings. His desire for harmonious viewing grew in proportion to his anxious awareness of an age which surrendered harmony to fragmentation, specialization, uniformity, boundless subjectivism, dulling luxury, an all-devouring acquisitiveness, and the hustle of metropolitan life... And when Burckhardt spoke of such values as harmony and beauty and form, such words as "great" and "eternal" and "divine" also appeared.[8]

Fortunately, Burckhardt's work on the cultural interpretation of history was not confined to the realm of theory. He also studied and assessed many cultures in fact and in great depth, especially the historical cultures of Italy and Greece. In his book *The Civilization of the Renaissance in Italy* (*Die Kultur der Renaissance in Italien*), published in 1860, the breadth and depth of Burckhardt's knowledge, understanding, and vision of culture as a whole and individual cultures and civilizations as wholes and overall ways of life was revealed as immense and profound. This book is divided into six chapters dealing with the following matters: the state as a work of art; development of the individual; revival of antiquity; discovery of the world and of man (people); society and festivals; and morality and religion. These headings speak volumes about developments that were of utmost importance during the Renaissance in Italy and the crucial role culture played in the creation of the Renaissance in that country and the way it flowed, flowered, and flourished in many other countries and parts of the world.

In his book *The Greeks and Greek Civilization* (*Griechische Kulturgeschichte*), published in 1862, Burckhardt gave even more specific expression to the idea of life, culture, and cultures as "harmonious wholes." In the table of contents for his second book, Burckhardt attempted to visualize and view the cultural history of Greece in a series of nine ordered sections that commenced with the Greeks and their myths; state and nation; religion and cults; exploration of the future; the total balance sheet of Greek life; the fine arts; poetry and music; philosophy, science, and rhetoric; and especially "Hellenic man" in his chronological development.[9] Whereas many of these sections in this book are no more than 30 to 80 pages, the last section on "Hellenic man" and his chronological development constitutes a book in itself numbering more than 480 pages. In these two books, Burckhardt often uses images rather than words or arguments to make his case, feeling that pictures provide a more effective way of conveying such matters than words.

Burckhardt's views on the nature, meaning, and importance of the cultural interpretation of history generated many studies and publications on this subject by other cultural historians who followed in his footsteps, most notably Karl Lamprecht, Johan Huizinga, Oswald Spengler, Arnold Toynbee, Wilhelm Dilthey, Raymond Williams, Will Durant, Thomas Berry, and many others. However, studies of this type were also conducted prior to Burckhardt's time by such scholars as Voltaire, Herder, Vico, Gibbon, Möser, Macaulay, Adelung, and Klemm. All these scholars were interested in culture, cultures, and civilizations in the broader and deeper holistic sense, and therefore espoused an all-inclusive cultural interpretation of history, rather than the narrower and more materialistic and partial economic interpretation of history.

For cultural historians who are committed to seeing history from a holistic or cultural perspective, as well as the many people who are interested in culture, cultures, and the cultural interpretation of history, the most fundamental question of all is this: "How can a civilization or a culture (in the human sense) be understood and presented in all its complexity and yet as an intelligible and structured whole?"[10] This question is posed by Karl J. Weintraub, also an exceptional cultural historian and scholar, on the very first page of his book *Visions of Culture.*

Weintraub answered this rhetorical question by saying that the cultural historian is concerned with "the total way of life characteristic of a given social group at a given time," and can only "give form to it by conceiving this totality as a structured whole."[11] Weintraub makes this case in no uncertain terms when he states that "every cultural historian worth [their] salt will try to present the civilization [they have] selected for [their] investigation as a unity of interdependent parts, even if full of tension and contradiction. [They] therefore will search for a center, or a cluster of interrelated foci, from which the totality can be understood and presented as a *unified whole.*"[12] And what is true for selected civilizations in this sense is also true for cultures, when Weintraub goes on to make the following statement about the functioning of cultures as wholes:

> Sheer scope and the esoteric subtlety of subject matter pose problems, but the historian of culture is in addition challenged by its complexity. He [she] sees a culture not as a mere aggregate of traits but as forming an intricately interrelated pattern. In this delicately fashioned network the arts may have their ties to religion and economic values, morality may affect the constitutional arrangements and in turn be affected by political realities, a mood reflected in literature may also come to the fore in a social custom, and a scientific insight may work back upon a religious belief.[13]

Weintraub's views contrast sharply with the conclusions arrived at by Marx and most Marxian scholars. Whereas they believed that there is a unilateral and primarily irreversible relationship between the economic base and the non-economic superstructure—making economics the root cause and basis of everything in history—Weintraub contended that there is an interactive and multilateral relationship between all activities in cultures, and that these interactions and interrelationships flow in both directions and not just one.

Since insights like these are of crucial importance to the world of the future, it pays to persevere with Weintraub's keen and informative convictions about this crucial matter for a moment longer. Here is what he had to say at greater length about this situation, and with it, the interpretations and work of cultural historians:

> He [she] studies what a culture is and also how it develops. He [she] must be able to see a culture in the total, relatively static, configuration attained at a given time; but he [she] must trace as well its gradual transformation through time. This double concern ... implies, on the one hand, the study of connections between cultural factors in their structural relationship, and, on the other hand, the study of the gradual changes, either by the introduction of new factors or by a shift in emphasis among the existing relations, resulting in a modification of the cultural configuration. In the world of the cultural historian all things touch one another. He [she] is compelled to keep track of a host of intricately interrelated matters simultaneously.[14]

This statement has profound implications for the world of the present and the future. Whereas Marx's basic conclusion was that economics must be given the highest priority because this is the way the world works in real terms—something he argued that history confirmed and illustrated—the conclusion arrived at by Weintraub and many other cultural historians is that people have much more freedom to develop societies, countries, cultures, and civilizations as they see fit. In other words, history is an open book that is written and charted according to the needs and circumstances that confront people at specific times in history and the overall scheme of things.

There is something else of fundamental importance regarding the work of cultural historians and the cultural interpretation of history that needs to be dealt with here as well. It is the fact that the world is made up of culture and cultures—and not economics and economies—at its core and in its fundamental essence. This has become steadily more apparent as a result of globalization, the migration and interaction of millions of people throughout the world, interactions among all the different cultures, civilizations, and species in the world, the COVID-19 pandemic, and many other factors. What is most significant about this is that cultures are ways of life composed of countless interrelated parts that are weighed, prioritized, and valued differently by different people, groups, and countries. They are also constantly evolving, mutating, and changing over time. While this fact has been largely ignored over the last two centuries due to commitment to the economic interpretation of history, it is of crucial importance. Seen from this perspective, the challenge of the future is clear and unequivocal. It is to embrace the cultural interpretation of history and focus attention on developing culture and all the diverse cultures in the world as wholes and total ways of life in all their complexity and diversity, ensuring that they are sustainable in space and time.

One person who is keenly interested in matters like this and is undertaking a great deal of seminal research in the area is Mira Sartika, founder and director of the Chakra Cultural Foundation in Indonesia. Sartika believes that examining "the roots of culture and cultures"—and especially focusing on their origins, characteristics, features, and inheritances—provides an effective perspective on how culture and cultures are "complex wholes" in the human domain. As she puts it, "I believe there are two fundamental roots of culture that exist in human societies based on 'environmentally affected thresholds' and they are the sea environment and the land environment, and, as a result of this, the development of two distinctive types of cultures, namely '*sea people cultures*' and '*land people cultures*.'"

Through her research, Sartika has discovered that the Y chromosome has an interconnection with sea environments and sea people cultures, which are therefore more patriarchal, whereas mitochondrial DNA has an interconnection with land environments and land people cultures, which consequently are matriarchal in nature. In specific terms, this has resulted over the centuries in the development and manifestation of two distinct and different types of cultures with very different characteristics. Whereas sea people cultures are based largely on trade, maritime-oriented activities and economies, and social structures that are most often patrilineal and follow the father's lineage, land people cultures are based on agriculture, agrarian activities and economies, communal living, and social structures that are matrilineal and follow the mother's lineage. This explains the differences that exist in these two specific sets of cultures in terms of their actual sizes, geographical locations, diverse masculine and feminine skills, competencies, and characteristics, and types of societies and economies. In Asia where most of her research has been conducted, India and China, for instance, are manifestations of sea people cultures, and Mongolia, Kazakhstan, Myanmar, Cambodia, Thailand, and many others are manifestations of land-based cultures. According to Sartika, "Knowing who we are and our own identity as 'People are Culture' is the first concrete step in the creation and realization of a cultural age."[15]

Another Indonesian cultural scholar who plumbed the depths of cultures in this broader, deeper, and more fundamental holistic sense was Sutan Takdir Alisjahbana. He was convinced that it is impossible to overstate the importance of nature, the natural environment, and cultural landscapes in the creation and development of cultures in the human domain. This includes the size, variety, flora and fauna, and distinctive features of nature and the natural environment and their many diverse elements and ingredients:

The landscape which enters consciousness through the senses evokes a percept of landscape. The human mind sees the landscape as an organized, meaningful configuration... We can also say that the landscape evokes in the bearers of culture a certain basic attitude, which gives to their behaviour a constant tendency characteristic of the value system of the culture.[16]

In human terms, this is evident in cultures located close to the Arctic and Antarctic that have a much different character, quality, and feel about them than cultures at or near the equator. Moreover, where human cultures are situated in the world in terms of their specific location, surroundings, and proximity to oceans, lakes, rivers, mountains, natural resources, and so forth is of vital importance in determining the particular details and characteristics of cultures as well as all aspects of their lives as noted earlier. This is also true for where cultures are positioned with respect to other cultures—what may be called their geographical, geopolitical, or geocultural context or location, which is also extremely important in determining the overall character and features of cultures, their outlook on the world, and their worldviews and value systems. Cultures situated close to or right beside a major superpower, such as Ukraine to Russia or Canada to the United States, usually have a very different character and outlook on the world compared to cultures that are surrounded by secondary or tertiary powers, as is the case for many cultures in the world.

Other types of activities also play an important role in determining the character of human cultures, as we have seen in the case of town, city, regional, and national cultures. There is hardly a single aspect of the development and overall nature of these cultures that is not deeply affected by factors such as economic endeavours, educational pursuits, political processes, social conventions, communications systems, arts forms, religious practices, and many others.

In the final analysis, all cultures in the human realm must deal with the specific environments, locations, contexts, and diverse activities that confront and affect them, as well as work out suitable arrangements within and between them. In some cases, these arrangements can be and often are very challenging. When land is parched, soil is dry, and water is scarce, the development of cultures is usually exceedingly difficult, as it is for many African cultures. In other cases, when cultures enjoy access to a great deal of arable land, fresh water, favourable climatic conditions, and other benefits, their development can be and usually is much less demanding and strenuous. Nevertheless, in all cases, people are compelled to work out symbiotic relationships with their environmental surroundings. When and where these relationships and activities are realized with sensitivity, care, attention, and a great deal of cultural consciousness, the outcome will probably be positive, beneficial, and harmonious. However, when and where it is predicated on insensitivity and little attention and cultural consciousness, the result can and may well be negative and disappointing.

Cultural development can also be violent or peaceful. History has revealed time and again that when one culture imposes its will and military might on another culture, such impositions can be brutal and inhumane. However, the situation can be pleasurable and favourable when cultures are prepared to respect and accept the worldviews, values, convictions, and customs of others and learn from them. The result is likely to be a "win-win" situation for the people, cultures, and countries involved, providing a ray of hope for the future.

This brings us to the fact that over the course of history, cultures in the human domain have been dominated by different activities and themes. Whereas the dominant activity or theme in one culture or period of history may have been aesthetic, in another it might be religious, social, or political. An example was given by Sutan Takdir Alisjahbana when he said, "We know, for example, that the culture of the Middle Ages was dominated by religion, while our modern secular culture is dominated by science and economics."[17] The Dutch cultural historian, Johan Huizinga, not only agreed with this statement but carried it a step further. After undertaking an intensive analysis of the late Middle Ages, Huizinga concluded that "chivalry"—as an outgrowth of religion and the religious way of life—was *the* most important activity or theme in many cultures of Europe at this time. It was concern for chivalry as an important dimension of religion more than any other factor that governed the actions of individuals, institutions, and societies at large and therefore had a powerful effect in this period of history.

This belief that human cultures can and have been dominated by different activities and themes and not always the same activity and theme is consistent with much of the accumulated knowledge of history as well as a great deal of anthropological and archeological evidence. However, this should not be interpreted to mean that cultures are always *harmonic* in their activities and themes since this is not the case. In fact, they are often *disharmonic* in their activities and themes as well as their patterns and characteristics: highly developed and evolved in some areas; but less developed or underdeveloped in others. As a result, interpretations of history must be sufficiently broad, malleable, and adaptable to account for these differences. To do so, cultures should be seen in relative rather than absolute terms, varying from time to time and place to place in accordance with constantly changing and altered conditions as well as new environmental realities.

This is where the cultural interpretation of history is much more effective than the economic interpretation and all other partial or specialized interpretations of history. Whereas partial and specialized interpretations of history must interpret the past in terms of the same activity or theme, by virtue of its holistic capacity and flexible adaptability the cultural interpretation of history can interpret history in terms of different activities and themes. As a result, it makes sense to talk about the medieval religious culture, the Renaissance aesthetic and humanistic culture, and the present economic culture. All these cultures have been or are dominated by different activities, themes, and events at one time or another in their history that have played instrumental roles in coalescing around them all other activities and themes.

There is another dimension to the cultural interpretation of history that needs to be stressed here and emphasized in no uncertain terms. It is the fact that there is not only a positive and desirable side to the cultural interpretation of history but also a negative and sinister side that must never be forgotten. As indicated earlier, this negative side includes all the oppression, brutality, wars, human rights abuses, plundering, exploitation, and killing that has taken place in the world from the beginning of history to the present day. Like the positive and desirable side, the negative and sinister side has also existed in all parts of the world as well as in the past and the present. No group of people, country, culture, or continent is exempt from this. There may be no greater need confronting humanity than dealing with problems like this. Only in that way can culture act as a real beacon of the future with the ability to inform and alert as well as to illuminate and inspire.

Just as interpretations of history must be flexible, adaptable, and relative rather than deterministic, fixed, and absolute in order to deal successfully with such problems, so they must also be capable of giving credit, attention, and recognition to the creative achievements and beneficial contributions that all people, countries, and cultures have made and are making to the world and the cultural heritage of humankind. Not only must these achievements and contributions be documented in considerable detail as well as by the most effective and up-to-date methods and techniques possible, but also they must bring to an end the belief that is it only people, countries, and cultures in the Western and more affluent parts of the world that have made lasting contributions to the cultural heritage of humankind. This realization is also needed to bring an end to colonialism and colonization, thereby eliminating one of the greatest barriers of all to cooperative and peaceful developments in all parts of the world in the years and decades ahead.

The fact that all people, countries, and cultures have made and are making valuable contributions to the natural and cultural heritage of humankind is confirmed by the list of world heritage sites that is complied, confirmed, and updated on a regular basis by UNESCO. As of August 2022, UNESCO had recorded 1,154 official natural and cultural heritage sites in 167 countries throughout the world, of which 897 were cultural, 218 natural, and 39 mixed natural and cultural. These sites are located throughout the five major geographical regions of the world (identified by UNESCO as Africa, the Arab States, Asia and the Pacific, Europe and North America, and Latin America and the Caribbean).

This heritage includes an incredible array of diverse items, sites, and artifacts from every period in history, part of the world, and aspect of cultural life. This heritage is the birthright of all citizens and countries and belongs to the whole of humanity and not just specific peoples and countries, thereby providing a sense of collective identity, well-being, and belonging.

It is also a *living heritage* in the sense that it is constantly evolving, mutating, and growing in size and stature as well as over time and across space. A significant part of this heritage has been preserved, protected, and sustained by women over the centuries because they have been much more actively involved in, and deeply committed to, ensuring that the neighbourhood, community, local, municipal, regional, and national heritages of all people, ethnic groups, tribes, races, and countries are passed on from one generation to the next and one century to the next. In effect, this miraculous accomplishment is a precious gift from past generations to present and future generations.

In specific terms, the natural component of this heritage includes many places that are of great importance to humanity as a whole, most of which are now located in national parks throughout the world. Examples of UNESCO World Heritage Sites that are focused on the heritage of the natural world include the Los Glaciares National Park and Iguazú National Park in Argentina, Uluru and the Great Barrier Reef in Australia, Mount Kenya National Park/National Forest in Kenya, Dinosaur Provincial Park in Canada, Ilulissat Icefjord in Denmark, the Galápagos Islands off the coast of Equador, the Western Ghats in India, the Dolomites in Italy, Kinabalu Park in Malaysia, Monarch Butterfly Biosphere Reserve in Mexico, Sagarmatha National Park in Nepal, Jeju Volcanic Island and Lava Tubes in South Korea, the Danube Delta in Romania and Ukraine, the Central Highlands of Sri Lanka, Lake Baikal in Russia, Singapore Botanic Gardens in Singapore, the Grand Canyon and Yellowstone National Park in the United States, and many others.

The cultural component of this heritage includes buildings of unusual historic significance and value, the centres of many well-known towns and cities, special monuments, historic sites and venues, and such human-made creations as the Pyramids, famous forts and bridges, ancient ruins, and so forth. Examples of World Heritage sites in this realm include Angkor in Cambodia, the Pyramids of Egypt and related archeological sites, Persepolis in Iran, Chichen Itza in the Yucatán Peninsula in Mexico, the centre of Saint Petersburg in Russia, the Lahore Fort in Pakistan, Samarkand in Uzbekistan, the Great Wall of China, the historic centre of Prague in the Czech Republic, the Acropolis in Greece, the Mayan archeological site of Copán in Honduras, Masada in Israel, historical monuments in ancient Kyoto in Japan, the ancient city of Petra in Jordan, and many others.

While there was a tendency in the earlier decades to confine cultural sites of great international significance to those that were largely physical, material, and tangible in nature, pressure built rapidly throughout the world to extend this list to include many activities that are largely non-physical, non-material, and intangible in nature. This list includes such items and activities as stories and storytelling, athletic and recreational games, dances, folk songs, embroidery, falconry, boat races, oral histories, theories, ideas, calligraphy, festivals, fairs, carnivals, tea ceremonies, throat singing, and many others.

Nothing confirms the fact that all people, countries, and cultures have made and are making indispensable contributions to the world and its universal heritage more effectively than the tangible and intangible dimensions of the cultural heritage of humankind. Among countless other items, activities, and people, this heritage includes the architectural accomplishments of the Egyptians, Mayans, Aztecs, Incans, Asians, and Europeans; the music of Bach, Beethoven, and Heitor Villa-Lobos; the religious teachings of Buddha, Muhammad, Christ, and Moses; the activist activities of Gandhi and Marx; the philosophical, educational, and literary writings of Socrates, al-Jazari, and Gabriela Mistral; the scientific discoveries of Newton, Einstein, and Ibn al-Haytham; the technological innovations of the Japanese, Chinese, and Americans; the artistic masterpieces of Europeans, Africans, Asians, Latin Americans, Caribbeans, and countless others. It is all this and much more. It is also the even less tangible but equally essential ideals of humanity down through the ages: the pursuit of knowledge, wisdom, beauty, love, and truth; the struggle for justice, order, equality, and inclusion; the quest for peace, harmony, happiness, and perfection; and the search for sustainability, simplicity, and the sublime. As the crowning achievement of people from all parts of the world over the centuries, surely this precious heritage of hope should guide our footsteps and actions in the near and distant future.

If sustainable development is to be achieved and the welfare and well-being of all people, countries, and other species in all parts of the world assured, ideals and values like these are imperative. Providing grounds for optimism in this regard is the fact that the cultural interpretation of history makes it possible to see the big picture in far more expansive spatial and temporal terms, explain and interpret historical and contemporary events and developments much more accurately, impartially, and fully, learn from history and come to grips with the cultural baggage that people and countries have inherited from the past, and set humanity and the world on a very different developmental path in the future. Surely the time has come for the cultural interpretation of history to play a major role in the world as a more authentic, accurate, and sustainable interpretation of the past, a more objective and impartial evaluation of the present, and a more enlightened, inspiring, and enticing vision of the future. As Sutan Takdir Alisjahbana, the cultural scholar quoted earlier, pointed out:

In the great movement of time which we call human history, we must ask ourselves the question, "Where are we, and where is our road leading to?" in the hope that through an understanding of the growths and declines, of the successes and the failures of cultures, we will acquire some clues that will lead us to the right decisions in our time.[18]

With this valuable insight in mind, it is possible to progress to the next crucial requirement that needs to be addressed—the centrality of cultural development and policy. This likewise has a great deal to do with entrance into a cultural age and enabling it to flourish.

Chapter Nine

The Centrality of Cultural Development and Policy

Culture is the alpha and omega of any sound development policy.
—Léopold Sédar Senghor[1]

An historic event took place in Venice in 1970. It was the first world conference on cultural development and policy. It was convened by UNESCO and proved to be a harbinger of things to come. Since that time, culture and cultures in general and cultural development and policy in particular have slowly but surely begun to achieve much more prominence in the world.

This journey has not been easy, but it has been productive, informative, and revealing. While Venice, with its many architectural masterpieces, fascinating history, and romantic canals, was the ideal place to convene a ground-breaking conference like this, UNESCO found itself in a difficult position because of all the misunderstandings, controversies, and uncertainties that existed over the nature and meaning of culture. This was because there were many different ways to perceive, define, and deal with culture. This fact had been revealed by Alfred Kroeber and Clyde Kluckhohn, two American anthropologists, who conducted the first comprehensive investigation into this matter and showed that there were more than a hundred and fifty ways of looking at and defining culture in use throughout the world. Their findings were set out in their book, *Culture: A Critical Review of Concepts and Definitions*, published in 1952, eighteen years before the Venice Conference.[2]

While it was widely rumored that UNESCO had asked delegates attending the Venice conference to abstain from having any discussions or debates about the nature, meaning, and definition of culture for fear that the conference would degenerate into a rancorous semantic debate, a great deal was actually achieved at this historic conference despite the fact that the delegates steered clear of the evocative but elusive term *culture*. Many matters of crucial importance to culture and cultures as well as cultural development and policy were discussed by representatives of the member states of UNESCO, thus shining light on the role that culture, cultures, governments, and UNESCO were capable of playing in the world of the future. As René Maheu, first Director-General of UNESCO, stated during his opening remarks: "One day we shall realize ... that the essential options in any truly national development policy are cultural."[3] At last, culture was starting to be taken seriously by at least some people, organizations, and governments.

Having opened the doors to culture and cultures in general and cultural development and policy in particular at the Venice Conference, UNESCO followed up on this successful initiative by dividing the world into four distinct regions and convening conferences on cultural development and policy in each of them. Conferences were held for Europe and North America in Helsinki, Finland, in 1972; for Asia in Yogyakarta, Indonesia, in 1973; for Africa in Accra, Ghana, in 1975; and for Latin America and the Caribbean in Bogota, Colombia, in 1978. According to Herbert Shore, author of *Cultural Policy: UNESCO's First Cultural Development Decade*:

Each [of the four regional conferences] had its own cultural style, its own approach and distinctive focal emphasis.... Yet there were continuities from one conference to another, threads of universal concern that ran throughout. The sequence of discussions can be seen as an evolutionary process in the ever deeper consideration of concepts, problems and solutions. At the same time, they maintain, within that evolution, a constant dialectical interplay between the local and global, the specific and general, the particular and the universal.[4]

Nowhere was this "dialectical interplay" more in evidence than in the differences that existed between the delegates attending the European and North American conference compared to delegates attending the Asian, African, and Latin America and Caribbean conferences.

Generally speaking, the dominant concern of the delegates at the European and North American conference was the need to achieve what they called the *democratization* and *decentralization* of culture and cultures. This resulted from the fact that over the centuries, audiences at many artistic and related activities in Europe and North America had become very elite in character and concentrated for the most part in the largest cities in this region. (This situation was confirmed by a number of studies undertaken at that time which revealed that audience members at these activities were wealthy and well-connected, and that many artists and arts organizations were located in the largest cities in Europe and North America because this was where employment opportunities and funding sources were to be found.) The conclusion that was drawn from this was that cultural development and policy in this particular region of the world should focus on diversifying audiences at artistic and related events as much as possible (*democratization*), and move many of these activities and the organizations that provided them out of the largest cities and into smaller communities not only in this part of the world, but also to other areas of the world (*decentralization*). Many countries in Europe and North America immediately responded to these "dual requirements of cultural development and policy" and acted on them through governmental plans, policies, and practices.

A very different response to this situation occurred at the regional conferences in Asia, Africa, Latin America, and the Caribbean. In fact, quite the opposite was the case. Being on the receiving end of the export of artistic activities and products from Europe and North America—which appeared to them to be yet another form of cultural imperialism and colonization—delegates in these regions focused most of their time, attention, and funding on creating and developing viable alternatives to this. As a result, much more emphasis was placed in Asian, African, Latin America, and Caribbean countries on preserving and protecting their own cultures and cultural identities, cherishing their own cultural heritages and accomplishments and promoting them at home and abroad, fostering local, regional, and national cultural values and indigenous development policies and practices, and training cultural animators, administrators, and activists who were skilled at counteracting artistic exports from Europe and North America and generating much more interest in the cultures in their own countries. With this also came much more interest in culture and cultures as "wholes" and "overall ways of life" and not just the arts, humanities, heritage of history, and related activities, as was more the case in Europe and North America.

Once the Venice Conference and four regional conferences were over, UNESCO embarked on organizing a second world conference on cultural development and policy in Mexico City in 1982. By this time, it was clear that while some significant strides had been made in cultural development and policy throughout the world over the preceding twelve years, how culture was perceived and defined could no longer be avoided, downplayed, or ignored because it was causing a great deal of confusion for UNESCO as well as for most governmental cultural departments and agencies. The problem was that the substantially broader perception and definition of culture as a whole and a total way of life was beginning to be recognized and gaining traction throughout the world, especially in colonized parts of the world such as Asia, Africa, the Middle East, Latin America, and the Caribbean, where the most important factor of all was their overall way of life and how it had been changed.

Despite the importance of this second perception and definition of culture, most people, institutions, and governments continued to cling to the narrower and more traditional way of perceiving, defining, and dealing with culture. This was not only because this was the way culture had evolved over more than two thousand years, but also because it tended to treat culture in far more concrete, tangible, specific, and visible terms. This made it easier to understand and deal with culture. Plays and operas could be watched, music listened to, paintings seen and appreciated, books read, architectural and culinary masterpieces enjoyed, craft objects handled, and artistic commodities bought, sold, and traded in the marketplace. This was also true for what were starting to be called "the cultural industries," most notably publishing, radio, television, film, and sound recording.

This traditional and preferred definition of culture also made it much easier for corporations, foundations, and governments to determine which cultural activities, individuals, and organizations were eligible for financial support, as well as for departments and ministries of culture to create and develop cultural plans and polices. It was also much more consistent with the prevailing economic system because the value of cultural goods, commodities, and activities could be determined by the prices paid for them in the marketplace. This made it possible to determine the specific contribution culture was making to countries' economies.

Despite the attraction of this traditional and far more concrete and tangible way of perceiving and defining culture, interest in the all-encompassing holistic perception and definition of culture as a whole or total way of life was steadily escalating. As a result, delegates at the second UNESCO world conference on cultural policies in Mexico City in 1982 endorsed what came to be known as the "holistic definition of culture":

Culture may now be said to be the *whole* complex of distinctive spiritual, material, intellectual and emotional features that characterize a society or social group. It includes not only the arts and letters, but also modes of life, the fundamental human rights of the human being, value systems, traditions and beliefs.[5]

Interestingly, this definition of culture bore a striking resemblance to that created and advocated by Edward Burnett Tylor in 1871. Not only did the 1982 UNESCO definition provide official confirmation of Tylor's all-encompassing anthropological definition of culture, but it paved the way for its use in the years ahead.

As a result, this all-encompassing holistic definition played a crucial role in the World Decade for Cultural Development that was proclaimed by the United Nations and UNESCO and ran from 1988 to 1997, as well as in the work of the World Commission on Culture and Development from 1993 to 1995. This commission was headed up by Javier Pérez de Cuéllar, former Secretary General of the United Nations, and was committed to examining culture's role in development at that time and making recommendations concerning its future development, promotion, and use. The legitimacy and importance of this definition was asserted by Pérez de Cuéllar when he claimed:

Today, rethinking development is necessary on a world scale.... It was believed, not so long ago, that the economy was the base, the infrastructure. That is wrong: historians of the "long history" have shown that the decisive element is culture.... Without a large transformation, development is doomed to the destiny of ghost towns.[6]

When the commission released its report—*Our Creative Diversity*—in 1995, culture was defined in much broader terms than just the arts, humanities, heritage of history, and cultural industries (essential as they are), but, rather, as the whole and total way of life of people and countries, something that was consistent with the recommendation of delegates at the Mexico City conference.[7] As the title of this report indicated, a high priority was placed on *creativity* and *diversity*, which, by this time, were garnering much more attention than democratization and decentralization as the new twin engines needed to drive cultural development and policy in the future.

As far as creativity was concerned, it was manifested most conspicuously around this time in the work and publications of Richard Florida. He became well known for his research on "the creative class" and its dynamic role in urban development. His books on this subject—and especially his book *The Rise of the Creative Class: How It's Transforming Work, Leisure, Community and Everyday Life*—documented in detail the role that creative people such as artists, designers, architects, activists, inventors, advertisers, and so forth were playing and should play both individually and collectively in providing the impetus and innovations that were required to broaden, deepen, intensify, and enrich all aspects and dimensions of urban life. His work was embraced by many people in the cultural and other fields as yet another confirmation of the benefits that were and could be realized by treating culture as a generator of economic activity.

One of the best ways to do this was deemed to be through the development of the *creative economy*. According to the United Nations Conference on Trade and Development (UNCTAD), the creative economy is "an emerging concept that deals with the interface between creativity, culture, economics, and technology in a contemporary world dominated by images, sounds, texts and symbols." What was exciting about this idea for people in the cultural field was the realization that culture and creativity are intimately connected, should be situated at the core of the creative economy, and should be seen as "the driving forces" in the development of this specific type of economy (other types of economies often discussed were and are the "shared economy," "circular economy," and more recently the "green economy"). As UNCTAD stated in its *Creative Economy Report,* "adequately nurtured, creativity fuels culture, infuses a human-centred development, and constitutes the key ingredient for job creation, innovation and trade while contributing to social inclusion, cultural diversity and environmental sustainability."

While many people in the cultural field thought the focus in the future should be on culture's contribution to the creative economy, others thought it should be on culture's contribution as "the fourth pillar of sustainable development." This view arose when the idea of "pillars of sustainable development" surfaced after the Report of the World Commission on Environment and Development—the Brundtland Report—was released in 1982 and immediately embraced by many people in the environmental, corporate, governmental, political, and diplomatic fields.[8] While economics was seen, treated, and confirmed as "the first pillar of sustainable development," many people in the environmental field felt that the natural environment should be seen and treated as "the second pillar," and, as such, given a much higher priority in public and private planning, policy, decision-making, funding, and developmental activities. Not long after this, pressure was exerted to make social affairs "the third pillar." And lastly, and much more recently, culture was added as "the fourth pillar of sustainable development."

Just as Richard Florida played a seminal role in the development of the concept of the creative class, so Jon Hawkes played a seminal role in the development of the concept of culture as the fourth pillar of sustainable development. His book *The Fourth Pillar of Sustainability: Culture's Essential Role in Public Planning* was instrumental in convincing many authorities in government, politics, corporate affairs, and foundations that culture has an important role to play in global development and human affairs. This would not have been possible, however, without a great deal of support and advocacy from

UNESCO, Agenda 21 for Culture, the World Summit on Sustainable Development, and many others.

As far as diversity was concerned—the other major factor emphasized in the World Commission on Culture and Development's report *Our Creative Diversity*—its prioritization stemmed from a much different set of factors and forces. This had to do with the trend that was taking place in the world in the latter part of the twentieth century towards uniformity, and with this, the threat to diversity that was evident in most if not all parts of the world. Spurred on by Canada, France, and a few other countries, UNESCO became so concerned about this threat that it created a worldwide movement and network aimed at promoting interest in and protection of diversity in the official and legal sense. This initiative coincided nicely with the Intergovernmental Conference on Cultural Policies for Development convened by UNESCO in Sweden in 1998. While the Stockholm conference was devoted to integrating the human factor into development and cultural and developmental policies and practices—as well as creating more financial assistance programs, international cultural relations, and new administrative structures and frameworks to deal with these necessities—the conference's findings and recommendations were very timely and beneficial in laying the foundation for the Universal Declaration on Cultural Diversity in 2001 and eventually led to the signing of the UNESCO *Convention on the Promotion and Protection of the Diversity of Cultural Expressions* in 2005.

This convention is a legally binding international agreement that ensures that artists, cultural professionals, practitioners, and citizens at large have the right to create, produce, disseminate, and enjoy a broad range of cultural goods, services, and activities in every country and region in the world, **including their own**. It was adopted due to the urgency of establishing and implementing a global law that recognizes the importance of cultural goods, services, and activities as vehicles of identity, value, and meaning *in their own right* and not just as commodities, consumer products, and objects of trade, industry, and commerce.

By the time the UNESCO convention on cultural diversity was signed in 2005, climate change and the environmental crisis had become the most pressing issue in the world. The task was to achieve "sustainable" rather than "unsustainable" development. The origins of the idea of sustainable development can be traced back to 1983 when the World Commission on Environment and Development was created. The commission's report—*Our Common Future*, as mentioned earlier—was published in 1987 and asserted that all future development must be *sustainable*. In order to achieve this, it was deemed to be imperative to take the needs and interests of the natural environment and future generations and not just the present generation fully and forcefully into account. While it was realized that it would take time to create the transformation in worldviews, values, lifestyles, individual and collective behaviour, and overall ways of life that were required to achieve this, many public and private organizations and authorities immediately commenced the search for legitimate and effective ways to make sustainable development a high priority and concrete reality in the world of the future.

As a result of this, concern for sustainable development progressed on many fronts. This culminated with the passage of the Agenda for Sustainable Development, which was adopted by all member states of the United Nations in 2015. This agenda provided "a shared blueprint for peace and prosperity for people and the planet, now and into the future." At the heart of this blueprint were seventeen specific sustainable development goals (UN–SDGs), as well as an urgent call for action on these goals by all countries in a global partnership. At the heart of the agenda are the *5P's*: people, prosperity, planet, partnership, and peace.

The UN–SDG conference and goals were the result of decades of work by numerous people, organizations, agencies, and countries, in addition to the United Nations and its Department of Economic and Social Affairs. Included in this massive undertaking and contributions were the *Earth Summit* in Rio de Janeiro, Brazil, in June 1992 where more than 178 countries adopted Agenda 21, which was (and still is) a comprehensive plan of action to build a global partnership for sustainable development to improve human lives and protect the environment; the *Millennium Declaration* endorsed at the Millennium Summit in September 2000 at UN headquarters in New York; the *Johannesburg Declaration on Sustainable Development and the Plan of Implementation* adopted at the World Summit on Sustainable

Development convened in South Africa in 2002; the United Nations *Conference on Sustainable Development (Rio+20)* in Rio de Janeiro, Brazil in June 2012; the creation of the thirty-member Open Working Group to develop a proposal on the SDGs in 2013; and the adoption of the *2030 Agenda for Sustainable Development* with *17 Social Development Goals* by the General Assembly of the United Nations in 2015.[9] These goals extend all the way from ending poverty and hunger, ensuring good health and well-being, and providing quality education for all people to ensuring the well-being of other species and the natural environment.

These ambitious social development goals and ideals and their relevance *in cultural terms* were considered at the most recent UNESCO conference on cultural policies in Mexico City in September 2022. Titled the UNESCO Conference on Cultural Policies and Sustainable Development, or, in short, UNESCO Mondiacult 2022, this conference provided an opportunity to capitalize on previous conferences on cultural development and policy, as well as to make the case in much stronger, bolder, and more compelling terms that culture and cultures, which were relegated to a secondary or tertiary rather than primary place in development and the world for a very long time, have a crucial role to play in helping to achieve sustainable development in general and the 2030 Social Development Goals in particular. It was concluded at this conference that culture needs to be included "as a specific objective and topic in its own right" at the next United Nations conference and in its set of Sustainable Development Goals, because no specific mention was made of culture at the United Nations Conference on these matters in 2015.

While UNESCO and the United Nations were involved in the actions discussed above, important developments were also taking place in the private sector. It was in 2014 about this time that Merriam-Webster, the dictionary publishers, declared that culture was "the word of the year." As stated on the company's website, "it seemed that culture moved from the classroom syllabus to the conversation at large in 2014, appearing in headlines and analyses across a wide swath of topics."

Included among this wide swath of topics was the holistic perception of culture as the complex whole or total way of life that was starting to be taken more seriously in both the public sector and the private sector after a long period of neglect. When people talk about being "products of their culture" today, they no longer mean they are products of the arts, humanities, heritage of history, and cultural industries, but rather of their overall way of life or their culture as a whole. In some cases, this means using the holistic definition of culture espoused initially by Edward Burnett Tylor in 1871 and endorsed by numerous cultural scholars since that time. In other cases, it means using the variation on the 1871 holistic definition that was endorsed at the UNESCO Conference on Cultural Policies more than a century later at the Mexico City conference in 1982.

Over the last few decades, one of the most obvious and prevalent uses of the holistic definition of culture has been in the field of organizational behaviour. This is manifested most conspicuously in the research and writing of such scholars and educators as Elliott Jaques and his concept of corporate culture, John Kotter and his theory of the leadership and management of organizations, and most notably Edgar Schein, professor in the Sloan School of Management at Massachusetts Institute of Technology in the United States, who developed the concept of the cultures of organizations in his book *Organizational Culture and Leadership*. In recent years, the holistic definition of culture has been applied in many different kinds of organizations, from hospitals to sports teams.

According to Schein, organizations as cultures usually evolve over long periods of time. These organizational cultures consist of a "shared pattern of basic assumptions" which members of the organization acquire and develop collectively as they deal with internal and external demands, needs, aspirations, expectations, and the difficulties confronting them. Cultures in this sense include an organization's vision, mission statement, worldview, values, axioms, languages, environmental setting, customs, beliefs, ways of doing things, and so forth. In Schein's model, there are three main layers of organizational culture: *artifacts, espoused values*, and a basic *underlying assumption*. Especially important in this regard are employees' voices, leadership, creating a sense of belonging, and, most importantly, making culture the priority. Recognition of this fact is the single most important factor in the development of successful organizations, and involves countless organizations throughout the world.[10]

Added to the vast panorama of organizational cultures are the countless number of clans, tribes, and clan and tribal cultures that exist throughout the world, such as the Masai in Africa, the Wano in Indonesia, the San peoples of southern Africa, the Kurds in western Asia, the Magyars in Hungary, the Māori in New Zealand, and many others. This also includes all the diverse ethnic groups and their cultures that exist throughout the world, as well as collectivities such as Black Lives Matter and its various movements and Indigenous Peoples and their cultures and organizations. Many of these groups are calling for "systemic cultural change" and not just incremental change, as well as the need to "change the culture" because the existing way of doing things is not working.

As Maurice Strong, who was a forerunner in recognizing the environmental crisis as well as the founder of many environmental organizations and projects through his work over many years at the United Nations, wrote:

The root causes of the crisis are essentially systemic in nature. That is to say the cause and effect relationships take place within a complex system of interactions in which no single element can be isolated from the whole. Ignoring this simple truth is, in my view, one of the principal root causes of the past developments that have produced the current crisis.[11]

Viewed in totality, all these developments and the great cultural awakening that is taking place in the world display many elements of Thomas Kuhn's concept of the *paradigm shift* and Malcolm Gladwell's idea of the *tipping point*.[12] A paradigm shift is a transformational or foundational change in the way things are seen, experienced, and especially done, such as the paradigm shift that occurred from the agricultural age to the industrial age many centuries ago. The idea of the tipping point suggests that things build up until a specific point is reached, when an abrupt and powerful change occurs in the direction things are going. An everyday example might be when a goal is scored in a hockey game, causing a sudden and dramatic shift in the momentum of the game. Many people now believe a paradigm shift is needed in the fundamental premises underlying society.

So matters stand at present with respect to culture, its treatment at various conferences over more than half a century, and the initiatives of the United Nations and many other organizations in creating the Social Development Goals. Unfortunately, however, despite all the conferences that have been held, no in-depth or intensive attempt has been made to ascertain what is actually meant by the term *development* in general and *cultural development* in particular, in either the theoretical or practical sense. As a result, the underlying assumption persists that development at its heart is an economic process.

The origins of this economic perception and definition of development can be traced back to the inaugural speech President Harry Truman made to the United States Congress in 1949, when he divided the world into "developed" and "developing" countries and claimed that "production is the key to prosperity and peace."[13]

While this perception and definition have been enlarged somewhat over the last few decades by adding such components as education and lifelong learning, the natural environment, and a few qualitative pursuits to the list of key factors in development, culture and cultures are still treated in very narrow terms as far as development is concerned, as means to other ends rather than ends in themselves. As a result, we have yet to capitalize on the holistic way of seeing, defining, and dealing with culture and cultures. It doesn't require a psychic to predict the kind of world that will result from this neglect in the not-too-distant future. Not only will there be a great deal more environmental devastation, but the result will also be far more conflict, tension, and danger. What has become steadily more apparent is that development, cultural development, and cultural policy are concerned with the total spectrum of people's and countries' needs, aspirations, problems, accomplishments, and weaknesses. As Gérard Pelletier, former Minister of State for Canada, said many years ago, "[C]ultural development and policy are nothing more or less than a plan for civilization." It is a plan that includes *all* dimensions of development.

In order to come to grips with requirements so fundamental, interconnected, and complex, public and private organizations in general and governmental and international institutions and agencies in particular will have to make use of models of development that are cultural and holistic rather than economic and partial in character. These models must range all the way from basic ideas about how to deal with people's needs, problems, and concerns to highly sophisticated and specific methods and techniques for addressing and fulfilling these requirements in systematic, comprehensive, and sustained terms. To do this, development and policy in this cultural sense will have to be integrated, inclusive, and egalitarian rather than fragmented, exclusive, and partisan.[14]

It is important to emphasize here that no single activity (such as economics, science, technology, education, or religion) is singled out for special attention or exclusive treatment in the cultural model of development and policy. It is as essential to address people's environmental, social, educational, health, recreational, artistic, and religious needs as it is to address their economic, industrial, commercial, scientific, financial, and technological needs. Viewed from this perspective, economics would no longer be seen and treated as *the* most important factor in development, but rather as one important factor among many. It would no longer be a case of developing economics and economies first and foremost, and then assuming that everything will fall into place and work out for the best. Rather, it is a case of developing all diverse activities *simultaneously* rather than sequentially, albeit at different rates and in many different ways. Without this, people, the environment, culture, and cultures will always play a secondary role compared to products, profits, the marketplace, and the bottom line.

A very important aspect of all this is developing the component parts of culture and cultures *in their own right*, but always keeping in mind that they must be properly situated in culture and cultures as wholes and total ways of life if they are to function effectively. This is why the component parts of culture and cultures in the cultural model of development and policy are referred to as the "environmental culture," "economic culture," "social culture," "artistic culture," "political culture," and so forth, since they all share culture in common.

These component parts are developed best when that is done in terms of the uniqueness, creativity, excellence, integrity, and diversity that is inherent in them. This is as true for the artistic, humanistic, recreational, educational, social, and political cultures as for the economic, technological, financial, and commercial cultures. Given the highly specialized nature of the world we are living in today, a great deal is known about all these component parts of culture and cultures and how they can be developed most effectively, even if the capital and human resources are not yet available to realize this. Regrettably, however, much less is known about how to deal with all the complex relationships that exist between and among the component parts of culture and cultures. Going forward, for instance, what should be the relationship between the economic culture and the artistic culture, and how can this relationship be dealt with most successfully? Or, to cite another example among many, what should be the relationship between the technological culture and the spiritual and humanistic culture, and how can this be cultivated so that technology impacts favourably rather than unfavourably on spiritual, humanistic, and human affairs, especially when it comes to such matters as artificial intelligence, robotics, and the like? As these two examples indicate, a complicated set of relationships will have to be worked out and dealt with if culture and cultures are to be developed and function properly in the years and decades ahead. In order to achieve this, it will be necessary to develop culture and cultures in breadth and depth, as well as situate them effectively in the natural, historical, global, and cosmic environment.

Developing culture in breadth and depth means ensuring that all people and countries have access to a diverse panorama of options and opportunities, as well as the ability to participate actively and openly in all aspects and dimensions of cultural life. This is imperative because every person, gender, class, clan, race, tribe, community, and country has a great deal to contribute to culture and an enormous amount to receive in return. This also involves seeing that a high priority is placed on the *ideals* of culture—or what some call the *universals* or *absolutes* of culture—despite major differences in worldviews, values, value systems, and beliefs. Included in these ideals, universals, and absolutes are the quest for knowledge, wisdom, beauty, and truth; the importance of creativity, diversity, and excellence; the need for equality, ethics, justice, identity, inclusion, unity, and well-being;

conservation of the natural and cultural heritage of humankind; and caring, sharing, cooperation, empathy, and compassion. Interestingly, many of these ideals, and especially creativity, diversity, caring, sharing, equality, inclusion, and compassion, are now being seen as the keys to municipal, regional, national, and international development in the years and decades ahead.

It is impossible to achieve these ideals without also placing a great deal of emphasis on what are called the *particulars* or *parts* of culture, especially the arts, humanities, education, learning, spirituality, heritage of history, ethics, and other activities that have a close historical or contemporary affiliation, connection, and affinity with culture. These activities tend to put the ideals of cultures ahead of many other types of activities. In doing so, they communicate effectively across geographical divides and political boundaries as well as racial, ethnic, and linguistic barriers in profound, moving, and human ways, revealing most clearly what culture is actually all about, how it has evolved in space and over time, and what is most cherished. Viewed from this perspective, every country, culture, and civilization possesses a rich tapestry of artistic, educational, social, humanistic, and spiritual achievements that need to be much better known and utilized. It is this fact that makes it imperative to develop international relations and global relationships to the point where a high degree of parity, inclusion, and equality is achieved and maintained between all cultures, countries, and civilizations.

In historical terms, no one understood the value and importance of ideals, universals, or absolutes better than Plato. Unlike Aristotle, who tended to place more emphasis on the particulars or parts, Plato understood that regardless of what kind of particulars and parts exist, if there are no ideals, universals, and absolutes, particulars and parts have little or no meaning.[15]

What is true for culture is also true for cultures. Developing cultures in breadth and depth means not only developing ideals, universals, and absolutes, but also developing all activities and not just some, as well as achieving balanced and harmonious relations between and among them. While it is essential to develop commercial, industrial, financial, technological, scientific, and economic activities, it is equally essential to develop artistic, social, political, educational, spiritual, and recreational activities if fulfillment, happiness, and harmony are to be realized. We need strong economies, for example, to create the material resources and monetary wealth required to make improvements in material living standards and physical circumstances, as well as to yield the consumption, investment, and employment opportunities needed to make quantitative improvements in all aspects of life. However, we also need economies that are properly contexted or situated in cultures—and constrained and enriched by cultural ideals and values—if economies are to be pointed in the right direction and serve human, humane, environmental, and cultural functions in the future. In order to do this, it is necessary to achieve synergies and symmetries between all absolutes and particulars, thereby ensuring that cultures are cohesive, coherent and harmonious rather than disparate, disorganized, disharmonious, and disconnected.

This brings us to the need to situate culture and cultures effectively in the natural, historical, global, and cosmic environment or space and time. In order to do this, it is essential to walk more lightly on the land, reduce our ecological footprint, come to grips with the cultural baggage we carry with us and pass on from one generation to the next, and create many more connections, bonds, and links between all the diverse peoples, countries, cultures, and civilizations in the world.

Just as culture and cultures provide the context within which the component parts of culture and cultures and the maze of relationships between and among these parts are situated, so the natural, historical, global, and cosmic environment provides the context within which culture, cultures, and cultural development and policy are situated. History has confirmed time and again that when culture and cultures are not positioned properly in the natural, historical, global, and cosmic environment, the consequences of this can be and usually are disastrous.

Viewed from this perspective, there may be nothing more important in the world going forward into the future than situating culture in general and cultures and their development and policies in particular in the natural, global, and cosmic environment. This means ensuring that culture in general and all the cultures in the world in particular are predicated on worldviews, values, principles, policies, and practices that promote environmental preservation, conservation, and sustainability, attend to the welfare and well-being of all species, and create harmony between people and countries. In terms of the historical environment, this means protecting and preserving the precious legacy of ideals, artifacts, ideas, values, traditions, stories, architectural monuments, beliefs, and so forth that have been built up over the centuries, and sharing them with humanity as a whole.

This precious legacy is designed to provide people, countries, and cultures in all parts of the world with the knowledge, information, insights, and ideas they need to create a continuous bond between the past, present, and future, and therefore past, present and future generations. It also provides the means to differentiate between right and wrong, good and evil, valuable and valueless, and meaningful and meaningless. This is what makes protection of the heritages of all countries and the entire cultural heritage of humankind from the ravages of time so imperative. Without this, people and countries will not be able to learn from the past, maintain their distinctive identities and diversities in the present, and preserve their cherished ways of life in the future. As Winston Churchill put it many years ago, paraphrasing George Santyana, "Those who fail to learn from history are condemned to repeat it."

This also necessitates coming to grips with the cultural baggage we inherit from the past. This is especially important when this baggage is negative or destructive, since the hostilities and resentments it creates stand in the way of achieving real peace and harmony in the world. As Janie Cooper-Wilson, founder and director of the Silver-Shoe Historical Society in Ontario, Canada, put it, "[C]ultural healing will require far more than sugar-coating the truth and paying lip-service to the concept of equality, diversity and inclusivity; it will require honest self-evaluation and the willingness to participate in uncomfortable conservations."[16]

Seen from this perspective, the truth and reconciliation commissions that have been created throughout the world over the past few decades provide a ray of hope for the future. (Examples include the commission initiated in South Africa in 1996 at the end of apartheid which was authorized by Nelson Mandela and chaired by Archbishop Desmond Tutu, and the commission created in Canada in 2009 with Murray Sinclair as its chair, among others.) This is primarily because they indicate a willingness on the part of specific groups of people and particular countries, as well as powerful institutions, to admit their wrongs in the past and seek forgiveness and reconciliation in the present and the future. Some of the most important of these wrongs as far as colonized countries and peoples are concerned have to do with the Doctrine of Discovery and papal bulls that were created by the Roman Catholic Church in 1455 and especially 1493, that provided the religious, political, and legal justifications for colonization of the Americas and Australasia. These documents encouraged the dehumanization of the Indigenous peoples by expropriating their lands and waterways as well as forcing them to give up their original cultures, heritages, languages, and tradition. In Canada, this was compounded and aggravated by putting Indigenous children in residential schools that were specifically designed for the purpose of assimilation. These problems were addressed officially in 2022 when Pope Francis came to Canada for the express reason of meeting the Indigenous peoples of the country and apologizing to them. The pope carried this a step further in 2023 when he rescinded the Doctrine of Discovery, as requested by Indigenous peoples when they met with the pope in Canada in 2022.

What is true of truth and reconciliation commissions is also true of other developments dealing with the cultural baggage that people and countries carry with them and often pass on to others. Many other Indigenous peoples throughout the world are also engaged in attempts to right the wrongs done to them over the centuries. Whether it is the Māori in New Zealand, Indigenous Australians, or native peoples in the United States and Central and South America, efforts to resolve land claims are essential. So is recognizing in political and public terms that most of these lands were inhabited originally by Indigenous peoples, giving them a major stake in the development and use of these lands in the future, enabling them to reconnect with their original cultures, languages, and ways of life, preserving their distinctive identities, customs, and traditions, and asserting their right to self-government in the present and the future. These are all vital steps towards ensuring that these peoples and their cultures are situated in the appropriate historical and contemporary contexts, frameworks, and developments in the years and decades ahead.

While an enormous amount remains to be accomplished in these areas, what is taking place at present does indeed provide a ray of hope for the future, especially if these initiatives are accompanied by the necessary economic and financial resources.

It is impossible to plumb the depths of cultural development and policy without realizing that every country and culture in the world is immersed in a specific pattern and type of cultural development. Whether by design or default, this pattern and type affects everybody and everything, including worldviews, values, value systems, lifestyles, ways of life, positioning in the world, and directions for the future.

Speaking generally, there are three distinct and different patterns of cultural development when they are looked at and assessed from a holistic perspective. These are the *imposed*, *imported*, and *indigenous* patterns.

The imposed pattern is the most obvious one at present because it can be traced back many centuries and has affected most countries in the world in one form or another. It is based on the coercion, subjugation, and dominance of one group of people, region, community, country, or culture by another, and has usually been achieved by brute force and the imposition of a specific way of life by the victors on the vanquished. This is how most of the great empires and dynasties in the world were created and maintained, regardless of whether it was empires or dynasties created by the Chinese, Mongolians, Persians, Ottomans, Hungarians, and others, or by rulers such as Genghis Khan, Cyrus the Great, Sultan Osman I, Attila the Hun, and numerous others. Usually, no stone was left unturned in this process, as languages, religions, economic and social activities, and public and private practices were all employed, imposed, and implanted in the interests of the conquerors. This was especially true for colonialism, imperialism, and the ability of one country to impose its will, worldview, and value system on another country or countries due to its superior military might or economic, political, or military power. Hence the ability of the British Empire to "rule the world" at one time, as well as for Portugal, Spain, France, Holland, Belgium, and a few other European countries to impose their wills on much of Africa, Asia, North America, South America, the Caribbean, and elsewhere.

It would be a mistake to assume that the imposed pattern was always a unilateral affair. It was often an interactive relationship, especially at the beginning when the colonizers had to learn many things from colonized people about how to survive in specific environments and parts of the world and the colonized people were anxious to acquire objects and artefacts brought to or for them by the colonizers. However, in most cases, this eventually led to the imposition of a great deal of "cultural conditioning" by the colonizing peoples and countries. The history of colonial-imperial relations indicates that imperial powers usually ended up driving traditional cultural practices underground or out of existence in the colonial satellites they dominated and ruled. These activities affected millions of people, and fanned the flames of hate, anger, resentment, and discontent by making colonized people aware of all the rights and freedoms they were not able to enjoy or had to give up. Usually, the embers of discontent and resentment smoldered under the surface for centuries before there was any hope of throwing off the shackles of foreign domination, something which is now going on in many decolonized and decolonizing countries and parts of the world. This is not to suggest that imperialism has been erased from the face of the earth, but rather to stress that it now operates in much more subtle and less conspicuous ways.

Unlike the imposed pattern of cultural development that results from sheer force, military might, and external domination, the imported pattern of cultural development is much more difficult to detect because it is often hidden from view. This also tends to make it more dangerous. There is a seductive quality about it that results from the fact that it is easier to accept than the imposed pattern, since the dominating country is less conspicuous and therefore the illusion of independence rather than dependence exists. Nevertheless, once the imported pattern has been established and settles in, it is usually very difficult to get rid of it or shake it off. This is because it is consciously and unconsciously accepted by people in the receiving country through their embrace of another country's worldviews, values, attitudes, technologies, institutional arrangements, and way of life.

These practices are often imitated or imported with the belief that they are shortcuts to development and therefore it is possible for a country's citizens to enjoy its benefits of development without having to incur the costs. These advantages are transmitted through a variety of devices and techniques, such as international communications and media systems, the operations of multinational corporations, the influence that some governments and countries exercise over others, or the use of various economic, commercial, and financial enticements. However, once a foothold is gained, the result is usually the same. The importing or imitating country takes on more and more of the characteristics, techniques, and features of the dominant country, possibly even to the point where it may be difficult to differentiate between the two, except for who holds the upper hand and calls the shots. This pattern often manifests itself most profusely and prominently in countries that have geographical boundaries and languages in common, or share certain customs or historical experiences in common, such as the United States and Canada, England, Scotland, and Wales, and numerous others.

Finally, there is the indigenous pattern of cultural development. While this pattern is the least frequent and most difficult to achieve, it is also the most rewarding and exciting going forward into the future. This explains why many countries in the world are attracted to this pattern today and are striving to achieve it. Creativity, ingenuity, courage, and determination are the assets that are most required to establish and drive this pattern. However, it is not these assets *per se* that are required most, but rather how they are directed to a specific end or purpose, namely the desire to create a very distinct way of life and become masters in one's own home. This is imperative for many countries in the world because the imposed and imported patterns are not working and leave people feeling angry, frustrated, disheartened, upset, or unfulfilled. As a result, many people and countries in the world are coming to the realization that their original cultures offer much more knowledge, wisdom, relevance, and awareness of what is needed to live in harmony with nature, the natural environment, and other species than the people and countries who subsequently shaped and dominated them.

It is one thing to recognize and aspire to the indigenous pattern of cultural development; it is quite another to achieve it. Regardless of how much countries may want to be shapers of their own destiny, not every country in the world is able to realize this at present, either because it is too difficult to throw off the shackles of foreign domination and control, or because they lack the capabilities, collective will, and basic commitment necessary to find their own indigenous path to cultural development and make it a reality. In parts of the world that have been colonized by other countries, breaking away from deep-seated and long-established colonial practices, policies, and protocols and returning to their origins and roots will not be easy to realize.

Achieving authenticity in deeds and actions and not just words and theories is the key to achieving indigenous cultural development. This means uncovering, exposing, reconnecting, and being true to one's original culture and roots. For many countries, this not only means breaking the web of foreign domination, imposition, and imitation of other countries' most powerful characteristics, but also rediscovering, asserting, and committing to their own histories and ways of life. Unfortunately, the histories of many colonized countries often start in a printed and documented sense with the period of external domination and colonialization, either because their histories were written, promoted, and dispersed throughout the world by their colonizers rather than by themselves, or because their original origins and histories only exist in oral or verbal form rather than written form.

Until recently, for instance, the written histories of many African countries tended to begin with the arrival of Europeans in Africa, despite the fact that Africans were making history and building sophisticated cultures and civilizations for centuries prior to the arrival of the first Europeans. Likewise, the written histories of many Asia, North and South American, and Caribbean countries as well as countries such as Australia and New Zealand are often dominated by the arrival of the French, British, Portuguese, and Spanish in these parts of the world, despite the fact that these areas were inhabited for thousands of years before this by Indigenous peoples who created cultures, worldviews, values, and ways of life that were cultivated and enlightened.

Fortunately, problems like this are now being addressed and coming to an end. In the case of Africa, for instance, this problem was confronted when UNESCO and the publisher Heinemann decided to collaborate on publishing a *General History of Africa*. The first two volumes, *Methodology and African Prehistory* and *Ancient Civilizations of Africa* were published in 1981, with many other volumes added since then. What is needed now, especially for countries aspiring to achieve indigenous cultural development, is to write, re-write, or re-create their histories in original, authentic, and genuine terms. Not only do conviction and common sense compel it, but the quest for truth and justice demands it.

If authenticity is a prerequisite for indigenous development, so is cultural identity, especially *national* cultural identity. Clearly, there can be no real national cultural identity without sharing certain similarities, since, in part, identity is achieved by recognizing and celebrating common feelings and characteristics. Likewise, there can also be no national cultural identity without recognizing and accepting certain differences, since too much sameness can obliterate identity by destroying its uniqueness and distinctiveness. Consequently, national cultural identity is achieved and maintained by walking the fine line between similarities and differences. A slip in the direction of too much sameness can cause people to rebel, if only to protect themselves from the numbing effects of similarity, uniformity, and familiarity. However, a slip in the direction of too much distinctiveness can be equally dangerous, perhaps more so, because people mistrust and reject what is different and what they don't understand. This makes achieving the right mixture of sameness and distinctiveness—similarities and differences—one of the greatest challenges of indigenous cultural development.

Ultimately, indigenous cultural development can't be realized without a country having sovereignty or control over its domestic and international affairs. This means bringing all vestiges of *undue* foreign influence, domination, and power under control, as well as refusing to buckle under to foreign influences and pressures. This is not to say that countries must deliberately cut themselves off from foreign influences and external aggression. In the interdependent world we are living in at the present time, it is inevitable that decisions made in one country or one part of the world will have strong influences on countries in other parts of the world. Nevertheless, countries striving to achieve indigenous cultural development should always be aware of this and take the implications, benefits, costs, and consequences into account, but never to the point where this interferes with their right to make decisions for themselves when circumstances warrant and it is the correct thing to do.

Countries striving to achieve authentic cultural development and assert sovereignty over their own affairs may not be able to do so without going through a period of nationalism, since it is one thing to talk about shifting from depending on others to depending on one-self, but quite another to achieve it in real terms. During this transitional period, a great deal of introspection may be required. However, it should constantly be borne in mind during this time that this is not nationalism in the conventional sense, namely promotion of one's own self-interests or asserting one's achievements to the exclusion of everything else. Rather, it is nationalism in the best sense of the term—standing firm and apart from other countries for a time in order to create the forms of cultural expression, symbols, and structures of cultural life that are necessary to come to grips with one's own origins, roots, historical traditions, interests, and needs. As long as the appropriate steps are taken to ensure that this situation does not go on for too long or threaten other people's well-being, this is a positive and healthy development, one that is essential to achieve independent, sovereign, and indigenous cultural development.

Deriving and assimilating developments from abroad is also a crucial part of this process if countries and their cultures are to mature, evolve, and progress properly. If this fails to happen, countries can easily become parochial, stagnant, and possibly too nationalistic. It is impossible to blossom effectively and achieve high standards of cultural creation and activity if countries are not able to benefit from international experiences, relations, exposure, and scrutiny. This is the best defense of all against excessive nationalism, stagnation, parochialism, and provincialism.

With this we complete our examination of the centrality of cultural development and policy. Advances in all these areas in recent years offer hope for the future. This is because cultural development and policy provide the contextual, conceptual, theoretical, and practical framework that is required to make sensible choices and sustainable decisions about a variety of domestic and international matters. They do this by developing culture and all the diverse cultures in the world in holistic terms, situating them effectively in the natural, historical, global, and cosmic environment, and recognizing that cultural development and policy are active, interactive, egalitarian, inclusive, and holistic processes rather than passive, unilateral, exclusive, partial, and partisan processes. As such, they address two of the greatest shortcomings of the prevailing model of development and policy of all: failure to take the natural, historical, global, and cosmic environment fully and forcefully into account in all developmental planning, policy, and decision-making; and failing to adopt the indigenous pattern of cultural development as the most authentic and legitimate pattern of development going forward into the future. With this in mind, we can now turn our attention to what is needed to open the doors to a cultural age and enable it to flourish in the years, decades, and centuries ahead.

Chapter Ten

Opening the Doors to a Cultural Age

Development is not merely an economic and political concept; it is
more fundamentally a process of culture and civilization.
—Rajni Kothari[1]

Just as it was necessary at the beginning of this book to deal with the
nature and meaning of "culture" in view of all the different uses there
are of this evocative but elusive term, so it is necessary at the beginning of this chapter to deal with the nature and meaning of the term
"age" in order to prevent any misunderstandings.

When we talk about the economic age we are living in today, two
things stand out above all the rest. The first is that this age has existed for a long period of time, specifically from the publication of
Adam Smith's book *The Wealth of Nations* in 1776 to the present.
The second is that the highest priority in this age has been awarded
to economics and developing all the diverse economies in the world.

What is true for the economic age is also true for all other types of
ages, be they spiritual, technological, cosmological, or any other kind.
Ages usually extend over long periods of time, and place the highest
priority on a particular activity or perspective.

Such is also the case for the cultural age. Not only would it have to
exist over an extended period of time, but as well the highest priority
would have to be accorded to culture and to developing all the cultures in the world, not to mention any new cultures that might be created after this age commenced. As has been demonstrated throughout this book, not only is a cultural age needed to come to grips with
the world's most threatening problems, but also to create more peace,
harmony, happiness, sustainability, and equality in the world.

As badly as a cultural age is needed at this time, it should be
stated at the outset that such an age is not viewed as an "ideal age" or

the "be all and end all" to all ages. Rather, it is seen as the next step needed to come to grips with contemporary problems, as well as to put humanity in the strongest position to create the new worldviews, values, value systems, lifestyles, and ways of life that are necessary to deal with these problems. Once these problems have been dealt with and the requirements met, it is very likely that a new set of problems will exist that will require the creation of a different kind of age to deal with them. How long this will take is an open book, to be determined by the conditions and circumstances that exist at that time.

There is a related problem that must be addressed here as well. By contrast with the views of Karl Marx and other scholars who share Marx's beliefs about history in general and the economic interpretation of history in particular, it is not possible to embrace the conviction that determinism in general—and economic determinism in particular—lies at the heart of history and that humanity will therefore always be locked in an economic age. Looking back over the past, it is obvious that free will and freedom of choice have existed over the entire course of history. Things are no different now.

Without doubt, the biggest problem today and in the future—and quite possibly in all periods of history—is to decide what should be seen and treated as "the whole" and what should be seen and treated as "the parts of the whole." This decision affects everything and everybody. Given humanity's freedom to choose, there are many options available. We might continue to treat economics as the whole, or we might substitute science, technology, education, spirituality, or some other activity or field. Nevertheless, it is clear that culture has the most legitimate claim to be chosen and treated as the whole. It was first defined in this way more than a hundred and fifty years ago and that claim has been affirmed by countless anthropologists, historians, and other cultural scholars ever since.

In addition, from what has been learned about culture and cultures over the last two thousand years and particularly over the last hundred and fifty years, it is apparent that culture and cultures in the holistic sense have become the most important means of dealing with the present world predicament and future prospects. This does not mean, and should never mean, that this will always be the case. In fact, at some point in the future, culture as a holistic entity and powerful force in the world will likely be replaced by some other activity, field, or discipline, one that is not evident or predictable today, but which nevertheless will be required to open the doors to a very different kind of age to deal with the needs and challenges that exist at that time.

Finally, there is the problem of calling the future age a cultural age *before* rather than *after* the fact. Many people, scholars, historians, and organizations may take exception to doing so. Until now, we have labelled ages in retrospect not in advance, after looking back on the past rather than forward into the future. Most scholars believe that a considerable amount of time must elapse before any in-depth assessment can be made of any period in history, at which point it can be characterized in a certain overarching way.

This is consistent, for example, with labelling the period in European history from the late fifth to the late fifteenth centuries the "Middle Ages." Use of this term arose as early as 1469, and by the very use of the word "middle" implied that this age fell in between the Classical Age and the Modern Age, distinguishing it from both. It was impossible to label a period as the Middle Ages until a new age—the Modern Age—had begun.

This "after or before the fact" dilemma exists because it is difficult to predict with any accuracy or confidence how matters will turn out before they occur. The dilemma is also intimately connected to the current conviction that ages are always the *consequence of change* rather than the *cause of change*, and therefore it is not possible to predict with any certainty what will occur over the next few decades let alone the next few centuries.

While this may have been the case in the past, that doesn't mean that it will always be the case. Indeed, given all the problems that exist in the world today, we need a far better understanding not only of exactly what is wrong with the present age, but also, and much more importantly, what is required in specific terms to fix it and set ourselves on the right course in the future. We did this earlier when we carried out an impartial assessment not only of the strengths and benefits of the economic age, but also of its basic shortcomings and devastating costs.

Heading the list in this regard was the need to take the holistic approach provided by culture and cultures to global development and human affairs. If we don't do so, we will move ever closer to the point where the destruction of humanity and even the planet is inevitable.

This is why it is so essential to label the future age a cultural age now rather than waiting for more time to elapse to see if a cultural age does in fact emerge. It is also why it is necessary to label the future age a cultural age rather than (say) an ecological age or an environmental age, as some are doing at present. Doing so is imperative because *we* are the cause of the ecological or environmental crisis, and it is incumbent on us both individually and collectively to set this situation right. Surely this can only be achieved by creating the cultural changes and transformations that are required in worldviews, values, value systems, customs, beliefs, and ways of life in order to achieve this goal.

While there are numerous benefits to be derived from specialization and breaking wholes up into parts—benefits we have seen over the course of the economic age—what is desperately needed now is to bring those parts back together rather than splitting them up even further. In other words, it is necessary at the present juncture in history to *unite* rather than *divide* activities, since this makes it possible to take advantage of culture's most powerful and timely asset, namely its holistic quality. It is this all-encompassing capacity in culture in general and cultures in particular that will make it possible to achieve more unity, harmony, sustainability, cooperation, stability, and equality in the world. It follows from this that what specialization and reductionism are and have been to the economic age, holism and the holistic perspective and capacity are and must be to the cultural age.

This explains why culture and cultures as ideas, ideals, and realities have been organic, dynamic, flexible, and fluid over the centuries. As such, they have been progressively broadened, deepened, diversified, and intensified over the course of history to stay in tune with the most powerful developments and pertinent changes that have taken and are taking place in the world. Not only have culture and cultures been concerned with a vast array of disciplines, areas, fields, and activities over a very long period of time now, but there is now very little in the world that is not concerned with or connected to culture and cultures in one form or another in this all-inclusive sense.

Whereas most disciplines and activities derive their power, profundity, and utility from being perceived, defined, and dealt in one way and one way only—economics, for example, is perceived and defined as the "production, distribution, consumption, and accumulation of goods, products, and services as well as the creation of material and monetary wealth"—culture derives its power, potential, profundity, and utility from being perceived, defined, and dealt with in many different ways. No other activity, field, or discipline possesses the breadth of vision, depth of understanding, theoretical potential, and practical capabilities that culture does when it is visualized and dealt with in holistic terms.[2]

The longer we fail to recognize this fact and take advantage of culture's profuse capabilities and possibilities in this respect, the more devastating and destructive the consequences may be. This is what makes the relentless trend over the course of history towards ever more expansive and all-encompassing perceptions, definitions, and manifestations of culture and cultures so timely, rewarding, and relevant. Since culture in the holistic or anthropological sense began to assert itself in earnest in the latter part of nineteenth century, it has been strengthened and enlarged substantially with the addition of the biological, ecological, and cosmological perceptions, definitions, and manifestations of culture.

As we have seen, these more recent and far-reaching perceptions, definitions, and manifestations of culture are no longer confined to the human realm but include other species, the natural environment, and many aspects and characteristics of the universe and the cosmos as well.[3] This is most apparent in the case of the cosmological manifestation of culture because it is based on the belief that the cosmos is not only a whole, but also a *structured, ordered, regenerative,* and *harmonious* whole. We are learning that the cosmos possesses certain qualities, characteristics, and capabilities that human beings do not at the present time, including this capacity for regeneration, sustainability, and renewal that we must create, develop, and apply in the future.

All of this confirms the conviction stated earlier that it is time to enter a cultural age and enable it to flourish as the next great epoch in the history of humanity and the world. As Valerie Lynch Lee, editor of *Faces of Culture,* put it:

The future of humanity is one and the same with the future of culture, for culture is the chief means by which we adapt to our environment. Cultural adaptations have allowed us to build large cities, increase food production, and travel quickly to all parts of the world. In fact, human inventiveness has so changed the world that our old ways of living may no longer be suitable. *We have changed the world to such an extent that it may now be necessary to change ourselves if we are to survive in it.*[4]

Lee's words bring us face to face with what is undoubtedly the most important requirement of all: the need to evolve the state and level of *cultural consciousness* in order to change the way we see the world, organize ourselves, conduct our affairs, interact with other people and other species, enhance and embellish life, and position ourselves in the world, the universe, and the cosmos. This is the key to opening the doors to a cultural age, making it a reality, and enabling it to thrive.

It is one thing to visualize this in theoretical, idealistic, and conceptual terms. However, it is quite another to achieve it in practical, operational, and specific terms. Having dealt with the first requirement in the previous chapters of this book, the time has come to deal with the second requirement in the chapters that remain.

This requirement will not be achieved without proactive and powerful contributions coming from three very distinct groups: people and organizations working in the cultural field; people and organizations working in government, politics, and international affairs; and the general public.

Of these three groups, people and organizations working in the cultural field have the most immediate and essential role to play and responsibilities to assume in opening the doors to a cultural age and enabling it to flourish. Not only is this group actively involved in culture, cultures, cultural development, and cultural policy on a full-time basis as well as committed to advancing the cultural cause, but it is also needed to provide the leadership, inspiration, and commitment required to set this process in motion and enable it to be realized. While this group is spread across numerous disciplines, activities, and areas, what is required more than ever is to coalesce it into a cohesive and coherent cultural community and crucial force. If this group does not provide the necessary initiative, it is very possible that a cultural age will not become a reality.

A similar challenge confronted people and organizations working in the environmental field more than half a century ago. They were also spread across a vast array of disciplines, activities, and fields and had to be brought together into the aggressive and relentless environmental community as well as the powerful force and movement they are today. They did this primarily through the commitment of countless dedicated and committed environmentalists and ecological leaders, scholars, scientists, policy-makers, and activists, as well as numerous organizations that represent these people and this field throughout the world. This is what is most required in the cultural field today. A strong and vocal cultural community needs to be created that is capable of making culture and cultures the centrepiece of the world system and principal preoccupation of municipal, regional, national, and international development in the years, decades, and possibly centuries ahead.

The impetus for this should come from people and organizations deeply involved in and committed to the centrality of culture, cultures, cultural development, and cultural policy in the overall scheme of things, as well as those who work with cultural wholes and overall ways of life in their multifarious activities on a daily basis. This group includes anthropologists, sociologists, psychologists, artists, humanists, ecologists, biologists, botanists, zoologists, and all the myriad organizations that are associated with them, because these are the individuals and organizations familiar with and knowledgeable about what culture and cultures as wholes and overall ways of life are actually all about and designed to accomplish.

There are many ways people and organizations such as these can fulfill their roles and responsibilities in this area during this difficult and demanding period in the history of the world. They can, for instance, create educational courses, programs, and resources as well as aesthetic, artistic, humanistic, and heritage activities, works, and experiences. All these are required to broaden, deepen, and intensify humanity's individual and collective knowledge, understanding, and consciousness of the intricacies, complexities, and essence of culture and cultures. They can also enhance awareness and appreciation of the similarities and differences that exist between all the different cultures and civilizations in the world as well as the cultures of other species. And this is not all. They can enhance appreciation and use of the natural and cultural heritages of all the different peoples and countries in the world as well as the entire natural and cultural heritage of humankind. In addition, they can facilitate the development of the many different communications media required to celebrate the best in human nature, conduct, and character, contribute to reducing violence, conflict, racism, terrorism, and war, and create deeper interpersonal, interorganizational, and intergenerational relationships. While many resources already exist in most of these areas, what is needed now—and needed more than ever—is to take a more systematic, intensive, and integrated approach to producing, utilizing, and sharing cultural resources, materials, and activities like this, as well as extending them far beyond specific groups and organizations and making them accessible to all people and countries.

This group can also foster and activate many more interactions, interconnections, exchanges, and agreements between the diverse peoples, countries, cultures, and civilizations of the world. This is especially necessary with respect to countries, cultures, and civilizations that are experiencing major conflicts, open hostilities, festering animosities, and wars. Initiatives and activities such as these are desperately needed to pave the way for an improvement in intercultural, multicultural, and international relations, thereby promoting greater sensitivity to the similarities and differences that exist between the different peoples, countries, cultures, and species of the world. They can also spread the word that the time is ripe to enter a cultural age, explain why this is so essential, and suggest what this age can and will be like using their own activities in the cultural field as symbols, guides, illustrations, and examples. This is required to move culture and cultures in general—and cultural development and policy in particular—out of the margins and into the mainstream of public and private life in all parts of the world.

In specific terms, a great deal of effort should be made at key contact points to connect people, groups, and countries that have been driven apart, such as Israelis and Palestinians, Russians and Ukrainians, mainland Chinese and Taiwanese, Sunnis and Shī'ites, and numerous others. This is equally important within countries that are polarized and divided and require new cultural symbols due to the diverse composition of their populations, a situation that is becoming more commonplace. It is here that a very important question arises. Where will the *new* cultural symbols come from in the years and decades ahead that are needed to serve similar functions to the Nubian Monuments of Ramesses II and Queen Nefertari in Egypt millennia ago, the Eiffel Tower in France, the Great Wall of China, the fourteenth-century Boudhanath stupa in Nepal, Machu Picchu in Peru, Petra in Jordan, the Taj Mahal in India, the Statue of Liberty in the United States, and numerous others? If the past is any guide, many of these symbols will come from oppressed, colonized, and marginalized people who are anxious to make their contributions to their countries of origin despite centuries of subjugation, brutality, persecution, and prejudice.

Next to people and organizations working in the cultural field, people and organizations working in government, politics, and international affairs have the most important role to play and responsibilities to assume in opening the doors to a cultural age and making it a reality. They must also play a powerful and proactive leadership role, but in a very different way than the first group.

In order to achieve this, this group will have to recognize and pay close attention to the great cultural awakening that is going on in all sectors of cultural life today, understand why this is taking place at this particular juncture in history, and be aware of how it is manifesting itself in all parts of the world and not just some parts. Many of the problems people and countries engaged in the great cultural awakening are confronted with today do not receive the attention, priority, and funding they require from governments and international institutions. This is because these problems are seen as matters of secondary importance compared to the primary importance of production, distribution, consumption, and accumulation of goods and commodities, creation of material and monetary wealth, profit maximization, and the treatment of wealthy classes and privileged elites.

These problems are exacerbated by the fact that most governments in the world are in a very precarious financial position today.

Governments and international institutions have had to spend huge sums of money to increase the rate of economic growth and have rung up huge debts in the process.

Long gone are the days of John Maynard Keynes and his valuable advice that surpluses should be created in good times in order to have the funds necessary to spend on public works and other activities in bad times. As a result, many governments are now compelled to raise taxes and cut badly needed social, educational, health, artistic, and environmental programs at the very time when they are needed the most, thereby hampering their ability to act objectively, impartially, and in the public interest. As long as this situation exists, the environmental crisis will not be solved, excesses, imbalances, and disharmonies will be experienced in the world system and people's lives that are impossible to prevent, inequalities and disparities will persist in the distribution of income, wealth, and resources, and consumer demands and expectations will be created that are beyond the capacity of governments to deal with effectively and fulfil. This is not a viable scenario at present or heading into the future.

It follows from this that a *new system of government and politics* is required to deal with these problems and others.[5] We are not talking about a governmental and political system of the left, right, or centre here. Rather, we are talking about a system that will make it possible to make a great deal more progress in achieving the social development goals advocated by the United Nations in 2015, deal equitably and equally with all citizens and community groups, realize sustainable development, reduce the enormous disparities in income, wealth, and resources that exist, and yield a great deal more caring, sharing, and compassion in the world.

At the heart of this new system should be commitment to one of the greatest, wisest, and most quintessential ideals of politics and culture of all in principle if not in practice today. It is commitment to "the whole" and not just "a part" or "selective parts" of the whole, as well as constantly striving to create balanced and harmonious relationships between the parts and the whole in all the many different types of cultural relationships that exist. In order to realize this, it will be necessary to act in the best interests of all people, activities, countries, and species, as well as achieve cultural development and policy from the bottom up and not just from the top down, as has usually been the case. If this holistic ideal is not applied and achieved by political and governmental authorities as well as by such international organizations as the United Nations, World Bank, UNESCO, International Monetary Fund, World Trade Organization, Organization for Economic Cooperation and Development, World Economic Forum, and others, it will not be enacted at all.

This is because other people, organizations, groups, classes, and sectors in society are involved in and committed to developments in their own specific areas of interest. While they may be committed to the importance of the whole in principle and achieving vital, viable, sustainable, and harmonious relationships between the parts of the whole in general, philosophical, and theoretical terms, they do not see this as their primary responsibility in practical and concrete terms. Rather, they see it as the responsibility of governments, politicians, and the political process.

This commitment to the whole and not just specific parts of the whole is what governments, politicians, politics, and international relations must be concerned with first and foremost in the future, not only in philosophical, theoretical, and idealistic terms, but also, and much more fundamentally at this particular stage in history, in practical, tangible, and applied terms. As difficult as this is or might be, if governments and politicians do not stand up to powerful elites, wealthy classes, corporations, corporate executives, lobbyists, special interest groups, and similar individuals and organizations and assert the importance of "the whole" and the "public interest" over partial, sectoral, partisan, or specialized interests, the cultural age will not be created. The economic age will persist, creating demands and expectations that are impossible to fulfil.

Many major developments will be required by governments, politicians, and international organizations to realize this precious ideal in practice and not just in theory. One is conducting an all-out assault on poverty and unemployment in the world by increasing foreign aid and developmental assistance as a percentage of gross national product, especially by the wealthiest countries in the world. Another is decreasing the oppressive debt loads and dire financial conditions in many countries in Africa, Asia, Latin America, the Caribbean, and the

Middle East, where this is justified and confirmed. And still another is improving the terms of trade and eliminating high tariffs and large subsidies in Western countries that are imposing considerable hardships and difficulties on people and countries in the less fortunate parts of the world. This is also necessary to make it possible for poor people, classes, and countries to access the credit, capital, technological expertise, entrepreneurial acumen, and educational training they need to take control of their destinies and lives.

What is also necessary is to create a much more effective and efficient structure and framework for governmental and political administration, policy, planning, and decision-making. This structure and framework should be based on taking an all-encompassing, impartial, and equitable approach to governmental and political affairs and activities rather than a partial, biased, and unequal approach. This is imperative if sustainable development, human welfare, environmental well-being, and global harmony are to be achieved and maintained.

Developing administrative structures and frameworks such as ministries or departments of culture that are holistic, egalitarian, and inclusive rather than specialized, partisan, and exclusive is the way to achieve this objective. In order to do this, politicians and governments will have to shift from administrative structures and frameworks that are based on breaking the cultural whole up into many separate parts and creating vertical structures and specific sectoral silos. Instead, the need is for structures and frameworks that are horizontal and based on commitments to dealing with the cultural whole and situating culture and countries' cultures properly in the natural, historical, global, and cosmic environment. This will ensure that the principal focus will be on using a cultural rather than economic model of development, and implementing appropriate policies, practices, plans, and programs.

Just as new government administrative structures and frameworks will be needed, so will new types of political and governmental leaders. Going forward into the future, these leaders will have to take a much broader and deeper approach to decision-making processes and have a different vision for the future—a vision that is capable of opening the doors to a cultural age and enabling it to flourish.

The types of leaders that come to mind in this regard are Léopold Sédar Senghor, a prominent cultural activist, poet, and first president of Senegal; Ignacy Jan Paderewski, a pianist, composer, and former prime minister of Poland; and Václav Havel, a playwright, author, and last president of Czechoslovakia, as well as Angela Merkel, chancellor of Germany for many years, Jacinda Ardern, former prime minister of New Zealand, and Volodymyr Zelenskyy, president of Ukraine. Leaders such as these are needed more than ever to bring the age of culture into existence and guide it through its formative stages. For it is leaders such as these that have all-encompassing perspectives on the world, a better understanding of the realm of culture and cultures in the overall scheme of things, and the courage and convictions to award a high priority to the well-being of all people and species.

Developments such as these, and others, will make it possible to create cultural development policies and practices that are transformational, transcendental, and redistributive rather than piecemeal, partisan, partial, or sectoral in character. While these latter kinds of policies and practices are generally preferred by governments, politicians, and international organizations today because they are predicated on moving forward one step at a time, unfortunately proceeding in this fashion leaves little or no room for systemic cultural change. Instead, the emphasis is on preserving the status quo, chipping away at problems one at a time, and dealing with problems and issues sequentially and by sector rather than simultaneously and holistically. This is not a viable option moving forward into the future, since it will not solve the world's most pressing and urgent problems or create new possibilities, policies, practices, and prospects. This explains why cultural rather than economic models of development and policy need to be implemented. They involve changing directions significantly and simultaneously rather than slowly and cautiously and in a way that ultimately reinforces the existing order.

In specific terms, the future policies, procedures, and practices should be *transformational* in the sense that they bring about the fundamental changes in human behavior, lifestyles, and ways of life that are needed to reduce the demands we are making on the natural environment, as well as decreasing the severe inequalities that exist in society. They should be *transcendental* in the sense that they expand people's awareness, appreciation, and commitment to the non-material dimensions of development and life, as well as enhancing their commitment to achieving higher and loftier goals and ideals and living happier, healthier, and more fulfilling, spiritual, and compassionate lives. And they should be *redistributive* in the sense that they direct income and wealth to people and countries that really need it. This will only be achieved by governments, political parties, and politicians if they stand up and take ten steps to the left from where they are positioned today, because this will create a political and governmental system that places a much higher priority on distributing income and wealth more equitably than the one that exists in most countries today.

In order to deal with policies, procedures, and practices as ambitious and far-ranging as these as well as ensure that culture and cultures are used for constructive rather than destructive purposes, it will be necessary for governments and political leaders to develop a strong public sector to offset the size and power of the private sector, ensure that corporate, financial, political, and military power is not concentrated in too few hands, establish democratic and benevolent forms of governance rather than authoritative and dictatorial ones, create cultural agencies such as arts councils and media agencies that are situated at arm's length from government and the political process, and democratize and decentralize development, planning and decision-making processes, and opportunities.

Governments, politicians, and civic servants will have to make maximum use of all the policy tools and techniques at their disposal if they are to put themselves in this much stronger position. This is especially important with respect to legislation, regulation, consolidation, and progressive taxation. Legislation and regulation are required to exercise control and authority over corporations, developers, and commercial interests, as well as to focus on citizens, community groups, and the public at large. Consolidation and progressive taxation are needed to redistribute income, wealth, and resources more equally, eliminate corruption, patronage, duplication, and waste, restore the financial well-being and fiscal viability of governments, and strengthen the capacity for governments to address pressing cultural issues, problems, and needs. While care must be taken not to dampen economic enthusiasm or curtail investment, technological, and entrepreneurial opportunities, a great deal can be accomplished through taxation measures that impose heavier tax burdens on the rich and privileged classes in society. This will make it possible for governments to reduce their debt loads and play a more benevolent and beneficial role in society.

Unfortunately, no country or government in the world today is able to claim that culture and cultures constitute the foundation and principal preoccupation of their development in concrete terms. However, there are several countries and their governments that are moving progressively in this direction. The most obvious is Indonesia. In 2017, this government enacted National Law No. 5 on Cultural Advancement that includes several key articles that place culture at the core of Indonesia's development. It states:

[The] Principles for the Advancement for National Culture of Indonesia are tolerance, diversity, cross-regional participation, benefits, sustainability, freedom of expression, cohesiveness, equality, and mutual cooperation. As for the purpose, it is to develop the noble values of the nation's culture, enrich cultural diversity, strengthen national identity, strengthen the unity and integrity of the nation, educate life for the nation, improve the image of the nation, realize civil society, improve the welfare of free people, preserve the nation's cultural heritage, and influence the direction of development so that *Culture becomes the national development direction.*

While little is known about this legislation outside Indonesia, this development is not surprising in view of the fact that Indonesia has produced some of the world's most important cultural scholars and journalists in recent decades. Most notable in this regard are Sutan Takdir Alisjahbana, who is quoted in several places in this book and is the author of such books as *Socio-Cultural Creativity in the Converging and Restructuring Process of the New Emerging World* and *Values as Integrating Forces in Personality, Society and Culture*; Soedjatmoko, former rector of the United Nations University in Japan and a well-known international diplomat, cultural scholar, and historian with several publications to his credit including *Economic Development as a Cultural Problem, An Introduction to Indonesian Historiography*, and, co-edited with Kenneth W. Thompson, *Culture, Development, and Democracy: The Role of the Intellectual—A Tribute*; Mochtar Lubis, an outstanding and courageous journalist, media founder, and prolific novelist who was jailed on several occasions for his opposition to various political practices in Indonesia and is the author of *Twilight in Jakarta* and many other novels; and, more recently, Mira Sartika, cultural geneticist, founder and director of the Chakra Cultural Foundation and its Center for Cultural Studies, and author of *The Map of Civilization: A Geocultural Synthesis, Cultural Genetics*, and *Culture in Sustainable Development: Harmony through Differences.*[6] Also not surprising in this regard is that one of Indonesia's most cultivated and cherished cultural regions—there are many!—is Bali, which is well known throughout the world for the high level of its creativity and numerous artistic and cultural accomplishments, as well as being one of the most coveted tourist destinations in the world.

Indonesia is not the only country that is steadily and progressively moving toward the centrality of culture in general and its own culture in particular. Several other countries should also be noted, including Italy, France, Spain, and India. All deserve a great deal of recognition and credit for their remarkable cultural achievements over many centuries and have produced more than their fair share of cultural scholars during this time. Take India as the most obvious and prolific example of this over an incredibly long period of time. According to Rana P. B. Singh:

> A country (Bhārat/India) with at least an 8000-year old history in continuity and contrasts, adaptability and superimpositions, a frame of succession-sustenance-sustainability, and a civilization united by its diversities and distinctiveness, keeping live experiences of the richness of culture/s, the glory of the past, the turbulences and triumphs, nevertheless keeping all together leading the march in the cybernetic sphere, while preserving the landmarks of each era, the achievements of each age, the legacy of the regime—all those tied together

in its vast geography that was created, re-created, maintained, continued and passed on from one generation to another on the long passage of time—thus evolved India's heritagescapes.[7]

Bhutan, which initiated and instituted the concept of gross national happiness (GNH) as opposed to gross domestic product (GDP) as its most important official means of measuring the state of its overall development, has had an important role to play in this area but in a very different and innovative manner. This measurement assesses development from a holistic perspective based on four major factors—equitable socio-economic development, promotion and preservation of culture, conservation of the environment, and good governance—as well as subdividing these four factors into nine strategic domains and utilizing thirty-three indicators in its GNH Index to assess its progress.

Added to this list should be Singapore, which as a country and city-state has achieved a great deal in terms of the multiracial and multicultural character of its population and especially people's relationship with nature. The Singapore government committed in 1967 to making Singapore a "garden city" (and country) that has allocated 10 percent of its overall geographical area to creating parks and nature reserves. South Korea has made rapid strides in the development of popular culture and populist forms of artistic and cultural expression, receiving a great deal of respect and awareness around the world for this. Japan is recognized for its historical, contemporary, domestic, and international cultural successes and contributions. Hopefully, these countries, and others, will provide useful prototypes and models for people and organizations to study, examine, and emulate in the years and decades ahead.

And this brings us to the general public as the third and final group in this important triumvirate. While this group is not required to play as immediate or forceful a role as people and organizations working in the cultural field or in government, politics, and international affairs, ultimately its role and responsibilities are the most essential of all. This is because things will not change—and change substantially and for the better—until the general public advocates for systemic cultural change and not just piecemeal and partial change. In order to realize this, this largest group of all will have to participate actively in reducing the demands they are making on the natural environment by living lives that are more qualitative, non-material, creative, and balanced in nature. They will also have to commit to conservation of the world's natural resources, fight for more inclusion, equality, and justice in the world in general and especially for oppressed and marginalized people and countries, live their lives in communion, community, and solidarity with other people, countries, and species, and elevate life to a much higher state of existence and mindfulness as well as level of consciousness.

Is it possible for people and organizations in this third group to initiate and achieve these objectives? Without doubt it is. As the great cultural awakening has demonstrated convincingly in recent years, people in many parts of the world have achieved and are achieving remarkable changes in the world through their active and aggressive engagement in numerous environmental protests, as well as participation in initiatives commenced by colonized countries and oppressed groups that have been and are calling for major cultural reforms. In so doing, they have demonstrated that it is possible to get things done when acting persistently and collectively. People are no longer willing to accept colossal disparities in income and wealth, lack of political concern for their present conditions and basic needs, exploitation by powerful companies and wealthy elites, and procrastination on the part of governments with respect to global warming, the environmental crisis, health care, marginalization, exclusion, and polarization. While a great deal remains to be accomplished, the bottom-up, collective approach to problems shows that there are grounds for optimism and enthusiasm going forward into the future.

Over the last few decades, a profound change and seismic shift has been taking place in the world, from preoccupation with wealthy elites to concern for people in general, and with this, from elite culture to popular culture. This is evident in the changes occurring in the character and content of community and city newspapers, magazines, radio and television programs, social media platforms, advertisements, marketing materials, and other sources of information.

And this is not all. Many of these developments reveal that peoples and groups who have been marginalized, oppressed, and colonized are nonetheless capable of producing remarkable works in the arts, sciences, and many other areas of life that are outstanding in quality and connect with other people and groups in emotional, sensitive, and inspirational ways. This augers well for the future, since it confirms the conviction stated earlier that commitment to inclusion and recognition of the talents, abilities, and contributions of such people, groups, and countries far outweighs the costs.

With this we conclude this chapter on opening the doors to the cultural age and making it a reality. But even more is needed to ensure the cultural age will thrive and flourish. To realize this, attention will have to be focused on one of the most difficult challenges we all face. The time has come to examine this matter.

Chapter Eleven

Harmonizing Crucial Cultural Relationships

> I would then define the theory of culture as the study of relation-
> ships between elements in a whole way of life.... Analysis of particu-
> lar works or institutions is, in this context, analysis of their essential
> kind of organization, the relationship which works or institutions
> embody as parts of the organization as a whole.
> —Raymond Williams[1]

While shifting the focus from economics and economies to culture
and cultures is imperative to enter a cultural age because doing so
places the highest priority on the holistic perspective provided by culture rather than the partial perspective provided by economics, this
in itself is not sufficient to ensure that a cultural age will flourish and
function effectively. In order to achieve this, it is necessary to create
as much balance and harmony as possible between many key cultural
relationships.

No one recognized the necessity of shifting this perspective more
than Raymond Williams, the well-known cultural scholar and historian whose words open this chapter. He believed that such relationships play a crucial role in the development of culture and cultures
in the holistic sense. This was affirmed by Peter Brook, the talented British theatrical director, in an article he wrote for the UNESCO
Round Table on Cultural and Intellectual Cooperation and the New
International Economic Order in 1976. In the article, entitled "The
Three Cultures of Modern Man," he stated:

> The third culture is the culture of links [the first two are the in-
> dividual and the state according to Brook]. It is the force that
> can counterbalance the fragmentation of our world. It is to do

with the discovery of relationships where such relationships have become submerged and lost—between man [people] and society, between one race and another, between the microcosm and the macrocosm, between humanity and machinery, between the visible and invisible, between categories, languages, genres. What are these relationships? *Only cultural acts can explore and reveal these vital truths.*[2]

Countless cultural relationships such as these exist throughout the world. Among the most important are the ones concerned with the relationship between

- the arts and sciences,
- human rights and human responsibilities,
- unity and diversity,
- rich and poor people and rich and poor countries,
- males and females, and among all genders,
- traditional and digital technologies,
- technology and humans,
- the private sector and public sector,
- the self and the other,
- idealism and realism; and, most important of all, the relationships between
- the material and non-material dimensions of development and life, and
- humans and the natural environment.

This chapter is designed to demonstrate why creating balance and harmony between key relationships such as these and many others is the greatest challenge confronting humanity and the world at present and going forward into the future. In order to illustrate the quintessential importance of this, let's begin by examining the imbalance and disharmony that exists between the arts and the sciences. By examining this specific relationship in breadth and depth—particularly how and why it came into existence in the first place, all the difficult and complex difficulties that have arisen from it, and, most essentially, how to address this problem and ones like it—an incredible amount of light can be shed on how to come to grips with crucial cultural relationships like these and others.

What makes this relationship so essential is the fact that the arts and sciences underlie so many other activities. There have been many times in history when major imbalances and disharmonies have existed between the arts and the sciences. This is because the arts have grown and thrived during some periods of history while the sciences have grown and thrived in others. The most obvious example is the Renaissance and the period following it. During the Renaissance, which most historians describe as the period in the fifteenth and sixteenth centuries that saw the transition from the Middle Ages to the Modern Age, the arts grew in prominence and importance much more rapidly than the sciences. The Renaissance began in Italy and was marked by the incredible creativity that was manifested in literature, architecture, painting, music, and other art forms by such talented figures as Dante Alighieri, Petrarch, Brunelleschi, Michelangelo, Raphael, Leonardo da Vinci, Palestrina, Monteverdi, and others.

However, this period was followed by one in which the sciences far more than the arts grew and developed rapidly, beginning in the fifteenth century and continuing to at least the nineteenth century. The development of modern science saw major contributions by Nicolaus Copernicus, Robert Hooke, Johannes Kepler, Isaac Newton, Galileo Galilei, Carolus Linnaeus, and numerous others.

These phenomenal bursts of creativity and ingenuity in the arts and then the sciences (broadly defined) occurred in response to specific needs, an enormous amount of intellectual curiosity and imagination, and especially tenacity and devotion on the part of gifted artists and scientists. Developments like this have occurred frequently throughout history in many other areas as well.

A somewhat similar event occurred in the latter half of the twentieth century and first few decades of the twenty-first century and is still going on today, although it has involved the arts and sciences simultaneously rather than sequentially. This event took place in Great Britain first, then spread rapidly to other countries in Europe and North America, and finally ended up affecting the world as a whole. What makes this example so revealing in terms of the creation of a cultural age is that when balance and harmony is realized among key cultural relationships, such as the one between the arts and the sciences, it tends to give rise to and manifest itself in order, stability, security, happiness, and well-being in society in general. However, when balance and harmony between key cultural relationships is not achieved, it usually manifests itself in imbalances, disharmonies, disorder, polarization, and conflict.

Such is the case today with the present imbalance and disharmony between the arts and the sciences, which began in earnest following the publication of C. P. Snow's book *The Two Cultures and the Scientific Revolution* in 1959.[3] This book had a powerful impact on the relationship between the arts and the sciences and eventually on culture and cultures in the decades to follow. Thus it is a valuable example to learn from in understanding how a cultural age can flourish rather than flounder in the future.

In his book, Snow divided intellectual life in Great Britain and generally throughout the western world into two very distinct components or "cultures" as he called them: the *artistic-humanistic culture*, and *the scientific culture*. According to Snow, the artistic-humanistic culture was receiving far too much attention and funding and the scientific culture far too little attention and funding. Snow was convinced that much more attention and funding should be provided to the sciences and to scientific education in order to come to grips with the world's most pressing problems at that time.

Snow made such a powerful case for awarding a higher priority and more funding for the sciences and scientific education that a major shift occurred away from the arts, humanities, and an artistic-humanistic education and towards the sciences and a scientific education. It was not long after this that the sciences became characterized in most educational systems in the Western world as **hard** subjects, while the arts and humanities were viewed as **soft** subjects. This resulted in a substantial increase in funding for the sciences and a substantial decrease in funding for the arts and humanities.

If this practice had been confined to educational institutions, Snow's argument likely wouldn't have had the powerful impact it eventually did. However, that was not to be. Not long after this shift in the pendulum began, Snow's argument became popular in the western world generally, and not just in its educational institutions.

Science was linked to economics, economies, industry, politics, and technology, and therefore it was widely believed by corporate and political leaders that this held the solution to the world's problems just as Snow had proposed. It was also seen by these powerful elites as a way to strengthen the economic age, which had faltered in the first half of the twentieth century because of the Great Depression. Following the Second World War, it was time to get things back on track again, and those in power felt this was best achieved through committing to science, technology, industrialization, and economic growth.

As a result, it was no longer a case of treating the sciences as hard subjects and the arts and humanities as soft subjects in educational institutions. More fundamentally, it was a case of treating the sciences as *hard activities* and the arts and humanities as *soft activities* in all areas of life and all parts of the world. Not only were these attitudes and beliefs firmly entrenched in the minds of corporate leaders, politicians, and civil servants by this time, but also in the minds of most citizens. As a result, the "Snow thesis" became a societal and global phenomenon. Hard activities were concerned with the "basics in life" and what life and living were really all about; soft activities were concerned with the "frills in life"—what people did in their spare time. Seen and dealt with in this way, artistic and humanistic activities were appropriate as leisure time pursuits but had little or nothing to do with the necessities of life. Their purpose was to round people out, make them more sophisticated, and provide them with the experiences they needed to enjoy their leisure time.

When Snow saw what was happening and how the relationship between the arts and the sciences had become polarized after *The Two Cultures and the Scientific Revolution* was published, he decided to write a second book on this subject in 1963 called *The Two Cultures: And a Second Look: An Expanded Version of The Two Cultures and the Scientific Revolution.*[4] In this book, Snow explained why he made the case for giving the sciences and scientific education a higher priority, and also tried to rectify the damage that had been done by the imbalance and disharmony that had erupted throughout the world between the arts and humanities on the one hand and the sciences on the other. However, it was too late. The pendulum was swinging and swinging rapidly and relentlessly away from the arts and humanities and artistic-humanistic education and towards the sciences and scientific education. Neither Snow nor anyone else in the world could stop it.

In the decades following the publication of Snow's books, courses and programs in the arts and humanities were cut drastically in most educational institutions in Europe and throughout the world because a much lower priority was assigned to them compared to the sciences. This trend worsened in the final decades of the twentieth century and first two decades of the twenty-first century. Educators in the arts and humanities in most parts of the world found themselves in a very demoralizing and distressing position as they had to decide which courses and programs would be cut and which would be retained. Educators and others working in the arts and humanities were compelled to make the best of a devastating situation.

This was a very difficult problem to deal with because the *context* of the arts and humanities was now stacked against them. Nevertheless, they fought back, especially in arts education, where educators began to justify arts courses and programs not only for their ability to teach students to write stories, play musical instruments, paint pictures, act in plays, dance, sing in choirs, produce poems, and enjoy the arts later in life, but also for their capacity to address critical social and cultural issues and stimulate creativity, imagination, and ingenuity.

An excellent example of this "added dimension" of the arts and arts education was the creation of the Seoul Agenda by delegates attending the Second World Conference on Arts Education convened by UNESCO in Seoul, South Korea, in 2010. Included among the most important goals and objectives of this Agenda were:

- To apply arts education principles and practices to contribute to resolving the social and cultural challenges facing today's world;
- To support and enhance the role of arts education in the promotion of social responsibility, social cohesion, cultural diversity, and intercultural dialogue; and
- To affirm arts education as the foundation for balanced creative, cognitive, emotional, aesthetic, and social development of children, youth, and lifelong learning.

This general description sums up the overall situation, context, and character of education in most parts of the world at the present time. It is a situation, context, and character that is heavily oriented towards science, the sciences, and a scientific education as *hard activities* and that places a low priority on the arts, arts education, humanities, and artistic-humanistic education as *soft activities*. These matters are manifested most conspicuously by the emphasis on what are called *STEM* subjects—science, technology, engineering, and mathematics—and the view that an emphasis on these subjects provides the best education for young people. In Canada where I live, for example, students in their final year of secondary school are encouraged by guidance counsellors and teachers to take what is known as "the six pack"—three science and three mathematics credits—in order to get into a good university, eventually land a better job, and enjoy a higher standard of living and quality of life.

This trend has now been reinforced by countless parents who are reluctant to see their children get involved in the arts and humanities, receive an education in those fields, and especially pursue professions and careers in the artistic and humanistic domain. This attitude says a great deal about the image of the educated person that is entrenched and promoted at the present time. It is an image based on the idea of the "economic man" or "economic personality" mentioned earlier. This is a person or personality who is concerned primarily with the production, distribution, and consumption of goods and services and creation of material and monetary wealth, as well as maximizing their consumer satisfaction in the marketplace. All this is needed to keep economies functioning effectively and growing at a rapid rate.

This highly imbalanced, disharmonized, and polarized situation was especially apparent and most pronounced when the COVID-19 pandemic hit. On the one hand, it exposed the fact that when many artistic and humanistic abilities, skills, programs, and courses were needed to cope with this deplorable disease, they were largely absent and unavailable because of all the cuts that had been made in the arts and humanities, especially when it came to the need to assist other people, help seniors living in dreadful conditions in retirement homes, and be conscious of the health requirements of other people by using masks and maintaining safe distances. On the other hand, the pandemic prevented people from taking advantage of the fact that the arts and humanities are intimately connected with people's health and well-being as well as what are now called the *healing arts*, which will be discussed in a moment. This was especially evident in the arts because many artists, arts educators, and arts organizations were unable to respond to people's needs because they had lost their jobs and sources of income due to severe cuts in funding. This was especially detrimental because this imbalance had expanded well beyond educational systems by this time, adversely affecting government, corporate, and foundation grants and subsidies for the arts and humanities in general.

What is the problem here? Surely it is that major imbalances and disharmonies such as the one between the arts, humanities, and sciences can erupt at any time and without warning, escalate rapidly, and do an incredible amount of damage if they are not addressed. This can happen whenever too much attention and too high a priority are assigned to one activity or one side of a cultural relationship and too little attention and too low a priority to the other side. That is why it is so imperative in the future to confront problems like this before they get out of hand.

In order to avoid such polarizing and damaging pendulum swings, countervailing forces, plans, policies, and practices must be created and set in motion when needed. In order to illustrate how the need for this harmonization process can be addressed and the rift between the two components in a crucial cultural relationship like this can be reversed, we must consider two very specific steps that are necessary to get things moving in the right direction again. The first requires instituting measures designed to reverse the direction the pendulum is swinging and get it moving back toward the centre where it belongs, so that some semblance of balance and harmony is achieved. The second step involves assisting individuals and organizations that are working at the cutting edge and interface of the two polarized components in a cultural relationship by funding and supporting their particular programs and projects as the most important ones being undertaken at this specific point in time. This involves giving encouragement and financial support to people and organizations that are walking the walk and not only talking the talk, as well as helping them in very direct, meaningful, and pragmatic ways.

In order to illustrate how this two-step process functions and can be applied to dichotomized relationships in real terms, let's return to the rift between the arts and humanities and the sciences to see how it is possible to get the pendulum swinging in the right direction again. The first step in reversing the imbalance involves restoring the funding and support for the arts and humanities that has been lost over the last four or five decades. This will start the pendulum swinging back towards the middle. This will also produce many benefits for people and organizations working in the arts and humanities field, including transformational, transcendental, and transactional experiences and opportunities, regardless of whether this is on a part-time, full-time, casual, or concentrated basis.

The second and equally essential step involves identifying, developing, funding, and supporting initiatives by people and organizations that are working at the cutting edge and interface of the arts, humanities, and sciences, and are therefore engaged in activities that blend and help to harmonize relationships between these two polarized components.

One of the best illustrations of this is the pioneering work being conducted by the International Arts + Mind Lab: The Center for Applied Neuroaesthetics (IAM Lab) at the Johns Hopkins University in Baltimore. This multidisciplinary research-to-practice initiative at the Pedersen Brain Science Institute was established by Susan Magsamen and her colleagues in 2016. The lab is committed to "working to build the field of applied neuroaesthetics as the scientific study of how the brain and body respond to arts and aesthetic experiences to improve biological, psychological, social/cultural, or spiritual outcomes for individuals and populations." This field comprises the full spectrum of sensory, perceptual, and expressive experiences in the visual, literary, and performing arts, music, drama, dance and movement, media arts, traditional handcrafts, architecture and design, natural environments, and cultural experiences.

A body of evidence is rapidly growing out of this research-to-practice initiative that demonstrates that the arts of all types can improve mobility, memory, and speech; relieve pain and the after-effects of trauma; enhance mental health and learning outcomes; build resilience and prevent disease; and a great deal else. Beyond the value of these activities for individuals, the IAM Lab team also sees tremendous potential for arts interventions that engage stakeholders collectively in the pursuit of more equitable and resilient communities through its Impact Thinking Model and NeuroArts Blueprint.

The Impact Thinking Model is a consensus framework designed to help the field develop an interdisciplinary scientific method for translational work using the arts and aesthetic experiences. It was developed by the lab in collaboration with an interdisciplinary team of nearly three dozen scientists and practitioners, and is predicated on the fundamental values of collaboration, transparency, and follow-through, as well as the belief that applied neuroaesthetics can address intractable issues. Its nine-step process begins with a problem identification workshop and collaborative discovery process and concludes with dissemination, scaling, and evaluation for impact.

The NeuroArts Blueprint: Advancing the Science of Arts, Health, and Wellbeing is an authoritative, first-of-its-kind roadmap to move this specific field into widespread use throughout the world. Released in December 2021, it charts advances in brain science, identifies gaps in knowledge, policy, and funding, and documents effective and replicable practices in order to create the conditions for a deep commitment to neuroarts in all its transformative powers. Five core recommendations have emerged in the Blueprint: strengthening the research foundation of neuroarts; honoring and supporting the many arts practices that promote health and well-being; expanding and enriching educational and career pathways; advocating for sustainable funding and promoting effective policy; and building capacity, leadership, and communications strategies.

This worldwide initiative is led by the IAM Lab in partnership with the Aspen Institute in Denver, Colorado, and is guided by a diverse, interdisciplinary team of leaders and experts in science, arts, technology, design, health care, philanthropy, education, and community development. Working together, these two organizations are helping to drive the paradigm shift that is necessary to fully integrate arts and aesthetic experiences into activities that will advance individual and collective health throughout the planet. More information on the IAM Lab and its exciting programs, projects, and publications is available on its website, which includes valuable information on Susan Magsamen and Ivy Ross's recently published best-selling book *Your Brain on Art: How the Arts Transform Us.*[5]

The IAM Lab is not the only organization working at the cutting edge and interface of the arts and sciences. Many others are doing remarkable work in this area, such as the Aspen Institute itself, the Community NeuroArts Coalitions, the Creative Arts Therapies Consortium at New York University, the Scientific Institute of Spiritual Development of Man and its UNESCO Chair in Spiritual and Cultural Values through Education at Volodymyr Dahl East Ukrainian National University in Ukraine, Healing Arts Arabia in Saudi Arabia, the Rotman Arts and Science School, and many others.

One final development in this area should be strongly supported at this juncture rather than downplayed or ignored. In recent years, strenuous attempts have been made by many arts, humanities, and heritage educators and organizations to create a broader and more inclusive version of STEM (discussed earlier) throughout the world. Called STEAM, it is designed to add the _Arts_ to STEM so that the acronym now stands for *Science, Technology, Engineering, Arts, and Mathematics.* The arts are defined broadly to include the humanities and heritage of history as essential dimensions of education and learning for present and future generations. Unfortunately, reactions to these attempts to date have been mixed. Some educational institutions are now adopting STEAM in their educational and promotional endeavours and activities, while others are downplaying this development or ignoring it entirely and sticking with their original commitment to STEM. Doing so only serves to aggravate the underlying problem and swing the pendulum further in the direction of great inequality between the arts and the sciences rather than creating more compatibility and harmony between and among them in the future.

What is true for the imbalance and disharmony in the relationship between the arts and humanities and the sciences is also true for the relationship between human rights and human responsibilities, but in a very different way as this next illustration of the two-step harmonization process reveals.

In this case, the imbalance and disharmony in this area require a great deal of attention because human rights have been accorded a very high priority for the better part of a century now while human responsibilities have been accorded a very low priority and largely ignored until quite recently. This has resulted in an adverse and severe imbalance and disharmony between the two components in this relationship.

When the United Nations Universal Declaration of Human Rights was signed in 1948, it was only three years after the end of the Second World War. During this devastating and destructive war, many people had their rights taken away by oppressive government regimes and brutal military rulers. As a result, the most obvious need and concern at that time was to address and assert people's human rights in virtually all areas of public and private life, and to enshrine these rights in a comprehensive and powerful international agreement.

A great deal has been achieved in this area since the signing of the Universal Declaration of Human Rights, though a lot more remains to be accomplished. By identifying people's rights in economic, social, political, educational, and other terms, a significant step forward was taken.

Once people's rights were enshrined in the Universal Declaration, it is understandable that the bulk of attention would be focused on human rights and their realization, as well as creating similar declarations at the national, regional, and municipal levels and ensuring these rights were binding and enforceable in national, regional, and municipal courts of law and not just in international courts. This is largely where the matter stood until the final two decades of the twentieth century. Many countries around the world created declarations that possessed the potential to protect their citizens' rights and monitor them on a consistent basis both inside and outside their jurisdictions.

This has helped to ensure that (at least in principle) the rights of people are not violated and that, if they are, these violations can be dealt with effectively. At the international level, much work has been done by such legal institutions as the International Court of Justice, the International Criminal Court, and others. In practice, however, a very different situation usually prevails because of the actions of powerful dictators, authoritarian governments, and corrupt regimes, as well as the inability to ensure enactment and enforcement of legal decisions in the courts. Obviously, it is one thing to claim that the rule of law and people's human rights are sacrosanct and must be respected and enforced at all times and at all political levels; it is quite another to manifest this in fact and deliver it in legal, concrete, and official terms.

While significant strides have been made with respect to the recognition, articulation, and enforcement of people's rights since the Universal Declaration of Human Rights was signed more than seven decades ago, unfortunately the same cannot be said for people's responsibilities. In fact, so much time and attention has been focused on the articulation, establishment, and enforcement of people's rights since that time that very little time and attention have been devoted to similar developments in terms of people's responsibilities, except in select cases or esoteric places. Interest and commitment to the articulation of people's responsibilities really only commenced when Helmut Schmidt, the former chancellor of Germany, contended that "to achieve balanced societal development, human rights must be matched with human responsibilities" in the latter part of the twentieth century. He followed up on his commitment to this by chairing an informal group of philosophical, humanistic, political, and religious leaders and experts on this subject. This led to the creation of the InterAction Council in 1983 and eventually to the Declaration of Human Duties and Responsibilities (DHDR), which was written largely to support and reinforce the implementation of human rights under the auspices of UNESCO and the Office of the United Nations High Commissioner for Human Rights. This declaration was proclaimed in Valencia, Spain, in 1998 to celebrate the fiftieth anniversary of the signing of the Universal Declaration of Human Rights, and is known throughout the world today as the Valencia Declaration.

Unfortunately, people's responsibilities are often seen and treated as part of, or inherent and implicit in, the articulation of people's rights and therefore are not spelled out in detail or specific terms in the Valencia Declaration and other declarations. As a result, there is still a large void in this area that needs to be addressed. The time has come to focus much more attention on people's responsibilities as such, since both people's rights and responsibilities must be dealt with successfully and fully if an effective system of ethics and higher standards of human conduct, character, and behaviour are to be realized. While many individual experts and organizations have been working on this matter over the last few decades, it will take time and effort to achieve this in comprehensive and practical terms. Hopefully, this will lead in the not-too-distant future to the creation, proclamation, and signing of a *Universal Declaration of Human Rights* **and** *Responsibilities*.

What are people's responsibilities in the more comprehensive and practical sense? Included among them are:

- Concern and respect for other people, especially those who are elderly, sick, disadvantaged, distressed, poor, oppressed, or marginalized;
- Treating all genders, age groups, races, tribes, ethnic groups, and peoples equally and without prejudice;
- Learning about other people's cultures, civilizations, and ways of life, and showing an interest and respect for them at all times and in all places;
- Pursuing peace, harmony, liberty, security, democracy, and freedom of movement and expression;
- Manifesting cooperation, compromise, compassion, and peace rather than conflict, confrontation, war, and aggression;
- Protecting the natural environment and all other species at every opportunity and in every conceivable way, as well as committing to sustainability and ecological well-being;
- Conserving resources and never taking more from the natural environment than is necessary for a reasonable standard of living and decent quality of life;
- Giving back to the neighbourhoods, communities, and countries where people were born, grew up, or are living and working in at present;
- Making the transition from preoccupation with wealth for some to well-being for all, and
- Creating values, beliefs, worldviews, and lifestyles that are consistent with the state of the world at present, and prospects for the future.

These responsibilities, especially if and when they are stated clearly and asserted properly, taken seriously, and addressed fully, should ensure that people develop the sensibilities, sensitivities, capabilities, behaviours, personalities, and ways of life that are necessary to be responsible citizens in human and humane terms and achieve sustainability in the world at all levels.

Stating and cultivating these responsibilities in deeds and actions and not just words and ideas would go a long way towards creating the balanced and harmonious relationship that is essential between people's rights and responsibilities as the first concrete and significant step in this two-stage process. It will put the world in the strongest possible position to create a Universal Declaration of Human Rights and Responsibilities that is applicable to all people and all countries. Developments and commitments like these would go a long way towards creating the ethical standards, objectives, and ideals that are badly needed in the world at this time, as well as creating the system of global ethics that the World Commission on Culture and Development felt was imperative. This is confirmed by examining the principal ideas and ideals that the commission felt should constitute the core of this new ethical system, namely human rights and responsibilities, democracy and the elements of civil society, protection of minorities, commitment to peaceful conflict resolution and fair negotiation, and equity between and within governments.

According to the commission, this system, and the individual and collective modes of ethical behaviour that are incorporated in it, is compatible with the centrality and essence of culture and cultures and the need for balanced and harmonious relationships between and among culture and all the diverse cultures in the world in many ways. As the commission stated it in its 1995 report on *Our Creative Diversity*:

It is not difficult to see that the search for a global ethics involves culture and cultural aspects in numerous ways. To begin with, such an endeavor is itself an emphatically cultural activity, including questions such as Who are we?, How do we relate to each other and to humankind as a whole? and What is our purpose? These questions are at the centre of what culture is all about. Moreover, any attempt to formulate a global ethics must for its inspiration draw on cultural resources, on people's intelligence, on their emotional experiences, their historical memories and their spiritual orientations. Culture, unlike scarce resources, will in this process be invigorated and enhanced rather than depleted.[6]

The second step in this process should focus on people and organizations that are working at the interface and cutting edge between human rights and human responsibilities, and consequently the work of such organizations as the InterAction Council, the Campaign for Universal Human Responsibilities, the Forum for a New World Governance, and so forth, as well as individuals and scholars such as Ashutosh Kumar Singh. In an article he wrote on this subject entitled "Universal Declaration of Human Responsibilities: A Distant Dream in 21st Century," he asserted that there is still an enormous amount to be done before it will be possible to claim that this dream—which in his opinion is shared by many people around the world—will be realized on the "responsibilities" side and not just on the "rights" side in the present century.[7]

If it is imperative to focus a great deal of attention on and award a much higher priority to human responsibilities and human rights going forward into the future in order to create the requisite balance and harmony that is needed between them, it is also necessary to focus a similar amount of attention and assign a high priority to the two components in another crucial cultural relationship, namely the relationship between unity and diversity. Unfortunately, a serious imbalance and disharmony has opened up in this area throughout the world in recent years that also needs to be attended to if this problem is to be dealt with successfully at present as well as in the years and decades ahead.

This imbalance and disharmony is growing rapidly in many parts of the world today due to the changing demographic composition of the populations of many countries in the world, the intermingling of people, groups, and races with very different worldviews, value systems, lifestyles, and ways of life, and the desire of many colonized, oppressed, and marginalized groups and countries to create and pursue their own paths to development rather than follow the lead provided by more powerful groups, classes, and countries. Whereas the focus of attention and highest priority in most countries for a long period of time was on "unity in similarities" in order to keep people and countries together, increasingly a shift is occurring toward the need to achieve "unity in differences" due to all the many cultural disparities that now exist in the populations of most countries and the desire to achieve inclusiveness for more people, groups, and races.

While focusing attention on similarities was a legitimate objective and worthwhile ideal in view of how peoples and countries evolved in the past, many peoples and countries are discovering that when the pendulum swings rapidly towards diversity, it is accompanied by the loss of unity and identity and a feeling of isolation, estrangement, and separation rather than togetherness and belonging. The most obvious illustration of this at present is in the United States, where this problem has become highly politicized and polarized and created many violent protests and demonstrations. However, this is also true for many other countries in the world that are experiencing similar difficulties. This is a very complicated and dangerous situation that can easily intensify if it isn't dealt with and rectified.

This problem exists because unity can't be achieved without a commitment to sameness, since this requires sharing customs, traditions, and beliefs in common with many other people, whereas diversity can't be achieved without a commitment to differences since this requires respecting and accepting a panorama of different customs, traditions, and beliefs. As a result, harmonization in this specific cultural relationship can only be achieved by walking the fine line between unity and diversity, similarities and differences. A slip in the direction of too much sameness and too many similarities can alienate and exclude people, groups, and races that are different and diverse, whereas a slip in the direction of too much diversity and too many differences will alienate people, groups, and races that want and expect more sameness and similarities.

Is there a way out of this dilemma? Indeed, there is, and the first step in this process involves putting a great deal of emphasis on *unity in diversity*. While this is not a new term, it will require a great deal more acceptance, promotion, and use in the future if balance and harmony are to be achieved between activities that unite and activities that divide. The key to this balanced and harmonized process in this case lies in creating many more *cultural symbols* that possess the potential and ability to bring people together rather than split them apart. Many of these symbols may have to be created from scratch, or quite possibly come from people and groups that have been marginalized, oppressed, or colonized because the symbols that traditionally brought about unity and a strong sense of identity and belonging are no longer working or are too exclusive rather than inclusive. This will help to rectify the present imbalances and disharmonies that exist in this area, but in an entirely new and very different and more imaginative and creative way.

One organization that is doing a great deal of pioneering work in this area and is situated at the cutting edge and interface between these two polarizing opposites is Cultural Infusion in Australia. This organization was founded in 2002 by Peter Mousaferiadis, a well-known composer, conductor, music director, cultural animator, and current CEO of this rapidly expanding organization. He has become an international leader and ambassador by promoting intercultural understanding on a global basis as the key to peace, prosperity, and sustainability in the world in the future.

Cultural Infusion got its start in the early twenty-first century by delivering cultural programs to schools throughout Australia, and currently delivers these programs on an annual basis to more than 350,000 students. Its work in this area is now being employed more than ever, especially in light of UNESCO's finding that three-quarters of the conflicts that exist in the world have a cultural aspect or dimension. Since it was created, this organization has expanded its activities considerably by rolling out a "digital strategy" in 2011, a "Learning Lands Program" in 2016 with a range of educational products and resources, and a "Diversity Atlas" in 2019 that provides detailed information on organizations' cultural and demographic diversity, as well as several other key initiatives. Cultural Infusion's materials, and especially its Diversity Atlas, are now being used in 32 countries including Australia. With its massive "database of humanity" comprising more than 42,000 attributes, it enables organizations to understand, acknowledge, appreciate, and act on diversity, inclusion, and development strategies that value the richness and multifarious character of their employees as a major source of innovation, productivity, creativity, expertise, and inspiration. As well, the organization recently created the Cultural Infusion Foundation to afford opportunities for many people and organizations in Australia with diverse backgrounds to provide programs in public venues throughout the world that possess the capacity to unite rather than divide people from different cultures, civilizations, and ways of life.

What is true for organizations such as Cultural Infusion and others working at the cutting edge and interface between unity and diversity is also true for Canada. In 1971, the government of Canada declared that henceforth Canada would be officially designated "a multicultural country with an official policy of multiculturalism within a bilingual (French and English) framework." While there was some resistance to this official policy at the time, Canada has since moved steadily, deliberately, and progressively in a multicultural direction, so much so, in fact, that today many Canadians feel proud that Canada is the first country in the world to officially recognize and embrace multiculturalism and cultural diversity in the political sense. This is because this policy is consistent with the multicultural character of the country's population and its evolution in the past and at present. With this policy has come a commitment to unity in diversity and to being more inclusive and less exclusive. As a result of these developments, and others, there has been a robust outpouring of creativity among Canada's Indigenous peoples and the country's diverse ethnic groups in recent years compared to earlier periods in Canadian history.

And this brings us to what many people and organizations claim are the two most important cultural relationships in the world at present. The first is the relationship between the material and non-material (quantitative and qualitative) dimensions of development and life, and the second is the relationship between people and the natural environment. If balanced and harmonious relationships cannot be established here and established very soon, people and countries in all parts of the world and the world as a whole will pay a very severe price.

As far as the relationship between the material and non-material dimension of development and life are concerned, it is a well-known fact that all activities in the world are composed of material and non-material elements or parts, regardless of what cultural sector they are in or where they are situated. As a result, it is imperative to be conscious of the "material draws" and "ecological impacts and expectations" that all activities have on the environment and assess them carefully. As we have seen, most economic activities, such as agricultural, industrial, manufacturing, transportation, and technological activities, draw heavily on the world's resources because the material element in these activities is high and the potential for environmental damage and pollution is great. In contrast, most artistic, educational, intellectual, social, and spiritual activities draw lightly on the globe's resources because the material element in these activities is much lower and the potential for environmental damage and pollution is substantially reduced. Apart from paints, brushes, easels, and other supplies for visual artists, books and computers for educators, pulpits and religious venues for ministers, imams, cantors, and priests, as well as administrative amenities for social workers—to cite only a few of the most obvious examples among many—artistic, educational, intellectual, spiritual, and social activities do not make *excessive* demands on the world's finite supply of resources.

And this is not all. Whereas most agricultural, industrial, manufacturing, and technological activities create *products* that are high in material resource inputs and outputs and usually require long-distance transportation to reach their destinations and markets, a substantial number of artistic, educational, humanistic, intellectual, social, and spiritual activities create *experiences* that are significantly lower in resource and transportation requirements. As a result, many people have engaged in these latter activities over the last few decades because they involve events and processes that bring them a great deal of contentment and happiness while simultaneously reducing their resource consumption quite considerably. As such, they are diminishing their impact on nature and its resources and doing exactly what is needed to achieve a better balance between consumption and conservation. In global terms, this is making a significant contribution to swinging the pendulum back towards the centre while simultaneously producing more joy and satisfaction in the process.

As far as the second step is concerned, many scholars have been working at the cutting edge and interface of this relationship for some time now. One of the most important and active of these scholars is Thomas Legrand, especially with the publication of his valuable book *Politics of Being: Wisdom and Science for a New Development Paradigm* in 2021.[8]

In this book, Legrand makes this case for what he calls the transition from *having more* to *being more*, a transition that will not only reduce the demands made on the earth's resources but will also shift the focus from material consumption to human fulfillment and well-being. The potential this holds for achieving balance and harmony in this particular relationship is unmistakable and unequivocal. As world population increases and more pressure is exerted on the environment, more emphasis will have to be placed on activities that do as little damage as possible to the natural world and its finite resource legacy. In order to realize this, Legrand makes the case that it will also be necessary to capitalize on humanity's accumulated wisdom over the centuries, as well as the remarkable advances that have been and are taking place in the sciences, arts, humanities, culture, and many other areas of life, since this will bring a more enlightened and environmentally friendly approach to life and living in the years ahead, especially if corporations and governments alter their policies, practices, and priorities accordingly.

This will go a long way towards realizing what Johan Huizinga meant when he said, "[T]he realities of economic life, of power, of technology, and everything conducive to people's material well-being must be balanced by strongly developed spiritual, intellectual, moral, and aesthetic values." His words were quoted earlier in the book but are repeated here because of their relevance to the present global situation and the way forward in the future. Without doubt, this is *the* most urgent and essential requirement if an effective balance and harmony is to be realized between ourselves and the natural realm. Huizinga affirmed the relevance of this conviction when he said:

> The balance exists above all in the fact that each of the various cultural activities enjoys as vital a function as is possible in the context of the whole. If such harmony of cultural func-

tions is present, it will reveal itself as order, strong structure, style, and rhythmic life in the society in question.[9]

Pitirim Sorokin, another cultural scholar, confirmed and reinforced Huizinga's convictions on this matter and carried them further. In his book *Social and Cultural Dynamics: A Study of Change in Major Systems of Art, Truth, Ethics, Law and Social Relationships*, Sorokin claimed that there is an urgent need throughout the world to shift from "sensate cultures" to "ideational, idealistic, and mixed cultures."[10] He believed that whereas sensate cultures put a great deal of pressure on the natural environment and the world's finite resources because they are based on activities that are largely physical, tangible, and concrete in nature, ideational, idealistic, and mixed cultures put less pressure on the natural environment and the world's finite resources because they are based on activities that are primarily intellectual, emotional, spiritual, aesthetic, and non-material in nature. Not only do these latter activities strike a better balance and harmony between the material and non-material dimensions of development and life, but they also make it possible to shift from economies, which constitute the foundation of the economic age, to cultures, which form the centrepiece of the cultural age. This is why the second step in this process involves giving a much higher priority to those undertaking research at the cutting edge and interface that is needed to make the transition from resource and energy consumption to resource and energy conservation.

And this brings us to what is without doubt the most important cultural relationship of all. It is the relationship between people and the natural environment. When this relationship is working well, everything is in balance and harmony. However, when it is not working well, a great deal of imbalance and disharmony is experienced, something which helps to explain the state of the world today and prospects for the future. Everybody and everything depends on this relationship. Not only is it manifesting itself in climate change, which is becoming progressively more severe and unsustainable, but also in the many other environmental catastrophes that are occurring in the world today.

While the relationship between humans and the natural environment has existed for countless millennia, its importance has intensified incredibly over the last few centuries and especially over the last few decades. Just as people have been pressing harder and harder against the natural environment, so the natural environment has reached its limit and is now pushing back harder and harder against people.

This is causing the pendulum to swing towards the natural environment and away from people, thereby destroying the necessary and fundamental relationship that exists between the two. This is because the natural environment has an uncanny knack of striking back when it is exploited and abused due to the phenomenal demands that are made on it. As indicated earlier, this is manifesting itself throughout the world in more frequent and ferocious floods, hurricanes, tornadoes, and forest fires, as well as devastating droughts and many other environmental disasters. This trend will continue to accelerate until the adverse components in this highly volatile relationship are subdued and brought back into balance and harmony. This will not be possible, however, as long as we are living in an economic age because the demands made on the natural environment by this age will escalate more rapidly than humanity's ability to come to grips with them and bring them under control.

When the cultural relationship between people and the natural environment is working effectively, culture is in a state of equilibrium and therefore in balance and harmony. And this is not all. According to Huizinga:

A community is in the state of culture when the domination of nature in the material, moral, and spiritual (*geestelijk*) realms permits a state of existence which is *higher* and *better* than the given natural conditions; and when this state of existence is furthermore characterized by a harmonious balance of material and spiritual values and is guided by an ideal ... toward which the different activities of the community are directed.[11]

Think about this inspiring possibility for a moment. When the right decisions are made and actions taken, this could not only yield a state of equilibrium that would be a major achievement in its own right, but could also be a "higher and better" state of equilibrium as

Huizinga claims. Surely this is what we should be striving to achieve in the future. Rather than merely achieving a state of equilibrium between people and the natural environment, it could be greatly enhanced by an elevated state of equilibrium between the two components in this relationship. What a marvellous possibility this would be to pursue and achieve during the cultural age.

An excellent example of this elevated state is presenting artistic works, experiences, and events outdoors rather than indoors, beside rivers and streams, on or around lakes, and even in dense forests, because they enrich these natural settings even more. This is also true when exquisite gardens are created, such as some of the gardens that exist in Japan, China, England, Italy, the United States, and other parts of the world. This is the case as well when beautiful pieces of sculpture and various monuments and sites heighten and complement natural and ecological landscapes and surroundings. And these are only a few examples of the limitless possibilities that exist and could start the pendulum swinging in a much more desirable direction as far as this most important relationship is concerned, thereby helping to fulfil the first step in this two-step process.

There are many other ways to do this as well, and it doesn't take a great deal of imagination to conjure them up. We could focus more attention on improving the lives of other species and making it possible for them to live in the natural environment more confidently, comfortably, and pleasantly than they do at present. This would also make it easier for plants and animals to grow and develop, as well as enjoy their experiences more fully by having more of their basic needs and necessities met, which would enhance their relationship with people and the natural environment and move them farther away from a "survival of the fittest" mentality and closer to a situation where they are looked after with greater care and much more sharing, sensitivity, and compassion. What a breakthrough this would be if this matter was dealt with in far more systematic and generous terms and a higher state of equilibrium was achieved in the process.

If goals, objectives, and ideals as timely and worthwhile as these are to be met, much more attention and a much higher priority will have to be accorded to the individuals and organizations that are working at the interface and cutting edge of this most essential relationship, particularly in terms of climate change, reduction of plastic pollution, the creation of cities that are committed to achieving carbon neutrality and net-zero emissions, greater environmental preservation, conservation, and sustainability, and bringing an end to unnecessary deforestation. Included among the countless organizations, corporations, countries, and cities that are working at the cutting edge and interface of this human-natural environment relationship are such not-for-profit environmental organizations as Greenpeace International, the Environmental Defense Fund, Nature Conservancy, Climate Realty Project, and the World Wildlife Fund; corporations such as Unilever, IKEA, Nike, and Panasonic; carbon-neutral countries like Comoros, Gabon, and Guyana; carbon-negative countries such as Bhutan, Panama, and Suriname; and C40 Cities, which is a global network involving nearly one hundred cities and mayors in leading urban centres throughout the world committed to cutting emissions in half by 2030 and limiting the average global temperature increase to less than 1.5 degrees C.

While the relationships we have discussed here are not the only pressing relationships that exist in the world, it is clear from these examples that entering a cultural age and enabling it to flourish will not be possible until a great deal of progress has been made and far more expertise has been developed in coming to grips with difficult cultural relationships like these and many others and creating more balance and harmony between and among them.

Now that this issue has been examined, it is possible to focus our attention on another requirement that must be addressed if the cultural age is to thrive and flourish in the future, namely cultivating more spirituality and compassion in the world. As we will discover, this is also connected with the cultural relationship problem and is of vital importance as well in the overall scheme of things.

Chapter Twelve

Cultivating Spirituality and Compassion

As human beings, our greatness lies not so much in being able to
remake the world ... as in being able to remake ourselves.
—Gandhi[1]

This is a very difficult time for all people and all countries. Not only
have conditions been changing rapidly in all parts of the world and
all areas of cultural life, but humanity is also confronted with a number of life-threatening and debilitating problems that need to be confronted and solved.

Take the COVID-19 pandemic as an obvious recent example of
this. Few people or countries managed to escape the adverse consequences of this deadly virus and its many mutations, regardless of
where people live, how young or old they are, what jobs, professions,
and lifestyles they have or had, or their relations with family members, friends, and colleagues.

This is not the first time that humanity has been compelled to deal
with pandemics. In earlier times, there was the Black Death and the
Spanish Flu. More recently, there have been HIV/AIDS, SARS, Ebola,
and many other diseases. However, COVID-19 has had a particularly
devastating effect on people and countries throughout the world in
one form or another due to its persistence and the multiplication of
its variants. Countless seniors have been compelled to live out the
final stages in their lives in isolation, and then pass away without
having a chance to spend time with their family members and loved
ones. Doctors, nurses, and other health care providers have been
compelled to work many more hours a day in order to help extremely
ill patients, and have had to risk their lives on a daily basis. Millions
of people lost their jobs and sources of income and experienced

numerous difficulties making ends meet. And major hostilities have broken out in many countries between "vaxxers" and "anti-vaxxers" that have had and continue to have polarizing effects.

This pandemic has been especially hard on marginalized groups and people living in countries with huge populations and inadequate medical and health care facilities. These marginalized groups and people experienced a great deal of difficulty obtaining the vaccines and medications they need to deal with this rampant disease and pay for them. Many countries were unable to prevent the spread of this virus and watched helplessly as their citizens died on city streets and in back alleys without any notice or attention.

But the largest problem of all has been experienced by children, young people, and future generations. While they have been less susceptible to the coronavirus than older age groups, the evidence indicates that they have been hard hit by the pandemic in other ways and are less able to deal with the consequences of this. On the one hand, they were forced to come to grips with the closing of schools with little or no warning, the cancellation of classes and courses, and the need to develop online learning abilities on their own with little or no guidance. On the other hand, they have been confronted with rapidly expanding health issues, especially eating disorders, panic attacks, depression, and higher rates of suicide attempts. According to a study conducted by the internationally renowned Hospital for Sick Children in Toronto, between July 2020 and March 2021 the number of psychiatric appointments for children increased by 30 percent, mental health visits by 25 percent, and medical emergencies by 20 percent. Moreover, millions of children and young people around the world continue to experience loneliness, alienation, anxiety, and depression. With this has come an astounding increase in the use of different types of drugs, as well as what some are calling the "other pandemic"—the opioid crisis.

And waiting in the wings after this deadly pandemic was brought largely under control are all the other problems that exist, most obviously climate change and the environmental crisis, colossal disparities in income and wealth, systemic racism, conflicts between genders, races, ethnic groups, and regions, wars in the Middle East, Ukraine, Somalia, and elsewhere, as well as countries lining up behind United

States and NATO on the one hand and China and Russia on the other hand, a confrontation which increases the potential of another world war. These problems are compounding the sense of despondency, futility, and despair that many people and countries are experiencing at the present time.

What has become steadily more apparent as a result of these problems and others is that we can't go on dealing with problems like this in the same way we dealt with them in the past or are dealing with them at present. Fundamental changes are needed in our lives, lifestyles, values, ideals, and ways of life if these problems and others are to be addressed successfully and resolved in the years and decades ahead.

As Mary Catherine Bateson, an American anthropologist and collaborator with her father Gregory Bateson, pointed out in her book *Composing a Life*:

> Today, the materials and skills from which a life is composed are no longer clear. It is no longer possible to follow the paths of previous generations.... Our lives not only take new directions; they are subject to repeated redirection.... Just as the design of a building or of a vase must be rethought when the scale of life has changed, so must the design of lives. Many of the most basic concepts we use to construct a sense of self or the design of a life have changed their meanings.[2]

Given this undeniable fact, it is imperative to make a fundamental change or paradigm shift in the way we live our lives at this crucial juncture in history. One of the most effective ways to do this is to become deeply immersed in culture and cultures as advocated earlier, and especially to cultivate *spirituality and compassion* as yet another major cultural relationship where balance and harmony are required. Developing and manifesting these abilities and characteristics is of utmost importance in preparing ourselves for living in a cultural age and enabling it to thrive and flourish in the future.

Doing so is bound to broaden, deepen, enrich, and enhance our lives in numerous ways. It will make it possible for us to experience a great deal more joy, happiness, fulfillment, and well-being in life, walk more lightly on the land, learn much more about all the remarkable cultures and civilizations in the world, achieve our most desired goals and cherished ideals, enhance our understanding of what is most essential and worthwhile in life, and discover what it is like to live life on a fuller and more human and humane level of existence. And the most interesting thing of all is that the more we become immersed in culture and cultures, the more our lives will become spiritual and compassionate in nature.

Let's start with the cultivation of spirituality. Clearly there is no single path to spirituality. There are many paths to spirituality, just as there are many paths to experiencing happiness, ecstasy, and contentment in life.

For many people, spirituality is achieved most effectively through religion. Not only is this the key to living a full, upright, moral, and ethical life, but also it is the key to experiencing higher and higher levels and states of spirituality, and with this, feelings of the sublime and occasionally even the divine. Central to virtually all religions in the world—Buddhism, Hinduism, Islam, Christianity, Judaism, Jainism, Baháí, and others—is the belief that spirituality is achieved by making a strong commitment to the tenets, values, and teachings of the faith and adhering to these tenets, values, and teachings as fully and frequently as possible over the course of our lives.

To achieve spirituality in the sense is to devote ourselves to religion and a religious life in the fullest and most complete sense of these terms. It is important to emphasize here that spirituality in this ultimate sense has a vaulted "quality, lift, presence, and feel about it" that is experienced and appreciated in all religions and religious pursuits. This is because spirituality emanates from a much higher, nobler, ethereal, and divine place, and therefore embodies a certain dimension that exists far beyond and above all life and living on Planet Earth. A good illustration of this are all the masterpieces that have been created in religious music, painting, dance, architecture, and so forth over the centuries, such as the great gothic cathedrals in Europe, the exquisite mosques in the Middle East, the beautiful Buddhist and Hindu temples and shrines in Asia, the "ascension paintings" created by such artists as Giotto and Tintoretto, the sacred music composed by Palestrina and Monteverdi, the whirling dances in the Sufi religious tradition, and myriad others. These works, and countless others like them, are designed to give people a sense that there is something far more powerful and profound than themselves and humanity at work in the world, as well as in the universe and the cosmos.

This comes at a time when ideas and thoughts about the role of a single God or many gods in our lives as a divine source or sources residing in heaven or some other ethereal place are changing and changing very quickly. It is becoming more commonplace in some parts of the world today to believe that God or gods exist in everything and everywhere—as has been maintained by some religions for centuries—and therefore is or are all around us and possibly even within us. According to Diane Butler Bass, author of the best-selling book *Grounded: Finding God in the World—A Spiritual Revolution*, this revolution that is occurring in the world:

> ... rests on a simple insight: God is the ground, the grounding, that which grounds us. We experience this when we understand that soil is holy, water gives life, the sky opens the imagination, our roots matter, home is a divine place, and our lives are linked with our neighbors' and with others around the globe. This world, not heaven, is the sacred stage of our times.[3]

One person who has contributed a great deal to expanding our understanding of the nature, meaning, feeling, and sense of spirituality at present is Maya Spencer. She expressed her views on this matter in an article entitled "What is Spirituality? A Personal Exploration," which was posted on the Internet in 2016. In this article, Spencer stated:

> [S]pirituality is the indefinable urge to reach beyond the limits of ordinary human existence that is bounded by unconscious forces and self-interest, and to discover higher values in ourselves and to live them consistently in our relationships and roles. It involves developing practices that aid us in rising and expanding, perhaps beyond the merely good to the tran-

scendent, in the process of looking inwards rather than outwards for our own morality and guidance. Above all, it means
becoming a more loving and compassionate human being, in
thought, word, and deed.[4]

With this statement in mind, let's delve more deeply into some of
the other matters that are connected to the cultivation of spirituality
and the possibility of living a spiritual life.

While many people prefer to see spirituality in religious terms and
involvement in specific religions or religious sects, others have a different "take" on this subject. They believe spirituality can be and often
is achieved in many other ways as well, such as through mindfulness,
meditation, yoga, expanded, enhanced, and more enlightened states
of consciousness, Tai Chi, the teachings of Eckhart Tolle, Deepak
Chopra, and Wayne Dyer, and the preachings of countless mystics,
evangelists, and others who possess powerful thoughts, ideas, feelings, emotions, and convictions about spirituality and how it is best
achieved in real terms. This is also possible through involvement in
many other types of activities, such as the arts, humanities, sciences,
education, lifelong learning, sports, recreation, reverence for nature
and the natural environment and more frequently interactions and
intimate connections with them, as well as virtually all other types of
activities if we take the time and make the effort to find and cultivate
spirituality in them.

Reaching above and beyond ourselves is without doubt one of
the most essential requirements for cultivating spirituality, much
as it is for most if not all religions and all other approaches to this
matter. In order to achieve it, it is necessary to go "inside the self" and
work out for oneself why it is so necessary to transcend the self, take
advantage of that vaulted quality and spiritual presence, as well as
realize that there are many things in life and the world that are much
greater and more significant than ourselves. In today's world, it may
also be necessary to break out of the "me generation mentality" that
is so conspicuous, commonplace, and deeply rooted in the world and
our lives today, as well as to embrace "the other" as one of the most
essential actions and relevant developments of all in the cultivation of
spirituality and practice of living a spiritual life.

Whenever I reflect on these matters, which is often, I immediately think of Martin Luther King, Jr. Not only did King identify far more with "the other" and the needs of other people than himself, but he conveyed this in much of his work as well as his remarkable speech—"I Have a Dream"—that was delivered to the colossal mass of people that were assembled on the Mall during the March on Washington for Jobs and Freedom on August 28, 1963. While this speech called for civil and economic rights and an end to systemic racism in the United States, it revealed King's powerful commitment and insight into causes in general, and one cause in particular, that were far greater than himself.

Obviously, there is an enormous amount of spiritual fulfillment to be gleaned from making commitments to causes that are greater than ourselves, as has been the case not only for Martin Luther King, Jr. but also for millions of other people. Myriads of people throughout history and around the world have experienced an incredible amount of spirituality in their lives by devoting themselves to a single cause or several different causes, regardless of whether this is concerned with helping other people or improving the health, welfare, and well-being of family members, close friends, neighbourhoods, towns, cities, countries, and the world as a whole.

Unfortunately, little attention has been paid in the past or is being paid at present to the role that culture and cultures can play in opening the doors to spirituality. This is because culture has been perceived and defined in many different ways over the course of history, as noted earlier, and this has caused a great deal of confusion, misunderstanding, and controversy throughout the world over its nature, meaning, and character.

Nevertheless, every perception of culture—from the artistic and humanistic to the biological and cosmological—possesses the potential to open the doors to spirituality. In combination, they make it possible to move from *specific moments of spirituality* to *more permanent states of spirituality*. This is revealed through the thoughts and experiences of many cultural scholars over the years. By introducing a great deal of happiness, exuberance, and exhilaration into people's lives and making it possible for them to reduce the demands they are making on the natural environment and world's scarce resources, culture and cultures in general—and living a full and fulfilling cultural life in particular—have profound implications and consequences for life, living, and spirituality in the twenty-first century.

One of the best ways to cultivate spirituality is through the arts since they constitute one of the most important dimensions of culture and cultures. This is because the arts possess the ability to lift people to great heights and transport them to ethereal places and sublime spaces. When George Bernard Shaw said, "You use a glass mirror to see your face; you use works of art to see your soul" in *Back to Methuselah*, he opened the door to connecting with many artistic activities that possess the potential to do this by digging deep into ourselves and especially our souls, spirits, feelings, and emotions.

For many people, this is possible through music, since it possesses an incredible ability to lift us out of the commonplace and project us to very lofty heights. This is not confined to adults or people in their twilight years. In fact, it can be experienced by people at all ages and in all walks of life and often in profound, moving, and very mystical and magical ways. And what is true for music is also true for all other art forms, it must be quickly added, such as paintings, plays, dances, poems, stories, and the like that can also produce spiritual experiences and states that are profound and profuse, and possibly even border on the marvellous and magnificent.

Earlier in this book, I mentioned some musical masterpieces that rank very high on my list of preferences because of their beauty. However, here are also a number of pieces that rank very high in my list in terms of spirituality: Gounod's *Sanctus*; Fauré's *Cantique de Jean Racine*; Handel's *Zadok the Priest* and *Ombra mai fu;* Richard Strauss's song "Morgen!"; Wagner's *Prelude to Lohengrin* and *Prelude to Parsifal*; Mahler's *Adagietto* from his *Fifth Symphony*; the second movement of Beethoven's *Fifth (Emperor) Piano Concerto*; Liszt's transcription of Schumann's song *Widmung;* Dvořák's "Song to the Moon" from his opera *Rusalka*; Schubert's *Impromptu No. 3 in G Flat*; and Ennio Morricone's "Gabriel's Oboe" from *The Mission*.

While classical music ranks highest on my list of favourites as far as spirituality is concerned, it is by no means limited to this. I also find folk music from many parts of the world, songs from musicals, and popular and film music very spiritual in nature, such as Romanian,

Hungarian, and Middle Eastern folk music; Richard Rodgers and Oscar Hammerstein II's songs "If I Loved You" and "You'll Never Walk Alone" from *Carousel*; "Give Me My Song" by Benny Andersson; "You Raise Me Up," "Ladies in Lavender," and "Wind Beneath My Wings"; Ennio Morricone's *Dinner* from his *Lady Caliph Suite*; and John Lennon's "Imagine."

One night, I had a remarkable experience with music that was very spiritual in nature. Here is how it came about. For many years, I have been in the habit of setting my radio to a specific station before falling asleep. This station plays soft and soothing music, which helps me and probably many others to end their day on a peaceful note.

On this particular night, I set my radio to the usual station and fell into a deep sleep. I don't know how long I was sleeping, but I slowly became aware that I was listening to one of the most spiritually uplifting pieces of music I have ever heard in life. As I lay there in a semi-conscious state—stupor would likely be a better word to describe this half-awake, half-asleep state—I remember thinking that I had died and gone to heaven because the music was so exquisite! Then, quite suddenly, I heard a voice say, "You have been listening to 'Grant Us Thy Peace' by Felix Mendelssohn. It was sung by the Corydon Singers." As soon as I heard the announcer's voice, I realized that I had not actually died and gone to heaven, even though it felt like it that night.

The piece in question has a captivating melody like many of Mendelssohn's musical masterpieces. This melody is sung by one section of the choir first, then another section joins in, and finally the melody is sung by all sections. I have often felt this piece should be humanity and the world's "universal anthem." Not only is it extremely beautiful and spiritually uplifting, but it would also serve a very useful purpose at this crucial time in history. With so much violence, terrorism, conflict, and war going on in the world, its plea to "grant us thy peace" would be timely to say the least.

While there are many pieces of music that are very spiritual in nature, there are also some pieces that were written specifically with spirituality in mind, such as numerous African American spirituals such as "Swing Low, Sweet Chariot"; Sufi music, which is well-known for inducing trances and spiritual states; much of the music of Hildegard of Bingen (1098–1179), a well-known nun in an abbey in Germany and a saint, composer, and poet; as well as some of the music of Gustav Holst (1874–1934). I am thinking here of Hildegard of Bingen's uplifting composition *Symphony of the Harmony of Celestial Revelations* and Gustav Holst's orchestral suite *The Planets* and particularly the movements devoted to three of the planets, namely "Venus, the Bringer of Peace," "Jupiter, the Bringer of Jollity," and, most notably, "Neptune, the Mystic." These pieces elevate my life substantially whenever I listen to them. Small wonder Beethoven said, "Music is indeed the mediator between the spiritual and sensual life."

What is the case for me with respect to specific pieces of music is also the case for certain paintings, poems, and many other artistic works. Paintings such as Joseph Mallord William Turner's paintings of Venice, of Rouen Cathedral at many different times during the day, and especially his late Swiss water colours, Monet's *The Garden in Flower at Giverny* and *Water Lilies and Japanese Bridge,* Van Gogh's *Starry Night,* Emily Carr's *Forest, British Columbia,* Keats's poem "On First Looking Into Chapman's Homer," Byron's "She Walks in Beauty," Rumi's *Divan-i Shams* and many others, as well as architectural masterpieces such as the Dilwara (Jain) Temples in India, the Blue and Pink mosques in Iran, and others, lift me to high heights because they are sublime and, in some cases, divine. As John Keats said, "A thing of beauty is a joy forever." It can also be incredibly spiritual forever.

This is true for many other art forms as well. The world of literature is packed with many works that are spiritual in character—works that run the gamut of possibilities from short stories to long novels and great epics as indicated earlier. This is also true for theatre, film, dance, opera, and the natural world, especially plays by Shakespeare and Molière, films like *Doctor Zhivago* and *Gandhi,* dances like the ones from *The Rite of Spring, Swan Lake,* and those performed in the Andalusian caves in Spain and by dance troupes in Africa and Latin America, and operas such as *La Bohème, La Traviata,* as well as many others. Nature, too, is filled with millions of exquisite elements and ingredients, such as lovely trees, shrubs, forests, flowers, rivers, streams, waterfalls, mountains, meadows, sunrises, and sunsets. The list goes on and on.

This is where things stood for me for many years with respect to spirituality and my quest and commitment to cultivating it. My experiences in these and other areas were limited to *specific moments of spirituality* that tended to occur when I was exposed to exceptional works of art or captivating cultures in the world. However, what I was not experiencing is what might be called a *permanent state of spirituality*.

This began to change when I grew deeply immersed in the natural world, which can be traced back to a time when I felt extremely depressed and was experiencing some very difficult health problems. I first went to doctors to get some help with these problems, much as most people do. When this didn't work as well as I had hoped, I sought the advice of some family members, close friends, and read several books and many articles on the specific health problems I was experiencing. While this helped a little, it didn't provide the lasting solution I was searching for and hoping to achieve. Finally, in a fit of desperation, I turned to nature and the natural world. I started taking long walks in the countryside near our home. There seemed to be nothing quite like "getting out in nature" and experiencing everything nature had to offer—much as Beethoven often did by leaving the hustle and bustle of Vienna and getting out into the countryside (that is what his *Pastoral Symphony* or *Symphony No. 6* is all about). Slowly but surely being immersed in nature produced a more lasting solution to my health problems. The process of enjoying the spring, seeing all the beautiful flowers, birds, trees, streams, rivers, animals, and especially watching the leaves turn many delicate shades of green and yellow in the spring and gold, orange, red, yellow, and brown in the fall, provided the elixir that was required to restore my health to normal.

Since that time, I have been actively engaged in nature and the natural realm in numerous ways. I take frequent walks with my wife Nancy and daughters Charlene and Susan in many local parks and conservation areas near our home in Markham and across the York Region, as well as enjoy the paintings of many of Canada's Group of Seven that depict the country's magnificent landscapes and wilderness areas. I also take long walks in forests whenever I am able to do so, especially the long trail in the Durham Region forest that is

subdivided into shorter oak, maple, birch, and pine trails that provide many opportunities to enjoy specific types of trees and make it
possible to engage in what the Japanese call "*shinrin-yoku*" or "forest bathing." On one level, this is about achieving and maintaining
good health, physical fitness, and happiness in life. However, on another level, it goes much deeper and farther than that. It can create
an incredible amount of spirituality, as well as allowing a person to
live life on a much higher and more profound plane of existence and
consciousness, on occasion even encountering moments that go far
above and beyond this. In the final analysis, this may be one of the
best sources of all of experiencing and cultivating spirituality. There
is simply no substitute for it, which is why we need to revere, savour,
and cherish nature and the natural world as much as possible and not
just preserve, protect, and conserve it. When I am doing this, I often
think of John Muir, founder of the national park movement in the
United States, who saw nature as a great teacher, "revealing the mind
of God," in the words of one of his biographers.

Speaking of finding one's soul, this is yet another route to cultivating spirituality. While this also varies greatly from person to person,
the thoughts of many well-known authors and cultural scholars on
this subject can be helpful, uplifting, motivating, and meaningful. The
advice "Find a job you enjoy doing and you will never have to work
a day in your life" has been attributed to everyone from Confucius to
Mark Twain to Winston Churchill; loving one's work can indeed bring
its own kind of spirituality. Carl Jung contended, "The privilege of a
lifetime is to become who you really are." And Herman Hesse said,
"Within you there is a stillness and a sanctuary to which you can re-
treat and become yourself," while Swami Vivekananda, the cultural
guru from India, believed that "There is no other teacher than your
own soul." These connections between spirituality and the soul are
fascinating and reassuring because, as we saw earlier in the book, it
was more than two thousand years ago that Marcus Cicero claimed,
"Culture is the philosophy or cultivation of the soul."

Insights, activities, and experiences like these and many others
are very beneficial in encouraging people to take deep descents into
themselves as well as numerous forays into the world in order to come
to grips with who they actually are and what they are meant to do with

their lives and accomplish in life. Not only can this lead to achieving and sustaining better health, fitness, and well-being, but it can also lead to realizing a permanent state of spirituality and not just specific moments of spirituality.

This is why learning about culture and all the different cultures in the world can also be very helpful in experiencing higher levels of spirituality and possibly even permanent states of spirituality. As Jin Li pointed out in her book *Cultural Foundations of Learning: East and West* when discussing the quintessential importance of culture as an activity and a discipline, "Culture, as the largest human created system ... penetrates so profoundly into all spheres of human life that it alters human cognition, emotion, and behaviour... Culture is like the air we breathe; we are completely dependent on it."[5]

Like the phenomenal breakthroughs now occurring in science, which comprise a fundamental dimension of culture and cultures and are designed to broaden our personal and collective knowledge of everything from the smallest particles to largest galaxies in the universe, both the tiniest and most expansive understandings of culture possess the potential to produce ever higher states of spirituality and consciousness with respect to virtually everything that exists in the human, natural, and cosmic realms. Whether these states have something to do with the divine may only be revealed in the fullness of time, if at all. However, this doesn't alter the fact that most areas of culture and cultures have a great deal to do with spirituality in its many profuse forms and fascinating manifestations.

From the most exquisite works of art and the artistic perception of culture to the cosmos and all the exquisite images of it that are now being projected back to earth, there is no doubt that culture possesses the capacity to act as a gateway to spirituality in countless ways because everything is there in one form or another when it is added up and considered in totality. Culture makes it possible to move horizontally and vertically, as well as in breadth and depth, across virtually every conceivable domain, activity, and discipline in the world, from the human to the non-human, the simple to the profound, the individual to the collective, the local to the global, and the mundane to the magnificent.

While I have yet to experience a permanent state of spirituality, I have the feeling that I have been moving in the right direction in this respect in recent years because the way of life I am living at present is slowly but surely evolving into an ongoing spiritual state. I hope this is the case, because culture is without doubt one of the best vehicles of all for cultivating spirituality and unlocking the secrets of the sublime and possibly even the divine.

In order to cultivate specific moments of spirituality, permanent states of spirituality, or live a spiritual life, it is necessary to descend deep into "the self," as mentioned earlier. This is because spirituality is largely an internal rather than external affair, despite the fact that it may involve activities, experiences, and events that exist outside rather than inside the self, such as listening to beautiful music, revering the arts, walking in forests, exploring captivating cultures, and helping other people.

Unfortunately, there are risks as well as rewards that can be experienced by getting immersed in the self, regardless of whether it is part of a quest to experience momentary or permanent states of spirituality. As a quest that is largely *within* rather than *without*, there is the potential danger that people will get so caught up in "the self" when they go deep inside themselves that they become self-centred and egocentric rather than other-centred and altruistic.

It is the process of looking inward into the self rather than outward on the world that helps to explain the development of the "me generation" over the last few decades, something that is so conspicuous in the world today. In the process of going inward, it is easy to get so preoccupied with oneself that this becomes the answer to all questions and the solution to all problems. This can end up causing people to neglect other people as well as any needs and problems that exist beyond the self, and to believe that one's own interests, requirements, concerns, and preoccupations are sacrosanct and take precedence over everything else. Hence the imbalance and disharmony that now exists in many parts of the world between "the self" and "the other," one of the most difficult and dangerous relationships in the world to deal with at the present time.

Fortunately, this is not the case with compassion, spirituality's close companion in many ways. In fact, compassion possesses the potential to counteract and reverse egoism, egocentrism, and the negative effects of the "me generation," as well as restore a much better balance and harmony between the self and the other and, in doing so, produce a great deal more kindness, goodness, thoughtfulness, generosity, and unity in the world.

Just as cultivating spirituality requires going deeper and deeper into the self, so cultivating compassion requires going deeper and deeper into the other and the world at large, primarily by identifying and dealing more with others than oneself. While in many ways this differs greatly from spirituality and living a spiritual life, a great deal of fulfillment, happiness, contentment, and spirituality can also be derived by cultivating compassion and living a compassionate life.

Just as many experiences and activities come to mind when we think and talk about spirituality and living a spiritual life, so do many experiences and activities come to mind when we think and talk about compassion and living a compassionate life. While the two are intimately interconnected and interwoven, I usually think first of Albert Schweitzer and the type of life he lived as an excellent illustration of cultivating compassion and living this type of life.

In 1913, Schweitzer left his promising and productive musical career in Europe behind and went to Africa to create and develop the Hôpital Albert Schweitzer in Lambaréné, French Equatorial Africa, which is now in the country of Gabon. He spent many years and thousands of hours there treating patients with many different types of illnesses and diseases, especially leprosy (also known today as Hansen's disease), risking his life and his health in the process.

When it was no longer possible for Schweitzer to do this due to his advancing years and several difficult medical problems, he divided his time between Africa and Europe for the remainder of his life. In 1952, he was awarded the Nobel Peace Prize for his individual achievements and professional commitment to "reverence for life" and "the necessity of ethics and ethical behavior in society." While he has been criticized for his paternalistic attitudes and treatment of Africans as well as the lack of proper sanitation and ventilation in his hospital, Schweitzer laboured for more than fifty years in Africa as a medical doctor and humanitarian, dealing with extremely sick people and very difficult working conditions. He also fought against the proliferation of nuclear weapons, feeling they were contrary to his belief that all life is precious and that everything that advances life is good while everything that degrades life is bad. For Schweitzer, all living things are valuable, and therefore deserve to be treated with dignity, compassion, sensitivity, and respect.

By expanding and enriching life in virtually all directions and in every possible way, Schweitzer provides a remarkable example of how our personalities and lives can be enhanced, enriched, and transformed by cultivating and manifesting compassion and concern for "the other and others" and not just "the self and oneself" as the foundation for our lives. As one of the greatest proponents of reverential thinking, reverential action, and empathy and kindness for others that are less fortunate than oneself, Schweitzer described what life and living can and should be like:

> The ripeness that our development must aim at is one which makes us simpler, more truthful, purer, more peace loving, meeker, kinder, more sympathetic ... that is the process in which the soft iron of youthful idealism hardens into the steel of a full-grown idealism which can never be lost.[6]

People like Albert Schweitzer and Martin Luther King, Jr., who both led exemplary and compassionate lives in many ways, are not the only people that come to my mind in this regard. I also think about Mahatma Gandhi and Mother Teresa. Whenever I think of all the painful experiences Gandhi and Dr. King had to endure over the course of their lives—and how their lives were snuffed out brutally, instantly, and without warning—I recall King's saying towards the end of his life that "I seek nothing more than to leave behind me a life wholly dedicated to a cause." It was a cause dedicated to helping others much more than himself. This is also true for Mother Teresa, who felt it is imperative to give to others and to worthy causes until it hurts and you feel and experience real pain from this.

There is an enormous amount of fulfillment that can be derived from having sympathy, empathy, and compassion for other people and commitment to causes greater than ourselves. While Schweitzer, Gandhi, King, and Mother Teresa are among the best known examples of this, there are millions of people all over the world who exhibit an enormous amount of compassion by devoting themselves to a single cause or many diverse causes. While spiritually is usually a personal feeling that is confined to people as individuals, compassion can be and usually is a public feeling that can and often does affect hundreds if not thousands of people.

While involvement in a single cause or many causes can help immensely in cultivating compassion and living a compassionate life, it is not the only way to manifest this. There are many other ways as well. An essential dimension of this involves recognizing and having empathy for people whose situation and circumstances are far worse than our own. This necessitates "getting out of your own skin" and feeling empathy for people who are in a much more precarious situation than we are, as well as assisting them with their problems and helping them as much as possible with their needs and recovery processes.

In fact, having or feeling empathy for other people is often the most important step we can take to cultivating compassion because it means recognizing that other people are or may be experiencing problems that are much more severe and serious than the problems we are experiencing and therefore need our help and maybe the help of others to get their lives sorted out and back on track. When exercised on a global scale, cultivating compassion could be one of the most promising ways of coming to grips with the life-threatening problems facing the world today. As Canadian cultural scholar Max Wyman pointed out in his recently published book *The Compassionate Imagination*:

Developing compassion for each other is our best chance at finding a way out of the mess the world is in. Seeing the world through someone else's eyes, by the simple act of reading a book, watching a movie, or listening to a song, is the first step away from fear and demonization of the Other. Sharing our imaginations through creative activity—letting our own imagination out to play for other people to share—lets us explore other people's realities. We tiptoe into a world that is private and precious to someone else, and, in so doing, we get a hint as to why that world is special. At the same time, we make space in our minds and hearts for people who don't think the way we do. Sharing someone else's vulnerability—recognizing their humanity—empowers us to show ours, and trust has a chance to flower.[7]

One of the most interesting things about being involved with a cause or cultivating compassion is that actions, deeds, and commitments like these may not only help people whose problems are much worse than our own, but also create feelings, emotions, and states of exuberance in ourselves that border on the sublime and are therefore very similar to those experienced through spirituality. In fact, this is where compassion and spirituality come together, intersect, and interact, thereby resolving the imbalance and disharmony that can result between the self and the other and producing a great deal of synergy and synchronicity in the process. One of the most important aspects of this is that a great deal of spirituality and compassion can be realized that produces "highs" naturally through embracing culture, cultures, the arts, and many other activities, rather than having to resort to dangerous substances to achieve this.

The best way to realize this is to recall the wise counsel provided by Pierre Teilhard de Chardin when he said, "We are not human beings having a spiritual experience, we are spiritual beings having a human experience."[8] To do so is not only to manifest a great deal of spirituality and compassion in life, but also to experience much more harmony, happiness, and fulfillment. This helps to put ourselves in the strongest possible position to not just think or dream about a cultural age, but actually make it in reality and enable it to flourish, as spirituality and compassion are two of the most important qualities and capabilities to cultivate and exhibit in such an age.

Chapter Thirteen

Living in a Cultural Age

Live in the whole, in the good, in the beautiful.
—Goethe[1]

Have you ever asked yourself what it might be like to live in a cultural age? I have often asked myself this very question. Moreover, I have been working in the cultural field for so long that other people are beginning to ask me this question as well. Would it be possible (they ask) to provide them with some thoughts, ideas, and insights that might be helpful in understanding what living in a cultural age would be like and how this would improve their lives and way of life in the future?

As I was wrestling with how to answer this question for the purposes of this book, I recalled coming across a very brief, wise statement by Goethe, the renowned German author, poet, and cultural scholar, that I felt summed up this matter better than anything else I had encountered. The statement was, *"Live in the whole, in the good, in the beautiful."* I came across it quite by accident one day when I was reading a book by John Cowper Powys on *The Meaning of Culture*. Like many remarkable authors and especially poets, Goethe possessed the ability to convey profound thoughts and ideas like this one in but a few simple words that are nonetheless packed full of wisdom, knowledge, insight, and understanding.

Goethe's statement hit me like a ton of bricks the moment I read it. It seemed to say what I felt living in a cultural age would be all about and designed to accomplish, in a way that was not difficult to understand, and, much more importantly, to put into practice. I recall thinking at that time that I would have to write about this incisive and sage statement at some point in my life. Now, many years later, I am attempting to do so, largely because I think this statement has an enormous amount to say about what life and living in a cultural age would be like, how it can be achieved in fact, and how we might experience all the joy, happiness, and benefits that can come from this.

In order to come to grips with this task, it is probably best to begin by breaking Goethe's statement down into its three main components—live in the whole, in the good, in the beautiful—and to write at first about each of these components separately. Following this, it is possible to tie these components together to demonstrate how they relate to living in a cultural age. It is my hope that this approach to the task espoused here—and the many implications and consequences that can be and are derived from this—will prove useful in providing some thoughts and ideas about what living in a cultural age might be like and all the rewards and possibilities that emanate from this.

As indicated at the beginning of this book, I believe we are living in an economic age at present that is based largely on focusing on and awarding the highest priority to a very important *part of the whole*—namely economics and economies—rather than *the whole*, and specifically in this case, culture and cultures. Living in this economic age means breaking the whole and wholes—virtually any or all wholes—down into many parts in order to capitalize on the economic benefits and material advantages that can be derived from doing so. While this process of breaking wholes up into parts has existed for thousands of years and probably from the beginning of human life on earth, it really only commenced in earnest as well as in a systematic and sustained manner when Adam Smith made a compelling case for "the division of labour" in his book *The Wealth of Nations*, which was published in 1776. This eventually led to dividing countless wholes up into parts and specializing in the production of these parts through the division of labour as the key to creating phenomenal increases in the quantity of goods and services as well as astronomical amounts of material and monetary wealth. As we have seen, this led to substantially improving standards of living and superior qualities of life for billions of people throughout the world since this book was published.

The problem at the present time in history is that this practice is having a devastating effect on the natural environment and is *divid-*

ing rather than *uniting* many things in the world because it places the highest priority on the parts and breaking wholes into parts, rather than on the whole and bringing the parts together to create integrated and holistic wholes (such as culture and cultures). This explains why it is so essential at the present time in history and going forward into the future to make the transition from focusing attention on the parts, as we do in an economic age, to focusing attention on the whole, as would be the case in a cultural age. As we have seen, culture, not economics, has the most legitimate claim to being seen and dealt with as "the whole." This has been the case ever since Edward Burnett Tylor perceived and defined culture this way in 1871, and this view has been confirmed by countless cultural scholars, historians, and practitioners since that time.

Admitting this fact in principle and committing to it in practice is the key to entering, realizing, and living in a cultural age, because the highest priority will be placed on culture in the holistic sense rather than economics in the partial and specialized sense. Not only will this mean focusing far more attention throughout the world and in people's lives on uniting rather than dividing things and dealing more effectively with divisions, polarizations, conflicts, and confrontations, but also it will mean creating more inclusion, togetherness, equality, and unity, and less exclusion, separation, inequality, and disunity in the world and in people's lives.

This doesn't mean that this will bring an end to focusing on the parts of wholes and specialization, especially when doing so plays such an important role in many activities in the world today and will continue to do so in all aspects of life in the future. What this *does* mean, however, is that partialism and specialization will be situated in a much broader and deeper *holistic context* and *cultural perspective* and treated this way in real terms. This is why holism and living in the whole possess the capacity to create the theoretical and practical foundations that are required for a cultural age, in exactly the same way that partialism and specialization provide these foundations for the economic age.

This is also true for ourselves as people, our worldviews, values, value systems, beliefs, lifestyles, and ways of life, how we live in the world and live our lives in the future, develop our families, educational systems, towns, cities, regions, countries, and their cultures, conduct our international relations and global affairs, see and treat other species, and visualize the universe and the cosmos. This is undoubtedly one of the most pressing and quintessential priorities in the world today since it is of vital importance to the survival and well-being of all species, countries, and the world as a whole. In a cultural age, people will not be seen in terms of their individual parts or specific characteristics such as their gender, race, religion, colour of their skin, educational credentials, income level, or any other single factor or feature. Rather, they will be seen and treated as "whole people" first and foremost. This will result in generating more respect, understanding, and appreciation for all the diverse people in the world, as well as creating more kindness, cooperation, compassion, and spirituality among people and countries in the world and in life generally.

Unfortunately, this is not the way we see ourselves and live our lives today. Rather than opening wide to the whole and wholes and embracing them at every opportunity, we tend to close ourselves off to the whole and wholes and downplay or ignore them. This is because we have been taught to identify more with the parts than the whole, not only in terms of ourselves, our education, our development, and our lives, but also in terms of virtually everything else. Nevertheless, to live in the whole—*really live in it*—it is necessary to make a quantum leap and concerted effort to expand our knowledge, understanding, and consciousness of the whole, wholes, wholeness, and all the many different wholes we encounter in the world as well as in our lives.

No one understood the importance of focusing attention on the whole and wholes rather than the parts and particulars better than Plato, the famous Greek philosopher. As Francis A. Schaeffer points out in his book *How Should We Then Live?*:

> Plato understood that regardless of what kind of particulars one talks about, if there are no absolutes—no universal—then particulars have no meaning. The universal or absolute is that under which all particulars fit—that which gives unity and meaning to the whole.[2]

A tremendous sense of satisfaction and fulfillment is experienced when we make the transition to holism, regardless of whether it is in the individual sense (the whole person), as is the case for Matthew Arnold and many others; the collective sense (humanity as a whole); the type of cultural development advocated by Johan Huizinga and numerous other cultural scholars (cultures as wholes and overall ways of life made up of many parts); neighbourhhoods, communities, towns, cities, regions, countries, and world cultures (municipal, regional, national, and world culturescapes or cultural landscapes); living in the whole (Goethe); as well as the natural environment, the universe, and the cosmos (ordered and regenerative wholes as seen by such scholars as Thomas Berry, Teilhard de Chardin, Wade Davis, Swami Vivekananda, Rana B. P. Singh, and many other eastern and western scholars and cosmologists).

It follows from this that to "live in the whole" as Goethe advised is to allow the whole in general and cultural wholes in particular to penetrate deeply into the interiors of our being and our consciousness, regardless of what specific type of cultural whole or wholes they are or might be. Not only should we see and understand ourselves and our lives in this way, but we also should see and understand our families and everything else in the world in this way as well. Whenever we step out our front, back, or side doors and connect with the world, this is how we should visualize and engage in it. When we walk around our communities—something that occurs so often in my case that children in the community call me "the walking man" because I am always out walking whenever they see me—we should become aware of our communities as wholes made up of many interrelated parts. Not only should they be visualized, treated, and dealt with in all-inclusive terms—much as Jane Jacobs did when she made the case for the crucial importance of neighourhoods and communities in the development of towns, cities, and our lives during the many years she lived in New York and Toronto—but we should also cherish them in this way.

A great deal of exuberance, excitement, and exhilaration can be experienced by treating neighbourhoods and communities as cultural wholes made up of many parts in all their diversity, complexity, richness, and vitality. And what is true for our neighbourhoods and communities is true for towns, cities, regions, and countries and their cultures as well as the human family. It is also true for the natural environment, the universe, and the cosmos. Each of these vast, complex, and remarkable entities when seen from the holistic perspective provided by culture are cultural wholes made up of millions of parts that are constantly changing, evolving, mutating, and impacting on one another in space and over time.

Rather than downplaying or ignoring cultural wholes in this sense, we should be constantly striving to learn as much as we can about and from them as possible, including how they function as wholes and how all their diverse parts are woven together in different combinations and arrangements to form these wholes. Living in the whole in this sense means embracing every culture in the holistic sense in this way and at every level. In the process, it is possible to understand what Goethe meant when he said "Live in the whole": it means to be conscious of culture as the whole and cultures as wholes at all times and in all places. This is especially important when and where culture and cultures are balanced and harmonious because this brings with it a great deal more coherence, cohesion, identity, harmony, and well-being.

Living in the whole in this sense as Goethe advised also makes it possible for us to take a major step towards understanding and experiencing how everything in the world is interconnected and what it means to talk about and experience the underlying unity, oneness, and connectivity that exists in the world, as countless scientists, philosophers, mystics, and others have stated over the centuries and written about to our benefit. It is culture, more than any other activity or discipline, that enables us to see and understand the interconnectiveness of everything and everybody when it is perceived and defined in holistic terms. As Jean Houston pointed out in her foreword to Robert Atkinson's book *A New Story of Wholeness: An Experiential Guide for Connecting the Human Family*, "We need the potential of the whole human race—and the particular genius of every culture—if we are going to survive our time."[3]

And this is not all. Goethe's thoughts on living in the whole in this vital cultural sense do not end here. Far from it. He also felt it is necessary to want "the best for the whole," as I discovered when I read that Goethe also declared, *"Who wills the highest must will the whole."* I interpreted this to mean that it is not only necessary to live in the whole and comprehend the significance of the whole, but also to make a commitment to improving the whole and wholes—such as culture and cultures—as one of the highest forms of holism of all for ourselves, others, and the world at large. This is not possible, however, without getting out of our own skin and doing the best we can for everyone and everything. To do so is not only to *"live in the whole"* and want *"the best"* for the whole and wholes, but also to *"live in the good,"* the second component in Goethe's profound and insightful statement.

We don't need to be a member or participant in a specific religion or religious or spiritual group to realize this, as was discussed earlier, despite the fact that participating in such groups can be very helpful and have its own individual rewards and collective advantages. Fortunately, living in the good can be achieved in many ways, such as committing to important activities and causes of one type or another, helping family members and friends with their problems, doing voluntary work and volunteering at a hospital, school, or seniors' home without expecting any financial remuneration in return, being a board member of a not-for-profit organization, creating a community event, festival, fair, or social occasion, preserving the natural environment, planting trees, conserving the cultural and natural heritage of our communities and urban environments as well as the cultural and natural heritage of humankind, or assisting at a local food bank. All these ways, and countless others, involve manifesting goodness, kindness, and generosity wherever possible, making a concerted effort to be friendly, setting a good example for others, and ensuring that empathy, spirituality, and compassion are a fundamental part of this holistic process and our overall lives.

It is difficult to see how the world will become a better, safer, more secure, and peaceful place, as well as overcome the colossal disparities that exist in income, wealth, and resources, and resolve the environmental crisis and deal with the aftermath of all too frequent natural disasters, without living in the good. Doing so requires commitment to causes that need a great deal of caring, sharing, teamwork, and collaboration with others. Countless people throughout the world are doing this on a daily and sustained basis, regardless of whether this means bringing an end to systemic racism, helping to improve the education of girls and terminating violence and the subjugation of women, or engaging in bringing more peace, harmony, equality, and happiness into the world. Appreciating the contributions that countless people in all parts of the world are making in these areas and myriad others is essential, as such contributions point the way both to entering and living in a cultural age in the years and decades ahead.

In talking about the need to "live in the good," we would probably be well-advised to leave the final word about this matter to Shakespeare, who, like Goethe, is one of the world's greatest poets and authors. Here is what Shakespeare had to say about such matters in his play *As You Like It*:

And this our life, exempt from public haunt,
Finds tongues in trees, books in running brooks,
Sermons in stones, and good in everything.
I would not change it.

If it is necessary to "live in the whole" and "live in the good," as Goethe advised, it is also necessary to "live in the beautiful," the last component in Goethe's simple and meaningful triptych. Many things in life and the world are unbelievably beautiful and are meant to be enjoyed, appreciated, and savoured because they bring so much happiness and fulfillment into the lives of people and the world at large. In so doing, they pave the way for a cultural age and make the world a better place for all—a world filled with much more love, contentment, and benevolence and much less hate, anger, discontent, and strife. Albert Einstein affirmed the importance of this view many years ago when he said, "The ideals which have always shone before me and filled me with joy are goodness, beauty, and truth."

If beauty is "in the eyes of the beholder," as the ancient proverb claims, it is fortunate that beauty manifests itself in the world in many different ways and not in just a few similar ones. For some people, beauty manifests itself in exquisite sunrises, sunsets, paintings, dances, stories, and musical masterpieces. For others, it manifests itself in magnificent parks and gardens, bonding with favourite friends and colleagues, having and loving pets, and much more. And for still others, it manifests itself in incredible discoveries, inspiring ideas, rare insights, evocative ideals, and productive innovations. It all depends on how people see, experience, and react to beauty in the world and in their lives. As Confucius said many centuries ago, "Everything has beauty, but not everyone sees it."

One of the reasons for this is that beauty is often defined for us by others and not ourselves. This is usually true as a result of what we were taught in school, the social classes we belong to, the upbringing we experienced in our families, climbing onto other people's band-wagons, or influences such as elitism and populism. Influences like these can be very powerful and have a remarkable effect on how we see beauty and assess beautiful things. How often have we heard people say that they like popular music but not classical music, a position that detracts from a person's ability to recognize and enjoy beautiful things. This is especially true for music, but can also be true for paintings, plays, poetry, dances, films, architectural creations, and many other types of activities. This makes it imperative to cut through the class distinctions, social trappings, educational teachings, and personal il-lusions that often accompany and encase beauty and beautiful things and decide for ourselves if things are beautiful or not, rather than hav-ing to rely on other people and groups to make these decisions for us.

In my own case, music provides the best illustration of how beau-ty works and can manifest itself in many areas of life, something I dis-cussed in the preceding chapter on spirituality and compassion. This began when I was very young, since I experienced beauty in many musical masterpieces, especially after I joined the choir at Grace Church-on-the-Hill in Toronto. Singing in the choir exposed me to an incredible amount of beauty in music through numerous hymns and anthems, as well as oratorios by Bach, Handel, Schubert, Mozart, and many other famous composers.

What made masterpieces by composers such as these and many others like them so beautiful for me was that when I experienced them in fact they transported me to ethereal places whenever I heard them. Beethoven's *Ninth Symphony* is a perfect illustration of this. Music like this evokes strong feelings and powerful emotions in me that border on the sublime and the divine. I feel that Beethoven was "walking with the gods" when he wrote this majestic piece of music and that I am "walking with the gods" when I listen to it. It is undoubtedly one of the most beautiful pieces of music ever written, and *the* most beautiful piece in the minds of many.

Of course, music is not the only art form that brings a great deal of beauty into our lives. The visual arts do so as well, especially artistic masterpieces that have some association with nature and the natural world. For me, this is especially true for the Impressionist painters of France, Canada's Group of Seven, and Chinese brush painters. Interestingly, music also figures prominently in this area as well. There is an incredible amount of music that has been written specifically with nature and its many exquisite elements and ingredients in mind. Think, for example, of Smetana's *Moldau*, Debussy's *Le Mer* and *Prélude à l'après-midi d'un faune*, and Vivaldi's *Four Seasons,* all of which are extremely beautiful and remind us of the exceptional beauty of nature and the natural realm.

What is true for music and painting is equally true for all other art forms, as noted earlier. For instance, literature is filled with many beautiful works—works that run the gamut of possibilities from short stories and poems to long novels and great epics such as Louisa May Alcott's *Little Women*, James Joyce's *Ulysses*, Emily Brontë's *Wuthering Heights*, and Miguel de Cervantes' *Don Quixote;* plays by such well-known playwrights as George Bernard Shaw, Anton Chekhov, Tennessee Williams, and Sophocles; operas such as *The Magic Flute, La Bohème, Tosca, Madama Butterfly, Aida,* and *Carmen*; films such as *2001: A Space Odyssey, La Dolce Vita,* and *Singin' in the Rain*; dances such as *The Rite of Spring* and *Swan Lake*; and architecture, including all the beautiful cathedrals, temples, mosques, pagodas, synagogues, and many others in existence around the world.

All these activities and experiences, and countless others, make it possible for people to live in the beautiful and not just in the whole and the good. They also make them aware of how essential it is to surround ourselves with beautiful things and make beauty a fundamental part of our world if we want to live happy, healthy, and contented lives. For beauty, and beautiful things play a key role in making us enthusiastic and excited about life and living, rather than despondent and depressed. And being enthusiastic and excited about life is what living in a cultural age should be all about.

Interestingly, Dostoevsky went a step further in this regard when he connected beauty with goodness, kindness, righteousness, truth, and many other qualities, as is evident in his novel *The Idiot*. In this well-known literary work, Prince Lev Nikolyaevich Myshkin, the protagonist, states, "I believe the world will be saved by beauty." For Dostoevsky, beauty not only manifests itself in the arts, aesthetics, and nature, but also transcends the arts, aesthetics, and nature by inspiring the best in everyone and connecting us with others. It also reminds us that regardless of how bad things are or might get, and no matter how much suffering, misery, chaos, and disorder there is in the world, beauty moves us to great heights and enables us to reach out and help others or request their help when it is needed. There is something deep down in our being and consciousness that enables us to do this. Perhaps this is why Mark Twain is supposed to have said, "Give every day the chance to become the most beautiful day in your life," leaving us with the feeling that beauty might just be what is most required to "save the world."

Without doubt, Goethe's insightful and evocative statement—"Live in the whole, in the good, in the beautiful"—conveys all this and much more and does so in simple, straightforward, revealing, and eloquent terms. As such, it gives us a deep sense of what it would actually be like to live in a cultural age and not just think, dream, or talk about it.

However, Goethe's statement is not the only one to convey in concise terms and simple words what it might be like to actually live in a cultural age. Joseph Campbell's succinct advice—"Follow your bliss and the world will open doors where there only walls"—does so, too. While Campbell is best known for his profuse research and writings on the great cultures and religions of the world as well as the importance of myths, mythmaking, mythology, and cosmology in this process, he also had many valuable things to say about life and living that are intimately connected to what is needed to enter a cultural age and enable it to flourish.

Many people think Campbell was talking about happiness when he said "Follow your bliss" in an interview with Bill Moyers in which Campbell talked about the need for people to do what they are intended to do with their lives. However, what he really meant was that people should strive to do the things in life they were intended to do: this will bring them the most fulfillment and happiness in life, despite the fact that following such a path can be very difficult. This quest is about accomplishing your real purpose, something that is hopefully possible for all people and not just some.

In order to come to grips with Campbell's astute advice, it is necessary to descend deep into ourselves and our being—much like cultivating spirituality—and draw from ourselves what is most imperative to realize in our lives. As a result, we should be constantly asking ourselves such questions as: What is the ultimate purpose of my life? What capabilities, skills, abilities, and characteristics do I possess that were meant to be realized in some way that may not or cannot be realized by others? And, perhaps most importantly of all, who am I at the very core of my being, consciousness, and essence?

In Campbell's view, following our bliss is the key to living a full, fulfilling, meaningful, and purposeful life. Once we discover what our true bliss is, we need only pursue it on a sustained and systematic basis to live in a permanent state of bliss, much like living in a permanent state of spirituality as discussed earlier. We can soar to great heights and fly with the eagles, so to speak, because we have taken the time and made the effort to determine who we are as people as well as what we were intended to achieve, and then worked diligently and relentlessly to realize it. It may be something large or small, simple or profound, admired by a few or admired by many, but it is right for us.

With insights as valuable and timely as the ones provided by Goethe, Campbell, and other cultural scholars uppermost in our minds, it is possible for us to live our lives in a manner as well as a state that we have never experienced before. This can be called *living a cultural life* or *living in a cultural age*, since everything fits together to form a balanced, harmonious, and integrated whole composed of many different and interconnected parts.

Living a cultural life, living in the whole, the good, and the beautiful, and living in a cultural age will broaden, deepen, intensify, and enrich our time on Earth in many ways. It will bring us a great deal more joy, pleasure, and fulfillment in life, increase our compassion, kindness, sensitivity, and respect for other people and their well-being, as well as broaden and deepen our knowledge, understanding, and appreciation for other people, countries, and cultures and their many different worldviews, values, customs, traditions, beliefs, and ways of life. It will also make us much more conscious of what can be learned from other people, countries, and cultures, which is helpful in enriching all aspects and dimensions of our own lives and the lives of others. This will make both our lives and their lives more expansive, as well as filled with much more awe, wonder, ecstasy, curiosity, and creativity.

What is needed more than anything else to bring this about is a great deal more inclusivity in the world. This is something that can't and never will be fully achieved in the economic age because this age is designed to channel most of the world's material and monetary wealth into the hands of the rich and powerful classes. The only way this can be changed is to open the doors to a cultural age and cross the threshold to it. A cultural age will be concerned with creating well-being for all people and for all countries, classes, and sectors of society. This in turn will enable people in all parts of the world to live cultural lives that provide more fulfillment, purpose, and meaning, to achieve their full potential, and to enjoy their experiences in life and the world to the fullest extent. This prospect is what makes entering a cultural age and enabling it to flourish so exciting, exceptional, and inspirational.

Chapter Fourteen

A Tale of Two Ages

It was the best of times, it was the worst of times, it was the
age of wisdom, it was the age of foolishness, it was the epoch
of belief, it was the epoch of incredulity, it was the season
of Light, it was the season of Darkness, it was the spring of
hope, it was the winter of despair.
—Charles Dickens[1]

This opening sentence of Charles Dickens' book *A Tale of Two Cities*
goes a long way towards describing the present world situation and
prospects for the future. For if one thing has become crystal clear over
the last few years, it is that we have arrived at a crucial turning point in
history. Where we go in the future will depend largely on the outcome
of the battle that is looming ahead between two very different types of
ages and worldviews—a battle that is manifesting itself in many of the
same signs Dickens saw when he wrote his popular novel but now on
a global scale rather than that of individual cities or countries.

On the one hand, there is the economic age we have been living in
for the last two hundred and fifty years, an age that is struggling to survive, be sustained, and remain intact. On the other hand, there is the
cultural age, which is beginning to take shape in the world but has yet
to see the light of day. The dawning of the cultural age is what this book
is all about. I have written about how a cultural age can be brought into
existence and flourish, not by striking a final blow to the economic age
but rather by incorporating this age along with a great deal else in a
far more all-encompassing age and compelling vision of the world of
the future. And "where there is no vision, the people perish," as was
proclaimed so prophetically in the Bible many centuries ago.

At the present time, most corporations, governments, international organizations, global leaders, wealthy elites, and powerful

countries are demonstrating by their deeds, actions, and policies that they are committed to maintaining the economic age but restructuring it in areas where it is deficient. However, a sizeable percentage of the world's total population, including all those involved in the great cultural awakening, are indicating through their actions, protests, interests, and work that they are committed to creating a very different type of age in the future. I have called such an age a "cultural age" in this book because it includes people and organizations from around the world that are actively involved in culture, cultures, and the cultural awakening, as well as millions of others who are exploring or working in many different areas of cultural life such as educators, scholars, world travellers, and the like.

Foremost among the quintessential requirements of this newly emerging cultural age is coming to grips with the life-threatening problems that exist around the globe, as well as creating more peace, harmony, happiness, and equality in the world. This includes making it possible for all people and all countries to enjoy reasonable standards of living and well-being without straining the globe's fragile ecosystems, natural resources, and finite carrying capacity to the breaking point.

Just as there is a great deal to be learned about the nature, functioning, and priorities of the cultural age from undertaking an impartial assessment of the economic age—as was demonstrated earlier—so there is much to be learned from Dickens' famous novel by seeing it as a metaphor for some of the most salient similarities and contrasts that exist between the economic age and the cultural age, and this despite the fact that the contexts for Dickens' novel and this tale of two ages are very different.

For one thing, *A Tale of Two Cities* moves back and forth between two very different countries and cities—England and France as well as London and Paris—just as this book has moved back and forth between two very different ages. Moreover, just as England and London in Dickens' novel epitomize the economic age in many ways because of the impact of the Industrial Revolution and the development of myriad industries, companies, financial institutions, and trade activities, so do France and Paris epitomize the cultural age with their remarkable achievements in the arts and letters and commitment to culture and cultural development. It is not surprising in this regard that two centuries later it was Jack Lang when he was Minister of Culture for France and Melina Mercouri when she was Minister of Culture for Greece who came up with the idea of "cultural capitals" and "cities of culture." This idea was initially limited to cities in Europe but has since spread to many other cities and countries around the world.

There are several other similarities between Dickens' novel and this book that should not be allowed to escape our attention. For example, Dickens' novel is very much concerned with human beings, wealth, poverty, inequality, and the need for economic, social, and political reform, especially in the sense of people who are better off helping those living in abject circumstances with very few opportunities. Interestingly, this is also what many of Dickens' other novels are about, including *A Christmas Carol, Great Expectations, David Copperfield,* and *Oliver Twist.* In much the same way, the cultural age is concerned with people and their present and prospective situations first and foremost, as well as helping those whose conditions are lamentable to experience much more equality, justice, well-being, and happiness in life.

Moreover, just as many interactions were taking place between England and France as well as London and Paris in Dickens' novel—interactions that affected both countries and their cosmopolitan cities—so too are many interactions going on in the world at present between the economic age and cultural age that are relevant to both ages. Ages are not independent from one another but, rather, intimately connected. Much as London and Paris were not completely independent of each other, so the agricultural age was not entirely independent from the industrial age that eventually followed it and that led to today's economic age. In fact, many elements of the agricultural age were incorporated into the industrial age, which profited from this immensely, just as much of the economic age will be subsumed into the cultural age and benefit from that incorporation as well. Not only is the cultural age needed to come to grips with the world's most dangerous and debilitating problems as well as the rapidly rising costs and shortcomings of the economic age, but it is also required to create a new vision of the future and produce the theoretical and practical foundations required to drive this vision forward.

No one at this very difficult time in history understood the need for this better than Sutan Takdir Alisjahbana, the Indonesian cultural scholar quoted earlier. Here is what he had to say about the state of humanity and the world at the beginning of the twenty-first century, a statement that is even more relevant, perceptive, and accurate today:

> Man [humanity] has arrived at a new turning point in his [its] existence. He [humanity] has to realize gradually that all societies and cultures will share equally in all achievements as well as in any catastrophes. Indeed, never was the concept of mankind [humankind] as a unity so urgent as in our time, because in the closely interlocked, often controversial political, economic, scientific, religious, and artistic life of the modern world there are almost no isolated solutions, valid only for a certain social group, or for a certain culture. It is no exaggeration to say that man [humanity] has to solve the problems of the *whole* world and the *whole* of mankind [humanity] or he [it] will not be able to solve any of them.[2]

This emphasis on the whole in terms of the world, humanity, people, the whole person, the entire human family, and, most importantly, the perception and definition of culture and cultures as "complex wholes and the total ways of life of people and countries" underlines and exposes many of the quintessential differences between the economic age and the cultural age. As we have seen, the highest priority of the economic age is accorded to economics and economies and breaking wholes up into many different parts through the processes known as *specialization* and *the division of labour*. While billions of people and numerous countries have benefited from these processes since *The Wealth of Nations* was published in 1776, the economic age that has delivered these remarkable achievements has also driven humanity and the world to the brink of disaster, largely because the natural environment was ignored for several centuries and the world is now confronted with an environmental catastrophe.

As we have seen, this problem and others like it have resulted from taking advantage of the *benefits* of the economic age while simultaneously ignoring the *costs* in terms of resource depletion and destruction of the natural environment at a devastating and escalating rate. It follows from this that the time has come to reconnect the parts of many activities and elements to form wholes and total ways of life that bring things together rather than splitting them farther apart. This can only be achieved by shifting the priority from economics, economies, specialization, and the parts as they were perceived and promoted by Adam Smith and affirmed by countless other economists, to culture, cultures, the whole, wholes, and holism as they were seen and defined by Edward Burnett Tylor and affirmed by numerous anthropologists, cultural scholars, and historians. This means that holism in general and culture and cultures perceived and defined in holistic terms in particular must be to the future cultural age what economics, economies, specialization, the parts, and partialism have been and are to the present economic age. This will not bring economics, economies, specialization, the parts, and so forth to an end, as discussed earlier, but rather incorporate them along with a great deal else in a substantially broader, deeper, and more all-embracing cultural perspective of the world and everything in it.

Like all ages, the cultural age will have shortcomings and costs as well as strengths and benefits. This is why culture has been seen and dealt with in this book as a *beacon of the future*. Doing so is necessary to ensure that every precaution is taken and safeguards established to minimize the shortcomings and costs of the cultural age, as well as to maximize its strengths and benefits by pointing out a safe, visible, viable, and vital path to the future, as all effective beacons do.

While the holistic perception of culture and cultures created by Tylor and elaborated upon by anthropologists and cultural scholars was used for more than a century to look *back* on the past in order to document and conserve cultures and civilizations that were on the brink of vanishing, the holistic perception of culture and cultures is needed now—and needed more than ever—to look *forward* into the future in order to create a new age and a very different perception of reality and way of life. Here again, Alisjahbana had something meaningful, relevant, and timely to say:

A new orientation must take place in our thinking in facing the new reality of our shrinking planet, and this must have its impact on the structure of our national states, on our economic relations, on our religious concepts, on our aesthetic expressions, and most of all on our solidarity relations to our fellow men [human beings] the world over.[3]

This new orientation is needed to open the doors to a cultural age and enable it to flourish. In order to do this, it must prove capable of doing two things and doing them extremely well. The first is to come to grips with the world's most life-threatening and debilitating problems; and the second is to provide a more all-encompassing, achievable, and viable vision of the future.

Is the cultural age capable of dealing with this first requirement? Indeed it is. When culture and cultures are defined and dealt with in holistic terms and utilized and applied properly, they possess the potential that is needed to reduce the demands being made on the natural environment and world's scarce resources by achieving a much more effective balance between people's and countries' material and non-material needs and expectations. Not only will this create a great deal more sustainability in the world, but also it will optimize rather than maximize economic growth and make it possible for people and countries to enjoy a great deal more well-being than they have today. Furthermore, by putting more emphasis on inclusion rather than exclusion, a major step will be taken towards decreasing the severe inequalities that exist in income and wealth throughout the world by distributing income and wealth on a much more equitable basis as well as across a much greater cross-section of the world's total population.

And this is not all. Broadening and deepening people's knowledge and understanding of culture and cultures and activating many more cultural exchanges, agreements, relations, and interactions between the diverse people, groups, races, countries, and cultures of the world will make it possible to decrease the numerous tensions and conflicts that exist in the world today. In addition, placing a much higher priority on harmonizing key cultural relationships—such as the ones between the arts and the sciences, human rights and human responsibilities, unity and diversity, and especially the quantitative and qualitative dimensions of development and life as well as people and the natural environment—will reduce the damage that is being done by erratic swings in the pendulums of these relationships. It will also decrease the divisions and polarizations that result from relationships, thereby producing more balance, order, harmony, and stability in the world.

Developments like these and many others will also shed a great deal of light on the way forward in the future by providing a more inspiring and overarching vision of the world of the future and everything in it. This vision will be set in motion and ultimately achieved by developing culture and cultures from the ground up, commencing with the cultures of children, parents, homes, and families, and concluding with the cultures of countries, international relations, the world, and the cultures of all other species. It will also be amplified and fortified by realizing a number of other crucial requirements, such as creating a cultural interpretation of history, committing to the centrality of cultural development and policy in the affairs of municipalities, regions, countries, and the world, and opening the doors to a cultural age and enabling it to flourish.

As this vision expands and evolves, it will pave the way for placing a much higher priority on people's and countries' overall well-being, being more rather than having more, living in communion, cooperation, and harmony with each other, other species, and the world at large, experiencing better health care and more creativity and contentment, living in the whole, the good, and the beautiful, following our bliss, walking in the corridors of peace rather than the catacombs of war, and realizing more equality, spirituality, and compassion in the world.

It is matters like these that make learning as much as possible about culture and all the diverse cultures in the world as complex wholes and total ways of life so exciting, rewarding, and compelling. This is because all the signs, symbols, technologies, creative works, and materials that are necessary to achieve this vision and holistic capability already exist and are manifested in some of culture's most essential and worthwhile activities such as the arts, humanities, heritage of history, ethics, and others. This includes beautiful music, exquisite paintings, superb plays, enticing architectural masterpieces, fascinating historic sites and monuments, compelling stories, savoury cuisines, timely ideas, admirable actions, impressive ideals, and many others. These are the *gateways* that are necessary to open the doors to culture, cultures, and a cultural age if we take the time and invest the energy that is required to have in-depth encounters with them.

Learning about culture and cultures in the holistic sense and expanding our knowledge, understanding, consciousness, and appreciation of them is what will make it possible for us to experience a real "paradise on earth." Brian Holihan paved the way for this possibility when he stated in his valuable and timely book *Thinking in a New Light: How to Boost Your Creativity and Live More Fully by Exploring World Cultures* that this paradise already exists in the world and is accessible to all of us. In Chapter 13 of his book, Holihan sets out a very effective way for broadening, deepening, discovering, and connecting with this paradise by "looking at, with, and beyond cultures," or what he calls "the AWB circle."[4] Through this method, we can learn much more about our own culture and the cultures of others. An additional advantage of this book is that he illustrates and applies this method through an intensive examination of many historical and contemporary achievements in several Southeast Asian cultures that are rapidly gaining prominence in the world and generating a great deal of international attention, interest, enthusiasm, and respect.

Opening the doors to a cultural age and enabling it to flourish also sets us on the right path to making the transition from the partial perspective, dualism, and all the divisions that exist in the economic age to the holistic perspective, holism, and understanding the interconnectedness of all things in the cultural age. This should eventually lead to achieving wholeness, togetherness, oneness, and unity in the world. As Robert Atkinson points out in his book *A New Story of Wholeness: An Experiential Guide for Connecting the Human Family*:

> Unitive narratives are needed now more than ever to lead us through a process of shifting the focus from individual wellbeing to collective wellbeing. In our time, the part no longer takes precedent over the whole. Both are completely interdependent. Exclusive emphasis upon any one part endangers the whole.[5]

This is all being made possible by the great cultural awakening that is taking place and spreading rapidly throughout the world, with more and more people now looking at the world and their lives from a cultural rather than economic perspective. This shift is manifested and confirmed by the remarkable outpouring of artistic and cultural works, accomplishments, and activities that are being achieved by numerous Black, Indigenous, colonized, and oppressed people, as well as many others who are connecting or reconnecting with their traditional cultures, worldviews, languages, customs, and ways of life. This is also the case for countless organizations that are re-creating their structures and cultures in order to make them more compelling and resilient as well as customer- and employee-friendly, numerous cultural scholars, historians, and practitioners who are producing much more research and writing on culture and cultures, as well as new forms of cultural creation, expression, and experience, not to mention millions of tourists who are travelling to different parts of the world to explore culture and cultures in detail, depth, and on location.

What is emerging as a result of all this activity is a very different way of looking at and living in the world. This is as it should be. For as John Cowper Powys pointed out many years ago, "The whole purpose and end of culture is a thrilling happiness of a particular sort—of the sort, in fact, that is caused by a response to life made by a harmony of the intellect, the imagination, and the senses."[6]

Without doubt, culture and cultures possess everything that is needed for all people and all countries to live full, fulfilling, and constructive lives, to produce a great deal more joy, happiness, well-being, and equality in the world, and to contribute to making the world a better, safer, and more stable place for everyone and everything. In the final analysis, this is what systemic cultural change and participating in the great cultural awakening are all about and destined to accomplish. The doors are opening to a cultural age. It is time we realize this, cross over the threshold to this age, and enjoy all the profuse opportunities and benefits that can arise from it. In so doing, perhaps in time we will all come to echo the words that end Dickens' *A Tale of Two Cities*; for in entering a cultural age, each of us might well say, "It is a far, far better thing that I do, than I have ever done; it is a far, far better rest I go to than I have ever known."

Notes

Epigraph
Jean d'Ormesson, *Cultural Policy Dossier*, No. 22–3/81. (Strasbourg: Council of Europe, 1981).

Chapter One
1. Eleanora Barbieri Masini (ed.), *The Futures of Culture*, Vol. 1 (Paris: UNESCO Publishing, 1994), p. 6.
2. Joel S. Khan, *Culture, Multiculture, Postculture* (London: Sage Publications, 1995), preface, p. ix.
3. For a detailed description of the origins, evolution, and mechanics of the economic age, see Part I of *Revolution or Renaissance: Making the Transition from an Economic Age to a Cultural Age* (Ottawa: University of Ottawa Press, 2008), pp. 9–118.
4. For an impartial assessment of the principal strengths and benefits as well as the fundamental shortcomings and costs of the economic age and a balance sheet on it, see *Revolution or Renaissance*, pp. 119–135.
5. John McHale, *The Future of the Future* (New York: George Braziller, 1969), p. 3 (italics mine).
6. It should be noted here that Adam Smith and Jeremy Bentham are often regarded as major contributors to the development of welfare economics by some scholars. In Smith's case, it was his commitment to improving the lot of citizens and the feelings he expressed in his book *The Theory of Moral Sentiments*; in Jeremy Bentham's case, it was his devotion to utilitarianism and the principle of the "greatest happiness for the greater number."
7. Alfred Marshall, *Principles of Economics* (London: Macmillan, 1890), Vol. 1 (insert mine).
8. Karl Polanyi, *The Great Transformation: The Political and Economic Origins of Our Time* (London: Farrar and Rinehart, 1944). It should be noted here that Karl Polanyi was training originally as an economic anthropologist and is probably remembered best (apart

from his famous book) as the originator of *substantivism*, which is a cultural dimension of economics that emphasizes the way economies are embedded in society and culture in a way that is consistent with the case made in this book.

9. Edward Burnett Tylor, *The Origins of Culture* (New York: Harper and Row, 1958).

10. *Ibid.*, p. 1 (italics mine).

11. Ruth Benedict, *Patterns of Culture* (London: Routledge and Kegan Paul, Ltd., 1963), p. 33 and p. 36 (italics mine).

12. For a detailed examination of the evolution of culture as an ideal and a reality as well as the perception and definition of culture and cultures over the centuries and going forward into the future, see: D. Paul Schafer, *The World as Culture: Cultivation of the Soul to the Cosmic Whole* (Oakville, ON: Rock's Mills Press, 2022).

13. The Jena Declaration states:

> We, the participants of the conference on "Humanities and Social Sciences for Sustainability" (October 21–22, 2020), organized in partnership with the Canadian and German Commissions for UNESCO, the International Council for Philosophy and the Human Sciences, the Social Sciences and Humanities Research Council of Canada, the World Academy of Art and Science, the Club of Rome, the Academia Europaea, and the International Geographical Union, having considered that the world is very close to the last chance to attain the broadly agreed Sustainable Development Goals Declare that:
>
> 1. Accelerating the progress towards achieving the Sustainable Development Goals and implementing the UN "Decade of Action" successfully requires a move from talking about sustainability to living sustainably. Such a shift implies the need to focus especially on peoples' everyday practices. This includes developing policies that enable, promote and support radical change in peoples' everyday actions.
>
> 2. Many sustainability policies stem from a human-nature dichotomy, understanding nature as humanity's surrounding environment. Yet with our body we are ourselves an integral part of nature, and we also incorporate it into our practices in

specific ways, depending on what we are doing. This premise inverts the perspective on sustainability from a nature-society opposition to a society-nature interdependent relation.

3. Most of the present crises find their roots in unintended, often foreseeable, problematic consequences of human actions that are, ultimately, of global significance. This implies the need to frame the crisis as primarily a societal rather than purely an environmental issue, and to expand what is understood to be its knowledge base.

4. Establishing long-term sustainable ways of living requires recognizing everyday practices as key drivers of the transformation. This calls for respecting those practices' cultural, social, and regional diversity, as well as past experiences of adaptation. In this context, the social sciences and the humanities must play a central role in shaping sustainability policies.

5. Transformations towards living sustainably will be broadly accepted if they are co-developed by everyday people, specific stakeholders, and policy-makers at all levels working together with academic experts and scientists. This implies a radical paradigm shift away from imposing "one size fits all" top-down strategies and towards specifically tailored approaches.

6. Cultural, social and natural dimensions of everyday practices are all inherently connected, locally embedded, and globally interrelated in specific ways. This insight requires scholarship that transcends disciplinary silos while benefiting from each discipline's findings, and is supported by new forms of research organization.

7. Genuine transdisciplinary research should provide information and insights in an accessible form and facilitate participatory knowledge production. This requires supporting bottom-up movements among relevant communities, allowing them to offer effective contributions and to take action.

8. A deep societal transformation across generations requires that young people are especially strongly involved in this shift from the start. This demands that they have access to

robust information and education, civic involvement, as well as political participation.

9. To establish culturally and regionally diverse ways of living sustainably, creativity and a new aesthetic are necessary. How we do things depends very much on what they signify to us, how we see the world and our place in it. The arts in all their forms, together with the humanities and social sciences are crucial for expanding mindsets, providing new perspectives on ways of living. This shall allow humankind to move from the age of extraction towards cultures of regeneration, to reach the SDGs with increased speed and depth, and to ensure measurable success.

10. To that end, we call upon all relevant political and scientific institutions, including funding agencies, to use the UN "Decade of Action" as a time to ensure that the cultural dimension is at the core of sustainability programs. This includes the need to:

- Reframe the basic perspective from an environmental issue to a societal challenge
- Complement solution orientated top-down strategies with more inclusive, regionally differentiated problem-avoiding bottom-up approaches
- Promote participation of younger generations in decision-making processes
- Reform sustainability research, its funding and organization
- Strengthen transdisciplinary cooperation in all domains of research
- Revamp the curricula of all educational institutions, focusing on global social emergencies and their mastering
- Establish universities, research and educational institutions as authentic examples for societal transformation
- Integrate the arts, as well as findings from the humanities and social sciences into the co-design of future, culturally and regionally diverse "ways of living sustainably".

Chapter Two

1. Meg Pier, *People Are Culture* and *Why Culture Matters*, 2021. More information on the philosophy and activities of Meg Pier, and on *People are Culture*, *Why Culture Matters*, and *Flip the Lens*, is available on the People are Culture website at http://www.peopleare-culture.com/.

2. James Feibleman, *The Theory of Human Culture* (New York: Humanities Press, 1968), p. 5.

3. Ruth Benedict, *Patterns of Culture*, foreword by Margaret Mead (New York: Mariner Books, 2006), p. 46.

4. Meg Pier, *People Are Culture, Why Culture Matters,* and *Flip the Lens*.

5. Matthew Arnold, *Culture and Anarchy* (Cambridge: Cambridge University Press, 1960), pp. 47–48 (italics Arnold's).

6. For a detailed account of the essential roles the arts can play in helping people to live their lives as wholes in general and harmonious wholes in particular, see D. Paul Schafer, *The Arts: Gateway to a Fulfilling Life and Cultural Age* (Oakville, ON: Rock's Mills Press, 2020).

7. For a comprehensive list of art forms that have specific characteristics and unique capabilities that may be helpful to people in living their lives and developing their personalities, see D. Paul Schafer, *The Arts*, pp. 26–32.

8. Matthew Arnold, *Culture and Anarchy*, p. 70 (italics Arnold's, inserts mine).

9. Karl J. Weintraub, *Visions of Culture: Voltaire, Guizot, Burckhardt, Lamprecht, Huizinga, Ortega y Gasset* (Chicago: University of Chicago Press, 1969), p. 216 (insert mine).

10. World Commission on Culture and Development, *Our Creative Diversity*, Report of the World Commission on Culture and Development (Paris: UNESCO, 1995), Chapter 1, pp. 24–51.

11. Karl J. Weintraub, *Visions of Culture,* pp. 219, 220, 216 (inserts mine).

12. Margaret Mead, *Letters from the Field: 1925–1975* (New York: Harper and Row, 1977), p. 16.

13. Yo-Yo-Ma, *Time*, October 21, 2020, quoted in Max Wyman, *The Compassionate Imagination: How the Arts Are Central to a Func-*

tioning Democracy (Toronto, ON: Cormorant Books, Inc., 2023), p. 219.

Chapter Three

1. Mary E. Clark, *Adriane's Thread: The Search for New Modes of Thinking* (New York: St. Martin's Press, 1989), p. 156 (italics Clark's).
2. Preamble to the Constitution of UNESCO, 1945 (insert mine).
3. Evelyn Kwong, "I finally saw myself in a main character," *Toronto Star*, March 19, 2022, p. C16.
4. Joshua Chong, "Musical magic in High Park," *Toronto Star*, June 15, 2022, p. B8.
5. Debra Yeo, "Welcome to the neighbourhood: Andrew Phung moves from 'Kim's Convenience' to the suburbs in 'Run the Burbs.'" *Toronto Star*, January 1, 2022, Section C, pp. 1 and 4.
6. "A culturally meaningful approach to building safe communities" (italics mine), Global Heroes website, https://www.globalheroes.com/muslim-resource-centre-safe-communities/. Article also appeared in the "Global Heroes" section of the *Toronto Star*.
7. More information on the Home for Humanity in France is available on its website at homeforhumanity.earth. Also see "Why Make Your Home a 'Home for Humanity',", Dr. A. T. Ariyaratne, founder, Sarvodaya Sri Lanka and Laureate of the Gandhi Peace Prize, homeforhumanity.earth/homes-for-humanity.

Chapter Four

1. Maria Montessori, https://quotefancy.com/quote/981132/Maria-Montessori-Culture-and-education-have-no-bounds-or-limits-now-man-is-in-a-phase-in.
2. Edward W. Said, quotation from *Orientalism*, https://www.goodreads.com/author/quotes/16770310.Edward_W_Said#:~:text=-Said%20Quotes&text=Every%20empire%2C%20however%2C%20tells%20itself,but%20to%20educate%20and%20liberate.%22.
3. Mahatma Gandhi, *Our Creative Diversity: Report on the World Commissions on Culture and Development*, p. 73 (italics mine).
4. Wole Soyinka, "Culture, Memory, and Development." *International Conference on Culture and Development in Africa*, April 2–3, 1992 (Washington: The World Bank, 1992), p. 21

5. Fernand Dumont, quoted in Bernard Ostry, *The Cultural Connection* (Toronto: McClelland and Stewart, 1978), p. 160 (italics mine).

6. Alfred Kroeber and Clyde Kluckhohn, *Culture: A Critical Review of Concepts and Definitions* (New York: Vintage Books, 1952), pp. 344–345.

7. Giles Gunn, *The Culture of Criticism and the Criticism of Culture* (New York: Oxford University Press, 1987), p. 95.

8. Robert Redfield, *The Little Community: Viewpoints for the Study of a Human Whole* (Chicago: University of Chicago Press, 1973), pp. 158–159

9. *Ibid.*, p. 161 (quotation marks Redfield's).

10. For a detailed account of these manifestations of culture and cultures, see *The World as Culture: Cultivation of the Soul to the Cosmic Whole* (Oakville, ON: Rock's Mills Press, 2022).

11. Jere Paul Surber, *Culture and Critique: An Introduction to the Critical Discourses of Cultural Studies* (Boulder: Western Press, 1988), p. 238.

12. Edward Hall, *Beyond Culture* (Garden City, New York: Anchor Press/Doubleday, 1976), p. 195.

Chapter Five

1. Amos Rapoport, "Culture and the Urban Order," in John A. Agnew, John Mercer and David E. Sopher (eds.), *The City in Cultural Context* (Boston: Allen and Unwin, 1984), p. 54.

2. Sung-Kyun Kim and Rana P.B. Singh, "Pung-Su: Evolving Cultural Landscapes and Placemaking in Korea" in Rana P.B. Singh, Olimpia Niglio, and Pravin S. Rana (eds.), *Placemaking and Cultural Landscapes* (pp. 39–59). Singapore: Springer Nature, 2023.

3. Rana P.B. Singh and Pravin S. Rana, Pravin S., "The riverfrontscapes of Varanasi, India: Architectural symbolism, transformation, and heritagization," *EdA Esempi di Architettura, International Journal of Architecture and Engineering*, Vol. 10, No. 2 (2023), pp. 244–269.

4. The culturescape methodology and process was developed for Ontario's Ministry of Culture and Recreation in 1975 and 1976. Designed to take a cultural approach to community development, it involved intensive probes into four communities in Ontario, and led to the publication of *Explorations in Culturescapes: A Cultural Approach*

to Community Development (Toronto, ON: Ministry of Culture and Recreation, Government of Ontario, 1976).

5. R. Murray Schafer, *The Tuning of the World: A Pioneering Exploration into the Past History and Present State of the Most Neglected Aspect of Our Environment: The Soundscape*. Toronto and New York: McClelland and Stewart and Alfred A. Knopf, 1977.

6. Charles Landry, *The Sensory Landscape of Cities* (London: Comedia, 2021), p. 7.

7. For a much more comprehensive and detailed statement on the culturescape methodology and process, see D. Paul Schafer. "The Culturescape: Self-Awareness of Communities," *Cultures*, Vol. 5, No. 1 (Paris: The UNESCO Press and La Baconnière, 1978).

8. See, for example, Michel Bassard. *"Culture et régions d'Europe"* (Lausanne: Presses polytechniques et universitaires romandes, 1990), and Biserka Cvjetičanin, "Cultural Change: Global Challenge and Regional Response," Razvoj Development International, Vol. 6, No. 2, July–December, 1991 (Zagreb: Institute for Development and International Relations, 1991), pp. 324–335.

9. D. Paul Schafer, "Municipalities and Regions: Powerful Forces in a Dynamic World," presented at the conference on "Decentralisation, Regionalisation et Action Culturelle," November 12–14, 1992 (Montreal: École des hautes études commercial, Université de Montréal, 1992).

10. Agenda 21 Culture, Newsletter, March 31, 2023, "Pact for the Future of Humanity: The Daejeda Political Declaration," 7th UCLG Congress in Daejeda, Republic of Korea, 10–14, October, 2022.

Chapter Six

1. Mahatma Gandhi, https://www.brainyquote.com/quotes/mahatma_gandhi_160857.

2. T. S. Eliot, *Notes Towards the Definition of Culture* (London: Faber and Faber, 1961). p. 31.

3. Paul J. Braisted, *Cultural Cooperation: Keynote of the Coming Age*, Hazen Pamphlets, No. 8 (New Haven, CT: Edward W. Hazen Foundation, 1945), pp. 5–6.

4. Mircea Malitza, "Culture and the New World Order: A Pattern of Integration," *Cultures*, Vol. 3, No. 4 (Paris: The UNESCO Press and la Baconniére, 1976), p. 102.

5. See D. Paul Schafer, "Towards a New World System: A Cultural Perspective," *Futures: The Journal of Forecasting, Planning and Policy*, Vol. 28, No. 1 (April 1996) for a fuller examination of what it means to see the world and international relations from a cultural rather than economic perspective. To see how this cultural perspective can be applied to a specific country, see D. Paul Schafer, *Canada's International Cultural Relations: Key to Canada's Role in the World* (Markham, ON: World Culture Project, 1996).

6. Paul J. Braised, *Cultural Cooperation*, p. 13 (insert mine).

7. RabindranathTagore, in Paul J. Braisted, *Cultural Cooperation*, p. 5.

8. Robert W. Wagoner and Donald W. Goldsmith, *Cosmic Horizons: Understanding the Universe* (San Francisco: W. H. Freeman and Company, 1982), p. 1.

9. Edward R. Harrison, *Cosmology: The Science of the Universe* (Cambridge: Cambridge University Press, 1981), pp. 10–12 (italics mine).

10. David Schenck, "Cosmology and Wisdom: The Great Teaching World of Thomas Berry," in *Thomas Berry's Work: Development, Difference, Importance, Applications*, in *The Ecozoic: Reflections on Life in an Ecological–Cultural Age*, 4 (2017), pp. 371, 373.

11. Milton Munitz, *Cosmic Understanding: Philosophy and Understanding of the Universe* (Princeton: Princeton University Press, 1986), pp. 4–5.

12. *Ibid.*, p. 6.

13. Pierre Pascallon, 'The Cultural Dimensions of Development,' *Intereconomics* (January–February, 1985), p. 7.

14. Fritjof Capra, *The Tao of Physics* (New York: Bantam, 1991), p. 130. It should be noted here that a great deal of attention has been focused in recent years on what is known as *cosmogenesis*, which is a specific branch of cosmology that deals with the origins of the cosmos as a whole. With this has come an escalating interest in the noosphere (that stage of evolutionary development dominated by the mind and consciousness), as well as what is called time-developmental consciousness. The latter starts with the origins of the cosmos and is concerned with its dynamic, evolutionary, regenerative, and expansive rather than static and unchanging character.

Chapter Seven

1. Alfred L. Kroeber and Clyde Kluckhohn, *Culture: A Critical Review of Concepts and Definitions* (New York: Vintage Books, 1963), p. 57.
2. For more detailed information on the intimate connection between all the various species in the world in general and plants, animals, and human beings and their cultures in particular, see D. Paul Schafer, *The World as Culture*, chapters 2, 9, and 10.
3. Kaj Birket-Smith, *The Paths of Culture: A General Ethnology*, translated from Danish by Karin Fennow (Madison, WI and Milwaukee, WI: University of Wisconsin Press, 1965), p. 9 (insert mine).
4. Peter Wohlleben, *The Hidden Life of Trees: What They Feel, How They Communicate* (Vancouver: Greystone Books, 2016), p. 3.
5. *Ibid.*, p. viii (insert and italics mine).
6. Hina Alam, "Chattiest schools are in the sea," *Toronto Star*, January 25, 2023, p. A10.
7. *Ibid.*
8. William J. Broad, "The tantalizing secrets of coral sex," *Toronto Star*, June 26, 2016, p. IN6.
9. Seth Borenstein and Mayuko Ono, "Feeling sluggish: These sea creatures found a solution," *Toronto Star*, March 13, 2021, p. IN3.
10. Frans de Waal, *Are We Smart Enough to Know How Smart Animals Are?* (New York: W. W. Norton and Company, 2016), p. 275 (italics mine).
11. *Ibid.*, p. 274 (italics de Waal's).

Chapter Eight

1. Alfred L. Kroeber and Clyde Kluckhohn, *Culture: A Critical Review of Concepts and Definitions*, p. 290.
2. P. Gardiner (ed.), *Theories of History* (Glencoe, IL: The Free Press, 1959), pp. 126–132 (inserts and italics mine).
3. Susan Hunt, "The Alternative Economics Movement," *Interculture*, Vol. 22, No. 1 (1989), p. 3.
4. John Gibb, "Sixty years after the prescient *Silent Spring*," *Toronto Star*, October 30, 2022, p. IN6 (insert and italics mine).
5. Oswald Spengler, *The Decline of the West* (New York: The Modern Library, 1962), p. 18.
6. While development of the cultural interpretation of history is far

beyond the confines of this book and a gargantuan task, it is important to point out that much of the material that is required for this interpretation already exists, especially in terms of the culture and cultures of all other species in the world and not just the human species. The challenge is really pulling all this material together and providing it in one place rather than having to produce it from scratch.

7. Karl J. Weintraub, *Visions of* Culture, pp. 117–118.

8. *Ibid.*, p.126.

9. *Ibid.*, p. 146.

10. *Ibid.*, p. 1 (insert mine).

11. *Ibid.*, p. 4

12. *Ibid.*, p. 6–7 (insert and italics mine).

13. *Ibid.*, p. 2 (insert mine).

14. *Ibid.*, p. 3.

15. See "The Roots of Culture, Cultures, and Cultural Genetics," Session 14, August 20, 2022, *Imagine: Culture as a Reality: Twenty Practical Steps Towards a Cultural Age* with D. Paul Schafer, author of *The World as Culture*, https://imaginezine.com/culture-as-a-reality/.

16. S. Takdir Alisjahbana, *Values as Integrating Forces in Personality, Society, and Culture* (Kuala Lumpur: Malaya Press, 1980), pp. 206–207.

17. S. Takdir Alisjahbana, *Socio-Cultural Creativity and the Converging and Restructuring Process of the New Emerging World Order* (Jakarta: P. T. Dian Rakyat, 1983), p. 23.

18. *Ibid.*, p. 12–13.

Chapter Nine

1. Léopold Sédar Senghor, in *Culture: A Critical Review of Concepts and Definitions*, p. 142.

2. Alfred Kroeber and Clyde Kluckhohn, *Culture: A Critical Review of Concepts and Definitions,* Papers, 1952, Peabody Museum of Archaeology and Ethnology, Harvard University, Vol. 47, No. 1, pp. viii, 223.

3. René Maheu, Address to the World Conference on Cultural Policies in Venice, 1970.

4. Herbert Shore, *Cultural Policy: UNESCO'S First Cultural Devel-*

opment Decade (Washington, DC: U.S. National Commission for UNESCO, 1981), pp. vii, viii (insert mine).

5. UNESCO *Second World Conference on Cultural Policies in Mexico City*, 1982 (Paris: UNESCO: 1982), p. 41.

6. Pérez de Cuéllar, Address to the *Inaugural Session of the Third Meeting of the World Commission for Culture and Development*, San Jose, Costa Rica, February 22, 1994, p. 1.

7. World Commission on Culture and Development, *Our Creative Diversity: Report of the World Commission on Culture and Development* (Paris: UNESCO, 1995).

8. The World Commission on Environment and Development (The Brundtland Commission), *Our Common Future: Report of the World Commission on Environment and Development* (New York: Oxford University Press, 1987).

9. The United Nations Social Development Goals (SDG's) to transform the world are: 1. no poverty; 2. zero hunger; 3. good health and well-being; 4. quality education; 5. gender equality; 6. clean water and sanitation; 7. affordable and clean energy; 8. decent world and economic growth; 9, industry, innovation, and infrastructure; 10. reduced inequality; 11. sustainable cities and communities; 12. responsible consumption and production; 13. climate action; 14. life before water; 15. life on land; 16. peace and justice, and strong institutions; 17. partnerships to achieve the goals.

10. Edgar Schein, *Organizational Culture and Leadership*, 5th ed. (New York: Wiley, 2016).

11. Maurice Strong, *Bridge of Hope*, unpublished book manuscript, p. 147.

12. See Thomas Kuhn, *The Structure of Scientific Revolutions* (Chicago: University of Chicago Press, fourth edition, 2012); and Malcolm Gladwell, *The Tipping Point: How Little Things Can Make a Big Difference* (New York: Back Bay Books, 2012).

13. For a detailed description and assessment of how the UN Decades of Development originated and evolved as a result of the inaugural address that President Harry Truman made to the Congress in the United States in 1949 where he divided the world into "developed" and "developing" countries and said, "Production is the key to prosperity and peace," see Wolfgang Sachs' series of essays for *New Inter-*

national in 1992, including an article titled "Development: A Guide to its Ruin." Also see Wolfgang Sachs, *The Development Dictionary: A Guide to Knowledge and Power* (London: Zed Books, 2010) for a more comprehensive assessment of "development" and how the idea of development was destroyed from the very beginning by equating development in the world with development that was taking place in the United States, which was seen and defined only in economic terms.

14. See D. Paul Schafer, *The Challenge of Cultural Development* (Markham, ON: World Culture Project, 1994) for a comprehensive discussion of the cultural model of development.

15. See Francis A. Schaeffer, *How Should We Then Live?* (Wheaton, IL: Crossway, 2005), pp. 144–165, for a much more comprehensive discussion of the importance and implications of "universals and particulars" and "the whole and the parts" in the historical evolution of philosophy and the sciences.

16. Jane Coopeer-Wilson, "Systemic racism has always been a real and present danger," *Markham Economist and Sun*, February 2, 2023, opinion section.

Chapter Ten

1. Rajni Kothari, *The Scheveningen Report—Towards a New International Development Strategy*, Scheveningen Symposium, July 25–28, 1979 (Nyon: International Foundation of Development Alternatives, 1980) p.7.

2. See D. Paul Schafer, *The World as Culture* for a detailed description of the evolution of culture as an idea and a reality over the course of human history and where it stands and how it is being perceived and defined today.

3. *Ibid.* See chapters on "Behaviour and Ways of Life of Other Species" and "Mythology, Worldview, and Cosmology," pp. 193–212 and 235–252 respectively.

4. Valerie Lynch Lee (ed.), *Faces of Culture: Viewers Guide* (Huntington Beach, CA.: KOCE-TV Foundations, 1983), p. 69 (italics mine).

5. D. Paul Schafer, "A New System of Politics: Government, Governance, and Political Decision-making in the Twenty-first Century," *World Futures: The Journal of General Evolution*, Vol. 61, No. 7 (October-November 2005).

6. See, for example, S. Takdir Alisjahbana, *Socio-cultural Creativity in the Converging and Restructuring Process of the New Emerging World* (Jakarta, Indonesia: Penerbit Dian Rakyat,1983), and *Values as Integrating Forces in Personality, Society, and Culture* (Kuala Lumpur: University of Malaya Press, 1986); Soedjatmoko, *Economic Development as a Cultural Problem* (Ithaca, NY: Cornell University Press, 1962), Soedjatmoko, *An Introduction to Indonesian Historiography* (Ithaca, NY: Cornell University Press, 1975), and Soedjatmoko and Kenneth W. Thompson (co-editors), *Culture, Development, and Democracy: The Role of the Intellectual, A Tribute* (Tokyo: United Nations University, 1994); Mochtar Lubis, *Twilight in Jakarta* (London: Darf Publishers, 2017); and Mira Sartika, *The Map of Civilization: A Geocultural Synthesis* (Indonesia: Mira Sartika, 2015), *Culture in Sustainable Development: Harmony through Differences* (Indonesia: Mira Sartika, 2018), and *Cultural Genetics* (Indonesia: CreateSpace Independent Publishing Platform, Mira Sartika, 2018).

7. Rana P. B. Singh, "Incredible India: Culture Heritage: Vision, Understanding and Preservation," in A. W. Tiwary, M. R. Tiwary, and A. K Rai (eds.), *India's Rich Cultural Heritage: Preservation, and Promotion* (Varanasi, IN: Shaurayam Publications, 2023), pp. 1–10. For references to other articles related to valuable contributions to cultural development over the centuries by historical and contemporary scholars in India, see Rana P. B. Singh, "Environmental Ethics and Sustainability in Indian Thought: Vision of Mahatma Gandhi," *Journal of Indian Philosophy and Religion*, Vol. 26 (2021), pp. 55–74; and Rana P. B. Singh, "Ecospirituality and Sustainability: Vision of Swami Vivekananda," in Editorial Board (eds.) *MANANAM (Reflection): Exposition of Vedantic Thought* (Piercy, CA: Chinmaya Mission West Publications, 2021), pp. 21–30 and especially pp. 23–25.

Chapter Eleven

1. Raymond Williams, *The Long Revolution* (London: Penguin, 1965), p. 63.
2. Peter Brook, "The Three Cultures of Modern Man," *Cultures*, Vol. 3, No. 4 (Paris: The UNESCO Press and La Baconnière, 1976), p. 144 (insert and italics mine).
3. C. P. Snow, *The Two Cultures and the Scientific Revolution* (Cam-

bridge: Cambridge University Press, 1958). This book was published following C. P. Snow's Rede Lecture on this subject earlier in 1959.

4. C. P. Snow, *The Two Cultures and a Second Look: An Expanded Version of the Two Cultures and the Scientific Revolution* (New York: New American Library, 1963).

5. The information in the text on the IAM Lab and its programs, projects, and publications was provided by Susan Magsamen, Executive Director of the Lab. More information on this organization is available on its website at https://www.hopkinsmedicine.org/pedersen-brain-science-institute/international-arts-mind-lab.

6. Commission on Culture and Development, *Our Creative Diversity: Report of the World Commission on Culture and Development*, p. 35.

7. Ashutosh Kumar Singh, "Universal Declaration of Human Responsibilities: A Distant Dream in the 21st Century," *PENACCLAIMS*, Vol. 9 (April 2020), pp. 1–9.

8. Thomas Legrand, *Politics of Being: WISDOM and SCIENCE for a New Development Paradigm* (N.p.: Ocean of Wisdom Press, 2021).

9. Karl J. Weintraub, *Visions of Culture*, p. 216.

10. Pitirim Sorokin, *Social and Cultural Dynamics: A Study of Change in Major Systems of Art, Truth, Ethics, Law, and Social Relationships* (Boston: Porter and Sargent Publisher (Extending Horizon Books), 1957), pp. 2–40.

11. Karl J. Weintraub, *Visions of Culture*, p. 219.

Chapter Twelve

1. Gandhi quotation, https://www.brainyquote.com/quotes/mahatma_gandhi_163698.

2. Mary Catherine Bateson, *Composing a Life* (New York: Grove Press, 1989), p. 2.

3. Diana Butler Bass, *Grounded: Finding God in the World: A Spiritual Revolution* (New York: HarperCollins Publishers, 2015), p. 26.

4. Maya Spencer, "What is Spirituality: A Personal Exploration" (2016), https://www.rcpsych.ac.uk/docs/default-source/members/sigs/spirituality-spsig/what-is-spirituality-maya-spencer-x.pdf?sfvrsn=f28df052_2.

5. Jin Li, *Cultural Foundations of Learning: East and West* (New

York: Cambridge University Press, 2012), p. 80.
6. Charles R. Joy, ed., *Albert Schweitzer: An Anthology* (Boston: The Beacon Press, (1947), p. 131.
7. Max Wyman, *The Compassionate Imagination: How the Arts are Central to a Functioning Democracy* (Toronto: Cormorant Books Inc., 2023). pp. 94–95.
8. Teilhard de Chardin, https://www.theclearingnw.com/blog/spiritual-beings-having-a-human-experience.

Chapter Thirteen

1. Goethe, as quoted in John Cowper Powys, *The Meaning of Culture* (New York: W.W. Norton and Company, Inc., 1929), p. 251.
2. Schaeffer, *How Should We Then Live?*, pp. 144–145
3. Robert Atkinson, *A New Story of Wholeness: An Experiential Guide for Connecting the Human Family* (Fort Lauderdale, FL: Light on Light Press, 2022), pp. i, ii.

Chapter Fourteen

1. Charles Dickens, *A Tale of Two Cities* (New York: Chartwell Books, 2021), p. 1.
2. S. Takdir Aalisjahbana, *Socio-cultural Creativity in the Converging and Restructuring Process of the New Emerging World* (Pulo Gadung, Jakarta: P.Yl Dian Kakyat, 1983), pp. 72–73 (inserts mine).
3. *Ibid.*, p. 73.
4. Brian Holihan, *Thinking in a New Light: How to Boost Your Creativity and Live More Fully by Exploring World Cultures* (Sunnyvale, CA: Full Humanity Press, 2016). See Chapter 13 (pp. 272–300) for a practical technique for studying and exploring cultures in depth and breadth as well as finding paradise in your own life and in the world.
5. Robert Atkinson, *A New Story of Wholeness*, "Prologue: A Pattern of Wholeness," p. vii.
6. John Cowper Powys, *The Meaning of Culture* (New York. W.W. Norton and Company Inc., 1929), p. 77.

Index